Palgrave Animation

Series Editors
Caroline Ruddell
Brunel University London
Uxbridge, UK

Paul Ward
Arts University Bournemouth
Poole, UK

This book series explores animation and conceptual/theoretical issues in an approachable way. The focus is twofold: on core concepts, theories and debates in animation that have yet to be dealt with in book-length format; and on new and innovative research and interdisciplinary work relating to animation as a field. The purpose of the series is to consolidate animation research and provide the 'go to' monographs and anthologies for current and future scholars.

More information about this series at
http://www.palgrave.com/gp/series/15948

Kristian Moen

New York's Animation Culture

Advertising, Art, Design and Film, 1939–1940

Kristian Moen
Department of Film and Television
University of Bristol
Bristol, UK

ISSN 2523-8086   ISSN 2523-8094   (electronic)
Palgrave Animation
ISBN 978-3-030-27933-2   ISBN 978-3-030-27931-8   (eBook)
https://doi.org/10.1007/978-3-030-27931-8

Image credit: Margaret Bourke-White/Contributor
Cover credit: New York World's Fair 1939–1940 records, Manuscripts and Archives Division, The New York Public Library

This Palgrave Macmillan imprint is published by the registered company Springer Nature Switzerland AG
The registered company address is: Gewerbestrasse 11, 6330 Cham, Switzerland

ACKNOWLEDGEMENTS

It is a great pleasure to be able to thank some of the many people who have helped in the research and writing of this book. The project benefitted enormously from the assiduous eye for detail and extraordinary research skills of Vicky Jackson. It was a great pleasure to work with Vicky on the "Idea of Animation" project, funded by the European Research Council. The research leading to these results has received funding from the European Research Council under the European Union's Seventh Framework Programme (FP7/2007–2013)/ERC grant agreement n° 338110. Research for the book was undertaken at a number of archives and libraries, including the British Film Institute, the Margaret Herrick Library, Yale University Library, the Harry Ransom Center, the Guggenheim Archives, the New York Public Library, the Archives and Special Collections at the University of Stirling, the New-York Historical Society, the Archives of American Art and the Rockefeller Archive Center. I would like to thank the many skilled archivists, librarians and assistants who helped make this archival research such a fascinating and rewarding experience. The publishing process has been a real pleasure thanks to the editors of the Palgrave Animation series, Paul Ward and Caroline Ruddell, and Lina Aboujieb, Ellie Freedman and Carolyn Zhang at Palgrave. The anonymous readers offered many insightful suggestions and ideas. Although I was not able to incorporate all of their comments, I hugely appreciate their input.

I am very lucky indeed to be able to work with such great colleagues in the Department of Film and Television at the University of Bristol, including Katie Mack, Alex Clayton, Sarah Street, Angela Piccini, Helen Piper, Peter Milner, Chris Barnett, Chris Jones, Jacqueline Maingard, Kate Withers, Deborah Gibbs, Pete Falconer, Nariman Massoumi and Jimmy Hay. I would also like to thank the wonderful students who have helped so much during many discussions and conversations, in class and out of class. Outside of Bristol, I have enjoyed a wealth of support from friends and colleagues. Gareth Evans has been a crucial help at many points during the writing of this book, keeping me on track when I needed it most and opening my eyes to new ways of seeing film, art and politics. I am tremendously grateful to Carole Zucker and Mario Falsetto for teaching me so much and for their kindness over the years. Sherry Kelley, Jonathan Tooke and Marguerite Valentine have been wonderful friends to exchange ideas with. Peter Krämer has been a source of constant support throughout the writing process, always ready to challenge assumptions and always ready to give warm-hearted encouragement. Many thanks also to Martin, Sookyung, Alan and Peter for introducing me to so much of New York.

Much of this book was written during trips to Alberta. I would like to thank the staff at the Medicine Hat College for giving me space to work, and especially Michael MacKenzie for our many delightful conversations. Concordia University of Edmonton was also a terrific place to work, particularly its welcoming and brilliantly run library. Thank you to Jasmina Odor for helping me to try and better understand the art of writing. Dan Mirau has been very important throughout the writing of this book, and I thank him profoundly for his insights and support. Finally, I would like to thank my mother, Carol, whose passion for art is a constant source of inspiration, and Paul Thibault, who is always there for me and always ready to share his wisdom.

CONTENTS

LIST OF FIGURES

CHAPTER 1

Introduction

In the late 1930s and early 1940s, New York City showcased an extraordinary panorama of animation. Walking through the city and ducking into a cinema, you were bound to catch a short animated film as part of the program, perhaps one featuring a major star such as Mickey Mouse or Popeye. But you could also settle in to watch one of the feature-length animated films which had begun to appear after the success of *Snow White and the Seven Dwarfs* (1937), with *Gulliver's Travels* (1939), *Pinocchio* (1940) and *Fantasia* (1940) playing in cinemas around Broadway. Along your walk, if you had timed it right, you might also watch animated films at a gallery such as the Museum of Modern Art, which was screening works ranging from contemporary Disney cartoons to the earliest animated films of Emile Cohl. If, like millions of others, you also wanted to take in the sights of the New York World's Fair, which ran from 1939 to 1940, a plethora of short advertising and educational films were on display—including a Mickey Mouse film advertising the National Biscuit Company's products, an animated three-dimensional film advertisement for Chrysler and an animated puppet film extolling the wonders of petroleum.

Animation had also spilled out from cinema screens to a wider visual culture, enlivening spectacles and displays. In a short stroll from Fifth Avenue to Times Square, you could gawk at the animated displays in the shop windows of the most prestigious stores, marvel at the scientific motion exhibits in the Hall of Motion at Rockefeller Center and gaze up at the animated

© The Author(s) 2019
K. Moen, *New York's Animation Culture*, Palgrave Animation,
https://doi.org/10.1007/978-3-030-27931-8_1

signs lighting up Broadway. The World's Fair offered another vivid landscape of motion, with the editor for *Display Animation*, I. L. Cochrane,
excitedly explaining:

> The great majority of all exhibits … will be made more fascinating and more
> impressive by means of motion and mobile light – and each will tell in drama-
> tized simplicity the story of an industry or a product! That is real achievement
> for all those who have striven for better sales expression through artistic Ani-
> mation. Approximately twenty percent of exhibits were animated in the great
> [Century of Progress] Chicago Fair of five years ago – and in those of next
> year *ninety percent will be animated!*[1]

Exhibits were awash with motion, yoking kineticism to the Fair's theme
of "The World of Tomorrow." If you were to visit the exhibit for the
Ford Motor Company, for example, you could see an enormous animated
mural depicting industrial machinery and science, an animated film playfully detailing the process of car manufacturing and a huge rotating display,
entitled the "Cycle of Production," that slowly revolved to show dozens
of animated models engaged in various activities of production and labor.
Amazed by such variety, a British visitor's account began with the observation, "A book could be written about the exhibit of the Ford Motor
Company at the World's Fair."[2] Writing in the journal *Display*, the visitor
was astonished by the extraordinary scope of motion: "This Ford exhibit
would suggest that these are really the days of animation."

This book is about these days of animation in New York City. Focusing
on the period from 1939 to 1940, I trace the diverse routes that animation
took during this dynamic period in its history. I explore "animation" in a
broad sense, common at the time, as a word that refers to giving motion
or the impression of motion to images and objects that would otherwise
remain static. Vivifying advertising and educational displays, creating new
forms of art, extending the boundaries of cinema and expressing the vitality
of modernity, animation was transformative. Whether using modes of producing animated films that had been in place for decades or experimenting with new technologies of mechanical movement, photoelectric cells
and hand-painted film, animators were opening up new vistas of motion.
Animation's expansive possibilities were evident across different exhibition contexts—projected in cinemas, displayed in galleries and department

stores and promoted in industrial exhibits. Not surprisingly, a vibrant conversation was taking place around these uses of animation, with the popular press joining artists, designers, advertisers, filmmakers and theorists in attempting to understand and explain animation's potentials.

Rather than approaching these disparate strands of animation as separate, I examine how they were interwoven in a distinctive animation culture. I use the phrase "animation culture" to refer to the ways in which animation is understood, created and used in a specific time and place. My focus on animation culture relates closely to established ways of understanding other cultural practices. The notion of film culture, for example, indicates how cinema is something more than a collection of individual films, made up of exhibition practices, theoretical explorations, audience experiences and a host of other facets. Instead of something that naturally developed around cinema, film culture has taken on different shapes in different contexts. For example, Malte Hagener argues that film culture's network of "film criticism and film theory, festivals and prizes, archives and repertoire cinemas, film schools and museums" emerges at a specific historical moment, in the 1920s and 1930s, shaped by a network of national contexts, institutional bodies and the efforts of an artistic avant-garde.[3] And there have been countless variations and permutations of film culture across the world throughout the last century, each situating film within their own distinct circumstances. Animation cultures can be similarly diverse, engaging with different uses, values and possibilities of animated motion in a myriad of ways. While sometimes related to film culture, an animation culture can also follow its own path, separate from a wider cinematic context.

Exploring an animation culture invites us to pay close attention to the ideas that circulate around animation, from theoretical discussions or artist statements to a broader cultural reception. These ideas of animation both reflect and stimulate creative practices. Such practices can involve the use of established production methods, but they can also engage with new technologies, innovative techniques or aesthetic experimentation. This multiplicity extends also to how animation is used in culture; for example, animation has been a delightful children's entertainment, a visionary form of art, a powerful means of advertising, an effective tool for education or a combination of these and other purposes. These uses of animation are inflected by the specific ways that animation is shown, whether in a cinema as a feature or a short film, or in other exhibition sites that have also played a significant role in animation cultures, such as galleries or displays. Tracing the ideas, creative practices and modes of exhibition that shape an animation culture—and seeing how they interrelate with one another—can reveal the multiple factors that determine animation's place in culture.

In his introduction to *The Culture of Print*, Roger Chartier discusses a "dual definition of print culture" that can help illuminate how an idea of animation culture might be understood, despite the obvious historical and material differences between a visual culture of the twentieth century and a print culture emerging after Gutenberg. Chartier first describes print culture, in what he terms its "classic definition," as "the profound transformations that the discovery and then the extended use of the new technique for the reproduction of texts brought to all domains of life, public and private, spiritual and material." With cheaper printing costs and a greater portability, "such new means of communication... modified practices of devotion, of entertainment, of information, and of knowledge, and they redefined men's and women's relations with the sacred, with power, and with their community."[4] By foregrounding the transformations of existing practices that print culture generated, Chartier offers a dynamic sense of how a wider culture is responsive and open to change. While animation cultures do not have quite such far-reaching implications, they can nevertheless offer a similarly rich diversity of effects. As well as taking on different forms in different places and times, animation cultures—and the ways that they become attached to changing experiences and values—are multifaceted.

One way that this can become obscured is by focusing on facets of animation culture that resonate with a contemporary sense of animation or that relate mainly to well-documented areas of its history. Chartier identifies a similar problem in his description of print culture. He writes, "All too long this culture has been reduced to reading alone, and to a form of reading that is common today or was practiced by the scholars in medieval and early modern culture."[5] Rather than relating print culture to these practices, Chartier argues for an expansion of its meanings to include "festive, ritual, cultic, civic, and pedagogic uses" (1). Chartier's approach to print culture brings to light aspects of historical experience that might seem, at first glance, to be marginal but which were still deeply significant. This approach is instructive in its attention to multiplicity rather than emphasizing singular forms or effects. The richness of animation history and the cultures that formed around motion's aesthetic expressions, within and beyond the cinema, call for a similar attentiveness to multiplicity.

There have been many different animation cultures, each with their own ways of understanding, creating and using animation. Every animation culture has different emphases, with certain features standing out as particularly prominent or characteristic. The Fleischer Studios in the 1930s, for example, had a distinctive animation culture which not only foregrounded the production of popular animated entertainment but also included exhibition strategies, an in-house newsletter, technological experimentation and extensions of animated characters into other media. Animation cultures also take shape in certain locations, such as the vivid entwinement of animation, art and advertising in Germany during the Weimar Republic, explored in Michael Cowan's work.[6] While animation cultures can be seen as part of a larger history of animation, as well as other fields including film, art and advertising, examining the particularities of different animation cultures can offer new perspectives on the diverse artistic, social and expressive potentials of animation itself.

"New York Is Not America"

In New York in the late 1930s and early 1940s, a particularly vibrant animation culture had emerged. This was, in many respects, enabled by New York's place not only as an enormous urban center, but also as a complex web of commerce, art, industry and entertainment with a vitalizing internationalism. While New York's animation culture was by no means isolated, it was hardly a typical or representative example of larger trends. Instead, New York offered an intensified and expansive animation culture. This was partly due to the city's distinctive qualities, a topic that was well recognized at the time. For example, an article in the trade journal *Department Store Buyer* stated bluntly in its title: "New York Is Not America."[7] The article warned retailers not to copy the shop windows that were appearing in New York as they relied upon conditions that were specific to a massive metropolitan area. Examples of this included the animated shop windows at Lord & Taylor's department store (discussed in Chapter 2), which were a major success partly due to the steady stream of pedestrians strolling along Fifth Avenue.

The admonition about New York not being representative of the United States was, of course, true far beyond the specific example of eye-catching advertising displays. In 1939, New York City was one of the largest cities in the world, with a population of over seven million spread across its five boroughs: Brooklyn, the Bronx, Queens, Richmond (named Staten Island since 1975) and Manhattan.[8] It was both "America's greatest commercial center" and its "major industrial city."[9] New York also faced extraordinary levels of poverty. In the late 1930s, almost ten percent of New York's residential areas were made up "of slums or blighted districts," with more than half of these "condemned as unfit for human habitation" (424). Accounts from the time highlighted the disproportionate impact that the Depression had upon certain communities within New York; the situation in Harlem was particularly distressing, with the newly created Federal Emergency Relief Administration finding "a majority of Harlem's population on the verge of starvation, as a result of the depression and of an intensified discrimination" that was deeply damaging to employment and educational opportunities (142). The Depression had hit New York hard, and by 1933, almost half of its factory workers had lost their jobs.[10] Recovery was sluggish and the 1937 recession "reversed four years of slow but steady improvements in the economy" (58). The effects of the difficult economic situation would last for years: "Despite gradual improvements in the economy after 1938, unemployment remained a heavy burden in the early 1940s" (60).

These economic hardships did not diminish New York's status as a globally recognized center of retail, culture and entertainment. The city's retail trade was by far the largest in the United States. Much of this activity took place in "the shopping mecca of the entire metropolitan district": the retail area of midtown Manhattan situated between Third and Eighth Avenue (Fig. 1.1).[11] The significance of this area was partly because it was a transportation hub, both for those who lived in the greater New York area and for the masses of tourists arriving at Penn Station or Grand Central Station. This part of Manhattan contained sites such as Fifth Avenue, Times Square and the Museum of Modern Art, offering a densely packed assemblage of venues for shopping, entertainment and art. It is hardly surprising that the dynamic expressions of New York's animation culture, dependent as they were upon commercial and artistic activities, were largely centered around this area of New York.

Just as "New York Is Not America," Manhattan—and particularly the retail center in midtown Manhattan—was hardly representative of New York more widely. The distinctive qualities of the area had become even more pronounced with the construction of the Rockefeller Center complex in the 1930s: "Covering twelve land acres in the fashionable mid-town shopping district, the project includes a vast skyscraper office center, a shopping center, an exhibition center, and a radio and amusement center."[12]

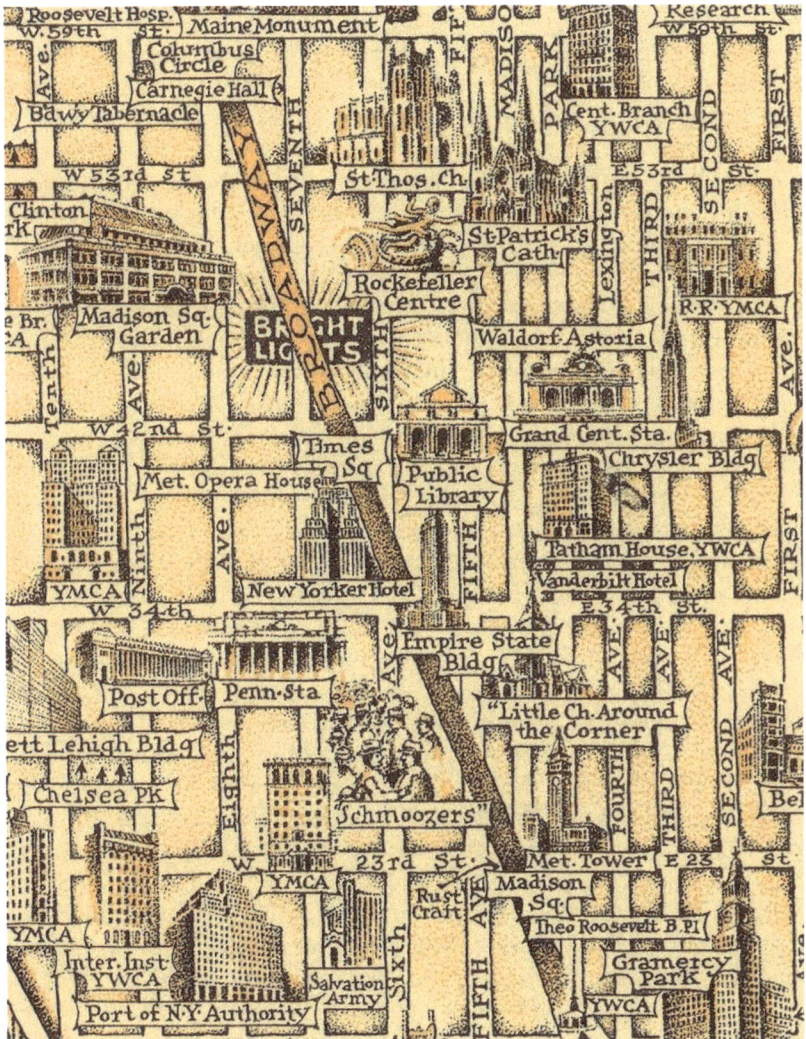

Fig. 1.1   Detail from Ernest Dudley Chase, "A pictorial map of that portion of New York City known as Manhattan," 1939. David Rumsey Historical Map Collection

Described at the time as "expressive of New York," Rockefeller Center was "an organization of amazing complexity, a city in miniature, where a tenant need not leave the premises in order to see the latest first-run movies, or buy a complete outfit of clothing, or study the newest manifestations of art and science, or engage passage to foreign countries with visas to match."[13] A number of the figures who were central to New York's animation culture had offices in Rockefeller Center, including the most prominent designer of animated signs, Douglas Leigh, the person running the marketing and advertising of Disney's tie-ins, Kay Kamen, and America's most well-known industrial designer, Norman Bel Geddes. Rockefeller Center also contained two of New York's largest exhibition spaces, Radio City Music Hall (seating 6200) and the Center Theatre (seating 3700); their regular screenings of films included the first two features produced by Disney, *Snow White* and *Pinocchio*. With its grand status as a meeting point for business, entertainment and culture, Rockefeller Center was a microcosm of the area surrounding it in midtown Manhattan.

The concentrated world of commerce and entertainment in Rockefeller Center would be joined by an even more elaborate site when the New York World's Fair opened its gates in Flushing Meadows, Queens. The Fair was another miniature world of commerce, entertainment, culture and art within New York. The Fair was distinctive in many ways, as Chapter 3 explores, and one of its characteristic features was the promotion of massive corporate exhibits that displayed new technologies and machine age spectacles. Terry Smith writes that "unlike previous fairs, no pride of place was given to foreign exhibits, their pavilions clustering in the far-flung precincts of the Federal Building."[14] Instead, "like no fair before or since," the New York World's Fair was "the province of a new breed of industrial designers." This included Norman Bel Geddes, Walter Dorwin Teague, Henry Dreyfuss, Donald Deskey and Egmont Arens, who designed exhibits for large corporations and major exhibitors. These designers used animation extensively in their exhibits, creating a dynamic vision of modern life that resonated with the fantasies of the Fair's sponsors and its corporate backers.

While the Fair, Rockefeller Center and the retail area of midtown Manhattan were all distinctive in many respects, one quality that they shared with the wider New York area was internationalism. In *Cue* magazine's 1940 guide to New York, George W. Seaton rather bluntly described the city's diverse population: "The most common complaint against New York, that it is not an 'American' city, is very true from the point of view of the visitor from other parts of the United States. But this is what gives the city its peculiar quality. You can take a trip abroad without ever leaving the three-hundred-odd square miles of the metropolis."[15] Institutional and commercial forces in New York embraced a sense of internationalism, though one that was carefully targeted to specific groups of people. For example, the "sort-of-success" that Rockefeller Center's La Maison Française and British Empire Building had with attracting European businesses as tenants influenced the construction of the International Building, which aimed to draw in "international trading firms."[16] A similar mixture of an international outlook mingled with commercial interests shaped the planning of the World's Fair. Reflecting this outward-looking quality, most of the key figures in New York's animation culture at this time had arrived from Europe and other parts of the United States, drawn to the city's cultural and commercial opportunities.

Manhattan was a beacon for entertainment and culture, with the *WPA Guide to New York City* reporting that in the late 1930s, there were "40 to 50 legitimate theaters," "73 art galleries," "29 museums" and "218 motion-picture houses."[17] In these cinemas, New Yorkers and tourists would have had the chance to choose from an array of Hollywood productions, from prestige pictures and star vehicles to genre films such as the musical and the Western. As Susan Ohmer writes, "In popular memory, 1939 stands as a banner year in Hollywood. The last year of the decade marked the release of such enduring films as *Gone with the Wind*, *The Wizard of Oz*, *Stagecoach*, *Young Mr. Lincoln*, and *Ninotchka*. The year is so celebrated that the U.S. post office has issued a series of commemorative stamps to recognize its importance."[18] Although Hollywood was producing artistically and commercially successful films, the industry was also facing significant challenges: "Financially, however, the year was anything but stellar, and 1940 was even worse. Antitrust investigations in Washington, a sharp drop in domestic box office receipts, and the loss of foreign markets due to the war in Europe all combined to put financial pressure on the studios."

Within New York, there were burgeoning alternatives to Hollywood's dominance. *New York Panorama*, a guidebook produced by the Federal Writers' Project, noted that "The comparatively discriminating tastes of New York fans have led to a marginal revolt against Hollywood on the adjacent fronts of exhibition and production."[19] Experimental and documentary films were having an impact, and New York was also a "mecca of the serious film student" with institutions such as the New York Public Library and the Museum of Modern Art offering educational resources for the study of cinema (288). In addition to the raft of Hollywood productions being shown in cinemas, foreign films such as *The Cabinet of Dr. Caligari* (1920) and *Battleship Potemkin* (1925) were being screened in venues associated with "the little cinema movement," which also provided a place where "esthetes rediscovered Charlie Chaplin, canonized Krazy Kat and well-nigh deified Mickey Mouse" (287).

In the wider context of mainstream cinema, animated films were thriving in popular appeal and critical estimation. Outside of the few feature-length animated films produced during this time, animated films were almost exclusively shown as supporting acts on film programs that included features and newsreels. Animated films exhibited in this manner were sold to exhibitors as part of packages set up by the major studios. Referring to an article about the state of the animated film industry in 1938, written by Bosley Crowther for the *New York Times*, Ohmer describes how "Each major served as exclusive distributor for one cartoon producer's output, and these films both enhanced the distributor's prestige with exhibitors and gained attention for its live-action releases."[20] Elaborating on the scale of production for animated films, Crowther explained that although Disney was the most well-known studio, "at least five other studios are regularly turning out as many, if not more, releases per year as the Disney organization."[21] Among these releases, Popeye and Betty Boop were being produced by the Fleischer brothers for Paramount, Porky Pig and Bugs Bunny were appearing in Leon Schlesinger's Merrie Melodies and Looney Tunes series for Warner Bros., and other studios including Universal, MGM and Columbia were producing a steady stream of animated shorts. Summing up the industry, Crowther writes "In all (and in short), somewhere between 175 and 200 animated cartoons are produced in the business in a year, and there is hardly a theater in the country which doesn't carry at least one on every bill. Contrary to reasonable supposition, this type of subject is quite as popular with grown-ups as it is with kids."

In this period, animation studios were facing financial pressures like the major Hollywood studios, with the added problems of labor disputes and uncertain distribution deals.[22] Nevertheless, there had been some astonishing successes. In particular, *Snow White*'s enormous popular and critical appeal had reverberated throughout the industry, with Crowther noting that that the "film industry" was now "regarding the lowly animated cartoon not only as a medium possessing vast artistic potentialities but (much more important!) as a mine of comparatively lightly worked ore."[23] The marvelous studio-produced animated films were part of a particularly vibrant period in the history of animated film, contributing to a cultural sensibility that valued animation's commercial and artistic possibilities. However, New York's most prominent animations often existed outside of the cinema, tied in with the life of the city in shop windows, billboards, exhibits and galleries. And even within the space of the cinema, animated films were going beyond their role as supporting elements within a film program—they were being exhibited as features and main attractions, becoming entwined with new exhibition practices. The liveliness of New York's animation culture drew upon the growing stature of animated film and animation beyond the cinema, further buttressed by New York's economic and retail power, its internationalism and its prominence in entertainment and culture.

THEMES OF ANIMATION

There was not a unified vision underlying the ideas and forms of animation that were circulating in New York at this time. Instead, a set of recurring and often interconnected themes were central to New York's animation culture: animation's capacity to transform existing media and arts by investing them with motion; explorations of the aesthetic potentials of movement; and attempts to understand "the inherent value of Motion" for different artistic and cultural contexts.[24] While these three themes are explored throughout the book, I want to first offer a brief outline of some of the ways they were taken up in New York's animation culture.

The first theme of how animation was used to transform arts and media was evident through the work of filmmakers, artists, designers and educators who experimented with the effects of animating static forms such as paintings, sculptures, displays and objects. This became a source of creative inspiration across different cultural fields, with articles and commentaries in the popular press marveling at the new arts and media that were being generated by animated motion. Gallery directors, shop owners and exhibitors joined the chorus that was celebrating motion; they began to encourage the creation of new kinds of animation. Partly because these activities of animation crossed between cultural fields, there was also a sense that animation was entwining different artistic and media forms. For example, as Chapter 2 explores, new technologies could create visual spectacles of animated advertising that combined aspects of cinema, theater, television and radio. These effects of animation were intermedial, a term which refers to "those phenomena that (as indicated by the prefix *inter*) in some way take place *between* media."[25] Intermediality could be generated by the disruptive or transformative potentials of animation, breaking down borders between established media or creating hybrid forms.

One example of motion's transformative power in this period was discussed in *Vogue*, which recounted Salvador Dalí's prophecy of "the first mobile jewels for evening – jewels that breathe, that become convulsed, that creep like ancient lizards; that are scintillating, terribly sensual, and swollen with sleep."[26] In order to achieve these wondrous effects, Dalí described how the jewels "will be fitted with an adequate mechanism" and "wound up like a watch." The article included an editor's note and annotations to Dalí's sketches in an apparent effort to help clear up any confusion caused by his "Delphic language," but some readers remained understandably suspicious of the whole idea. Geoffrey T. Hellman, writing in the *New Yorker*, noted that his "first instinct was to dismiss the entire article as part of the surrealist movement and as having no bearing on life," but "after seeing the Editor's Note... I began to suspect that *Vogue* really *means* that jewels ought to wriggle."[27] While this was both an extension of Surrealism's long-standing interest in animism and Dalí's engagement with commercial art in New York at this time—which included designing both a department store window and the "Dream of Venus" exhibit at the World's Fair—the prophecy was also an example of a wider interest in animation's transformative possibilities.[28] Dalí described the impact of motion, writing in all capital letters: "Mobile jewels will be to immobile jewels just what talkies are to the silent cinema."[29] Like the ruptures and changes caused by the introduction of sound in cinema, introducing movement to pieces of jewelry could significantly alter their identity. Although these mobile jewels were more imaginary than real, many other objects and forms were actually being transformed through motion.

The second theme noted earlier, regarding the exploration of animation's distinctive aesthetic and expressive potentials, was similarly vital to New York's animation culture. Different uses of animation—beyond its established associations with storytelling, humor or fantasy—were being explored. Giving animated life to non-human "characters," from cartoon animals to geometric shapes to industrial machinery, was one key effect of animation aesthetics, used to create dramatic expression with objects and things performing as if they were actors. More subtle effects of animation were also being developed and discussed. This included relationships between animation and other arts; for example, the temporal unfolding of music or the composition of paintings could provide models for animators to follow. Animation's capacity to show mutability was explored as well, from the metamorphosis of figures to fluid changes in color to visions of the dynamic flux of modernity. This scope of animation aesthetics had been developing over the course of decades, and New York witnessed a vivid extension of the manifold uses of animation aesthetics both on and beyond the cinema screen.

At the root of all this, there was, of course, animation itself. The third theme—how animation was understood at the time—was extraordinarily diverse. Offering an array of different effects and values, animation could accentuate entertainment or spectacle, it could be used as a tool for instruction or demonstration, or it could become a form of artistic or spiritually uplifting expression. No single principle underpinned these uses of animation. This may be partly due to the range of animation's applications that come to light by focusing on a specific milieu rather than the more cohesive framework of a particular animator or production company. But animation's diversity also has to do with the multifaceted quality of motion itself: animation can be animistic or automated, free-flowing or carefully composed, dramatic or mathematical, realistic or spectacular. The ways that these and other qualities could be found within animation—or even combined together—became a topic of considerable intellectual, creative and cultural interest. The conversations that circulated around animation were rich and varied; mainstream newspapers and magazines joined theoreticians and artists in discussions of animation's possibilities. Moreover, the wide-ranging uses of the term "animation" to characterize different kinds of moving images—sometimes in surprising ways—indicate the extent to which an idea of animation could appear in seemingly unlikely places.

Expanded and Micro Histories

Among those who were making animated films in New York, there was a burgeoning sense that new possibilities for animation were emerging. Mary Ellen Bute, whose work will be explored in more detail in Chapter 4, was an exemplary artist in this regard. Working with the cinematographer and producer Ted Nemeth in New York, she had established Expanding Cinema, "a production company doing research, experimental and creative work in cinematography."[30] In articles, interviews and publicity, Bute would highlight how her animated films—which she began producing in 1934—synchronized motion with light, sound and form to create an expanding sense of cinema's potentials. Bute's early films had been shown in different kinds of exhibition venues, including Radio City Music Hall and New York University's School of Architecture. Seeking further avenues to show (and support) her work, she engaged with New York's multifaceted culture of animation, approaching the Solomon R. Guggenheim Foundation in 1937, writing to the director of the motion picture division of the New York World's Fair in 1938 and meeting with the director of programming for CBS television in 1940.[31] While these various approaches were largely dead ends, it is telling that the possible sites for supporting or exhibiting her films were all engaged in novel ventures themselves: in 1939, the Guggenheim Foundation would open a new gallery in midtown Manhattan, the World's Fair would open its gates, and the CBS television station would begin broadcasting from the Chrysler Building. While "Expanding Cinema" referred to Bute's approach to film aesthetics, it also resonated with an expanding place for animation within a changing visual culture.

Animation continues to be expansive. Digitally animated films have been enormously successful in the last few decades, regularly topping box office tallies and end of year "best film" lists. And digital animation is ubiquitous in mainstream cinema, with computer-generated imagery creating spectacular effects for the most popular contemporary films. Beyond cinema, digital animation plays a major role in the wider context of contemporary visual culture, including video games, phone screens, television advertisements and scientific visualizations. Animation is, as Suzanne Buchan writes, "pervasive in contemporary moving image culture."[32] This has led to novel forms and uses of animation which are, Buchan continues, "implemented in many ways in many disciplines and on multiple platforms... artists increasingly incorporate animation in installations and exhibitions, and it has myriad applications across a wide band of creative, scientific and professional practice and industrial implementation." While digital technologies have opened up new spaces and uses of animation, the expansive potentials of animated motion are not new. In the nineteenth century, moving image technologies were refiguring culture. Spectacles such as the moving panorama, optical devices such as the zoetrope and visual technologies such as cinema were just a few of the many instances where motion offered new ways of showing and seeing the world. One effect of this was that established notions of art became immersed in a vitalized landscape, as Lynda Nead explains: "By 1900 art was part of a highly developed commercial entertainment world, organised around the logic of motion. The movement machines that often originated as amusements and spectacles within mass culture could also move across into the art gallery, transforming what looking at art meant and the concept of an aesthetic experience."[33] The impact of animation at different times indicates its adaptability in different contexts and its capacity to alter established media.

The early twentieth century and the contemporary moment are just two of many historical periods in which animation plays a significant role. While more limited in scale, animation had a similarly powerful impact in New York from 1939 to 1940. Focusing on this site of animation, I draw on the methods and implications of microhistory, a genre of history writing that foregrounds specific cultural events or formations as a way of drawing out their distinctive qualities and complexities. David A. Bell explains that one of microhistory's most important contributions is to "put the problem of scale itself at the heart of the historical enterprise, making historians aware that they cannot take their organizing frameworks for granted but need to adjust their scale of observation to the problem at hand."[34] In order to understand the multiple factors at play in an animation culture, a limited historical scope is often necessary. Of course, an animation culture does not exist in a bubble, and throughout this book I discuss other facets of animation's history. Rigidly adhering to the limits of a single place in a brief historical period can distort our understanding, and this is something that I take into account in my aim to balance specificity with a wider perspective. That said, by concentrating on a specific cultural environment, I hope to illuminate the diverse potentials of animation that can be found within a seemingly narrow purview.

A limited scope allows for a greater attention to examples and implications that might escape notice in a more expansive history. John Brewer uses the trope of "refuge history" to explain this key aim of microhistory:

refuge history is close-up and on the small scale. Its emphasis is on a singular place rather than space, the careful delineation of particularities and details, a degree of enclosure. It depends upon the recognition that our understanding of what is seen depends on the incorporation of many points of view rather than the use of a single dominant perspective.[35]

My examination of New York's animation culture offers a similarly sustained view on details and multiple perspectives. Paying close attention to a specific place and time also brings to light the productive possibilities that are created by what Brewer describes as "dynamic interconnections" (97). While Brewer is referring mainly to the interconnections between people, New York's animation culture was largely shaped by the interconnections between ideas, forms, places and creative practices. Rather than approaching this animation culture as something carefully planned, like a cultivated landscape, I approach it from the ground up—as a place of generative interactions and unpredictable liveliness. Instead of drawing sharp distinctions between different kinds of animation, such as art and advertising or displays and films, I explore how certain practices, ideas and values spanned this animation culture, generating a hive of activity that connected separate spheres—from corporate exhibits to abstract art—through a shared fascination with animation. My emphasis on these interconnections illustrates how animation is open to different formations and able to fluidly cross between different contexts. Rather than notions of a single identity or place for animation, this microhistory shows how animation's unfixed identity was productive for those who were developing, investigating and championing its potentials.

My emphasis on animation culture and my use of microhistory address the distinctive ways that animation history has unfolded. Esther Leslie writes,

> Animation is too obviously manifold to set out upon a single line of development. It begins with shadow play or with thumb cinemas, with zoetropes or magic lanterns, with lightning sketches or cel animation, with hidden wheels and pulleys or with stop-motion photography. It starts and stops in many places. It is at one and the same time a beginning and a culmination.[36]

Drawing on Leslie's insight, we can see that the significance of a moment in animation's history need not be absorbed by a large-scale or all-encompassing historical trajectory. Often, the most important or intriguing aspects of animation history are seemingly marginal practices. Rather than insignificant detours in a grand tour of animation, such practices can widen our understanding of animation's possibilities or reveal underlying aesthetic potentials of motion. Setting aside wider perspectives—such as the dominance of a particular studio—can help reveal the dynamic variety that operates in the substratum of animation history.

Microhistory can also provide a productive alternative to historical narratives that privilege large-scale trends. Brad S. Gregory writes that this mode of historical writing can "suggest that developments such as industrialization and bureaucratization should be rethought as contingent and uneven."[37] By focusing on "human interaction on the micro-scale," microhistory "suggests hope for an undetermined future insofar as it finds contingency in the past." This important value of microhistory informs my focus on the period between 1939 and 1940. By selecting these two years as the focal point of this book, I purposefully avoid other historical frameworks. For example, America's entry into the Second World War would be one logical end point if my emphasis were the relation between animation culture and American history. Similarly, if my concerns were focused on major trends in the production of animated films, the timeframe could begin with the release of *Snow White and the Seven Dwarfs* in 1937 and end with the Disney strike in 1941. While facets of American sociocultural history and the animation industry inform the discussion that follows, I do not approach these contexts as determining factors in New York's animation culture. Instead, I trace diverse forms of animation taken from a range of cultural fields, often with seemingly quite different interests and concerns. It is no coincidence, though, that these years coincide with the two seasons of the New York World's Fair. Not only did the Fair exhibit a staggering array of animation, it was also a major event within New York. As such, it offers a particularly useful timeframe, taken from the life of the city itself, from which to begin to explore New York's wider animation culture.

In order to illuminate the multifaceted scope of this animation culture, I investigate four central sites of animation: the city, the fair, the gallery and the cinema. Each site adapted animation to its own set of concerns and values. And, as we shall see, these concerns and values also crossed between places, establishing the larger network of animation culture in New York. I begin with a chapter, "The City," which explores how a wave of animated activity was creating vivid forms of dramatic and artistic advertising in two of the most prominent areas of New York's commercial culture: the shopping district on Fifth Avenue and the entertainment district around Times Square and Broadway. In these locations, advertising designers were embracing a new art of motion display, situating animation within the fabric of metropolitan life and exploring the impact of animated advertising. From debates over the acceptable use of motion in Fifth Avenue shop windows to publicity which heralded the intermedial qualities of animated billboards in Times Square, animated advertisements and displays became a major topic of creative and cultural interest.

Turning from the second chapter's focus on advertising and animation, the third chapter, "The Fair," examines the relationship between design and animation. New techniques of mechanized motion and automated display were astonishing spectators in animated exhibits at the New York World's Fair, from a massive diorama that depicted New York City in action to animated murals and sculptures created by major contemporary artists. Such exhibits engaged with the broader aims of the Fair, which celebrated industry, technology, progress and dynamism. The two most popular exhibits, designed by Teague for Ford and Bel Geddes for General Motors, exemplified the turn toward motion as an exhibition technique—using intricate and complex devices to create animated spectacles of labor and transportation, their exhibits seized on animation to visualize a modern age of movement. Developing their interests in how design could incorporate a sense of motion, from streamlined products to dynamic architecture, exhibits offered an opportunity to expand their creative practice into new animated contexts. Situating Teague's and Bel Geddes's exhibits alongside other animated exhibits at the Fair, this chapter explores how animation became a vital means for imaginatively promoting and designing the "World of Tomorrow."

A much different approach to the potentials of animation was evident in the art institutions of New York's animation culture. Animation and other arts of motion were appearing in New York galleries in the late 1930s, with the recently founded Museum of Non-Objective Painting screening and collecting abstract animated films. The fourth chapter, "The Gallery," explores how animators in New York who were working outside of narrative and commercial filmmaking—including Norman McLaren, Dwinell Grant and Mary Ellen Bute—engaged with this institutional context for animated art. Many of the films that they produced at this time, including *Scherzo* (1939), *Spook Sport* (1940) and *Themis* (1940), were funded or exhibited by the director of the Museum, Hilla Rebay, who saw them as relating to her vision of non-objective art. This kind of institutional backing allowed animation to take on an unprecedented artistic value in New York's animation culture. At the same time, these animators also resisted or diverged from established artistic contexts, aiming to develop new arts of motion. This chapter explores the shared concerns among these animators—in their creative practice and their theoretical writings—regarding the relationship between animation and other artistic forms, the aesthetic potentials of animated motion and animation's ability to offer new expressions and sensations that were distinct from existing arts.

Shortly after the premiere of *Snow White and the Seven Dwarfs*, three animated feature films—*Gulliver's Travels*, *Pinocchio* and *Fantasia*—were released between 1939 and 1940. After decades of being almost exclusively a supporting act, animated films were suddenly becoming the main attraction in film programs. The fifth chapter, "The Cinema," explores how this new place for animated film resonated with changing approaches to the status of animated film and its place in culture. Coinciding with their expanding place in cinemas, these films were marketed and exhibited in ways that expanded their place in culture. From gallery exhibitions of animated cels to window displays and museum exhibits, *Pinocchio* was situated in diverse sites within New York and presented as a work of art that entwined different media. *Fantasia* further developed this aim of expanding animation, with its exhibition linking it to the experience of attending a symphony concert through the development of new technologies of cinematic sound that first appeared in New York. Similar attempts to develop new paths for animated film were also appearing at the World's Fair, with promotional animated films using innovative technologies, forms and exhibition practices. Across the city and the Fair, animated film was transforming the cinematic experience.

Notes

1. *Display Animation, 1938: The Year Book of Motion Displays*, ed. I. L. Cochrane (New York: Reeder-Morton Publications, 1938), 7.
2. "Ford's Titanic Animation," *Display*, August 1939, 229.
3. Malte Hagener, "Institutions of Film Culture: Festivals and Archives as Network Nodes," in *The Emergence of Film Culture: Knowledge Production, Institution Building and the Fate of the Avant-Garde in Europe, 1919–1945*, ed. Malte Hagener (New York: Berghahn, 2014), 283. See also Hagener's introduction, 1–17.
4. Roger Chartier, "General Introduction: Print Culture," in *The Culture of Print: Power and the Uses of Print in Early Modern Europe*, ed. Roger Chartier, trans. Lydia G. Cochrane (Cambridge: Polity Press, 1989), 1.
5. Roger Chartier, "General Introduction: Print Culture," 2.
6. Michael Cowan, "Taking It to the Street: Screening the Advertising Film in the Weimar Republic," *Screen* 54, no. 1 (December 2013): 463–479.
7. "New York Is Not America," *Department Store Buyer*, February 1940, 23.
8. See George W. Seaton, *Cue's Guide to New York City* (New York: Prentice-Hall, 1940).
9. *New York Panorama* (New York: Random House, 1938), 373.

10. Robert P. Ingalls, *Herbert H. Lehman and New York's Little Deal* (New York: New York University, 1975), 35.
11. *New York Panorama*, 370.
12. *The WPA Guide to New York City* (1939; repr., New York: Pantheon Books, 1982), 333.
13. *New York Panorama*, 230.
14. Terry Smith, *Making the Modern: Industry, Art, and Design in America* (Chicago: University of Chicago Press, 1993), 409.
15. Seaton, *Cue's Guide to New York City*, 2.
16. Daniel Okrent, *Great Fortune: The Epic of Rockefeller Center* (New York: Penguin, 2003), 278.
17. *WPA Guide to New York City*, 53.
18. Susan Ohmer, *George Gallup in Hollywood* (New York: Columbia University Press, 2006), 92.
19. *New York Panorama*, 287.
20. Ohmer, *George Gallup in Hollywood*, 194.
21. Bosley Crowther, "Cartoons on the Screen; A Momentary Consideration of Who Makes Them, How Many and Why," *New York Times*, February 13, 1938.
22. For an account of the animation studios during this period, see Michael Barrier, *Hollywood Cartoons: American Animation in Its Golden Age* (Oxford: Oxford University Press, 1999).
23. Crowther, "Cartoons on the Screen."
24. *Display Animation, 1937: The Year Book of Motion Displays*, ed. I. L. Cochrane (New York: Reeder-Morton Publications, 1937), 8.
25. Irina O. Rajewsky, "Intermediality, Intertextuality, and Remediation: A Literary Perspective on Intermediality," *Intermédialités*, no. 6 (Autumn 2005): 46.
26. "Dali Prophesies 'Mobile' Jewels," *Vogue*, January 1, 1939, 88.
27. Geoffrey T. Hellman, "Oh, Where Is My Wandering Brooch Tonight," *New Yorker*, July 1, 1939, 34–36.
28. Dali's activities in New York were widely reported in the popular press at this time. For an account of these activities, see Lewis Kachur, *Displaying the Marvelous* (MIT Press: Cambridge, 2001), 104–163.
29. "Dali Prophesies 'Mobile' Jewels," 88.
30. Mary Ellen Bute to Solomon R. Guggenheim, August 9, 1937, box 3048, folder 14, Hilla Rebay Records, A0010, Series 2, Administration, Guggenheim Archives.
31. Bute to Guggenheim; Mary Ellen Bute to Claude Collins, June 8, 1938, box 1980, folder 1, New York World's Fair 1939 and 1940 Incorporated Records, VIII.B.5 Motion Pictures, General Correspondence, New York Public Library; Norman McLaren to his parents, November 6, 1940, folder 1, Norman McLaren Archive, Correspondence, Archives and Special Collections, University of Stirling.

32. Suzanne Buchan, "Introduction: Pervasive Animation," in *Pervasive Animation*, ed. Suzanne Buchan (New York: Routledge, 2013), 2.
33. Lynda Nead, *The Haunted Gallery: Painting, Photography, Film c. 1900* (New Haven: Yale University Press, 2007), 17.
34. David A. Bell, "Total History and Microhistory: The French and Italian Paradigms," in *A Companion to Western Historical Thought*, eds. Lloyd Kramer and Sarah Maza (Blackwell: Malden, MA, 2002), 274.
35. John Brewer, "Microhistory and the Histories of Everyday Life," *Cultural and Social History* 7, no. 1 (2010): 89.
36. Esther Leslie, "Animation and History," in *Animating Film Theory*, ed. Karen Beckman (Durham: Duke University Press, 2014), 26.
37. David S. Gregory, "Is Small Beautiful? Microhistory and the History of Everyday Life," *History and Theory* 38, no. 1 (February 1999): 101.

REFERENCES

Barrier, Michael. *Hollywood Cartoons: American Animation in Its Golden Age.* Oxford: Oxford University Press, 1999.

Bell, David A. "Total History and Microhistory: The French and Italian Paradigms." In *A Companion to Western Historical Thought*, edited by Lloyd Kramer and Sarah Maza. Blackwell: Malden, MA, 2002.

Brewer, John. "Microhistory and the Histories of Everyday Life." *Cultural and Social History* 7, no. 1 (2010): 87–109.

Buchan, Suzanne. "Introduction: Pervasive Animation." In *Pervasive Animation*, edited by Suzanne Buchan, 1–21. New York: Routledge, 2013.

Chartier, Roger. "General Introduction: Print Culture." In *The Culture of Print: Power and the Uses of Print in Early Modern Europe*, edited by Roger Chartier, translated by Lydia G. Cochrane, 1–10. Cambridge: Polity Press, 1989.

Cochrane, I. L., ed. *Display Animation, 1937: The Year Book of Motion Displays.* New York: Reeder-Morton Publications, 1937.

Cochrane, I. L., ed. *Display Animation, 1938: The Year Book of Motion Displays.* New York: Reeder-Morton Publications, 1938.

Cowan, Michael. "Taking it to the Street: Screening the Advertising Film in the Weimar Republic." *Screen* 54, no. 1 (December 2013): 463–479.

Crowther, Bosley. "Cartoons on the Screen; A Momentary Consideration of Who Makes Them, How Many and Why." *New York Times*, February 13, 1938.

"Dali Prophesies 'Mobile' Jewels," *Vogue*, January 1, 1939.

"Ford's Titanic Animation." *Display*, August 1939.

Gregory, David S. "Is Small Beautiful? Microhistory and the History of Everyday Life." *History and Theory* 38, no. 1 (February 1999): 100–110.

Hagener, Malte. "Institutions of Film Culture: Festivals and Archives as Network Nodes." In *The Emergence of Film Culture: Knowledge Production, Institution*

Building and the Fate of the Avant-Garde in Europe, 1919–1945, edited by Malte Hagener, 283–305. New York: Berghahn, 2014.

Hellman, Geoffrey T. "Oh, Where Is My Wandering Brooch Tonight." *New Yorker*, July 1, 1939.

Ingalls, Robert P. *Herbert H. Lehman and New York's Little Deal.* New York: New York University, 1975.

Kachur, Lewis. *Displaying the Marvelous*. MIT Press: Cambridge, 2001.

Leslie, Esther. "Animation and History." In *Animating Film Theory*, edited by Karen Beckman, 25–36. Durham: Duke University Press, 2014.

McLaren, Norman. Archives. University of Stirling.

Nead, Lynda. *The Haunted Gallery: Painting, Photography, Film c. 1900*. New Haven: Yale University Press, 2007.

"New York Is Not America." *Department Store Buyer*, February 1940.

New York Panorama. New York: Random House, 1938.

New York World's Fair 1939 and 1940 Incorporated Records, New York Public Library.

Ohmer, Susan. *George Gallup in Hollywood*. New York: Columbia University Press, 2006.

Okrent, Daniel. *Great Fortune: The Epic of Rockefeller Center*. New York: Penguin, 2003.

Rajewsky, Irina O. "Intermediality, Intertextuality, and Remediation: A Literary Perspective on Intermediality." *Intermédialités*, no. 6 (Autumn 2005): 43–64.

Rebay, Hilla. Records. Guggenheim Archives, New York.

Seaton, George W. *Cue's Guide to New York City*. New York: Prentice-Hall, 1940.

Smith, Terry. *Making the Modern: Industry, Art, and Design in America*. Chicago: University of Chicago Press, 1993.

The WPA Guide to New York City. New York: Pantheon Books, 1982. First published in 1939.

CHAPTER 2

The City

A few weeks before Easter, in 1937, Lower Manhattan's Trinity Church unveiled a diorama of Jesus praying in the Garden of Gethsemane. "A few Wall Street clerks and runners, several loafers, a handful of worshipers and some Roman Catholic nuns dropped in at odd times" to watch the astonishing scene: "Every four and one-half minutes the lights slowly dimmed and the haloed plaster head of Jesus raised slowly heavenward."[1] So unexpected was the motion of Jesus's head, one spectator reportedly fainted at the sight. According to the article in *Time* magazine that described this event, this was the first "animated diorama made of a religious subject," and while mechanized motion may have been unique in this context, it was rapidly gaining prominence in exhibitions, displays and advertising. Edward Heckler Burdick, the president of the company which had constructed this model, described how the "modern diorama" which presented a miniature three-dimensional scene was typically "animated and enhanced by lighting and sound effects," becoming a vivid new form of display.[2] The diorama was just one of many types of display that were being animated in the late 1930s; motion increasingly began to take center stage in department store windows, counter displays, outdoor signs and exhibition stands. Although these animations may have lacked the miraculous quality of Jesus raising his head, they offered other kinds of wonders for modern commercialism and exhibition.

© The Author(s) 2019
K. Moen, *New York's Animation Culture*, Palgrave Animation,
https://doi.org/10.1007/978-3-030-27931-8_2

Trade advertisements heralded a new field of "motion display," with companies describing how they could set up "Dependable, foolproof animation from the smallest mechanical motion to the largest exhibition machine."[3] New devices like the Stevenson Animotor, which could create multiple mechanical motions in a single display, entered the market.[4] And new ways of dramatizing sales messages through animation began to appear, such as a Dupont display which presented "two synthetic gentlemen" who "move their heads and arms and carry on a dialogue in praise of cellophane."[5] A whole industry was emerging around this flurry of motion, drawing upon the expertise of those working in many different fields, with display managers, artists, architects, lighting consultants, carpenters and engineers working together to create increasingly elaborate animated displays.

A series of *Display Animation* yearbooks, published between 1936 and 1939, cataloged this burgeoning industry of motion display. Their editor I. L. Cochrane, who also wrote the more technical *Motion Display Mechanics* (1939), documented a vast range of examples of how animation could be used in advertising and exhibition. Introducing the first of his yearbooks, Cochrane described the challenge of encapsulating the field of motion display: "There are no guiding precedents, no beacon lights beyond a few scattered articles in merchandizing and popular mechanic periodicals. Display Animation boasts no real trade literature, and the reason is simply that Animation as a scientific industry is so very new."[6] Cochrane offered several reasons for the rapid rise of animated displays, including the influence of Chicago's Century of Progress Exposition which ran from 1933 to 1934, technological developments that allowed for cheaper and more efficient animation, and a changing sensibility in which "display designers are becoming more Motion minded" and "getting away from the inhibition that static art comprises the one and only tool of the exhibition window and store decorator."[7] The new potentials that animation offered were taken up by display designers in many different ways. Cochrane's effort to catalog and explain this growing world of motion was an attempt to make sense of this diversity.

Rather than seeing animation as a passing trend in advertising or just another element for designers to exploit, Cochrane wrote that a new medium and form of art was coming into being: "The dramatization of merchandising displays, through the media of mechanical and light actions, is a relatively new art which has grown to its present maturity in less than a decade."[8] Others saw the rise of animated displays in a similar light. For example, observing the sudden surge of animation in the United States at the time, a British commentator wrote that "America's latest publicity theme is no ephemeral fashion, but a new medium which has come to stay."[9] Scholars of media formation point to several interrelated components that generate a sense of media identity: a technology or material that opens up the potential for new creative and expressive practices; a cultural recognition of a new medium that offers something different from existing media; and frameworks, institutions and discourses that begin to shape how a new medium might be used and understood.[10] These features of media formation were all developing around animated advertising in New York at the time, creating a motion-minded hub of creative and commercial activity.

During the late 1930s and early 1940s, the introduction of animated shop windows on Fifth Avenue and new animation technologies on Broadway signs had raised the profile of animated advertising to unprecedented levels. In these central sites of New York's commercial culture—the retail district in midtown Manhattan and the entertainment district around Times Square—innovative designers were embracing the new art of motion display, situating animation within the fabric of metropolitan life. The relation between motion display and existing advertising media became a topic of considerable interest for designers, advertisers and the popular press. This led to considerations of how animation could create vivid forms of dramatic and artistic expression that went beyond simply eye-catching appeal. Animation was seen to have a potentially transformative impact, creating new media of motion. Exploring how such ideas were circulating in New York, this chapter traces the multifaceted ways that animated advertising was being used, valued and reimagined on the streets of Manhattan.

Fifth Avenue's Animated Shop Windows

On November 29, 1937, the department store Lord & Taylor unveiled its latest shop windows. Each of the large windows facing Fifth Avenue displayed huge golden bells swinging back and forth, accompanied by the softly playing sound of chimes coming from inside the building. The windows were starkly lit and the moving bells cast shadows on the walls behind them, and underneath—in the bottom of each case—pedestrians could peer at the miniaturized depiction of a wintry landscape (Fig. 2.1). The windows were an extraordinary success: crowds gawked at them, the Galeries Lafayette in Paris copied them, and customers were enticed into the store.[11]

Fig. 2.1 Lord & Taylor's animated shop window. *Display Animation, 1938: The Year Book of Motion Displays*, 25

While shop windows for the large department stores on Fifth Avenue would typically be changed at least once a week, the bells kept tolling at Lord & Taylor well into December—advertisements in New York newspapers announced that there had been "thousands of requests" for them to be held over.[12]

Not showing any merchandise at all, the shop windows offered a kind of prestige display that stood apart from overt commercialism. By emphasizing elegance and seasonal qualities associated with the department store at Christmastime, the windows drew upon contemporary trends to "sell the store as well as the merchandise."[13] Their simple design and stark illumination also resonated with a modern artistic emphasis in window displays that had been developing over the course of the previous decade. Writing in 1932, Norman Bel Geddes described how he had "inaugurated the modern and simplified and abstract trend in window display in this country" at another Fifth Avenue store, Franklin Simon, when he used display windows as "a stage on which the merchandise is presented as the actors."[14] By doing so, Bel Geddes created dramatic emphases through the careful deployment of color, lighting and design strategies. Partly motivated by the success of innovators such as Bel Geddes, display departments at the most lavish Fifth Avenue department stores entwined their commercial interests with artistic and dramatic allures.

At the same time, the promotional budget spent on display windows was rapidly increasing, second only to newspaper advertising for department store publicity.[15] Merchants were realizing that it was imperative to use visually striking and elaborate displays in order to draw the attention of the "80,000 daily pedestrians" who would walk along Fifth Avenue; *Time* magazine described how the "Avenue Art" on show "has been conceived as such for only about a dozen years. It stems from a conception of fine art as the handmaiden of Industry, first popularized by the Paris Exposition of 1925. Its professionals are now at work in all the big cities of the U.S., but its greatest expenditure of money and ingenuity is on a mile-long stretch of Manhattan's luxury shopping street."[16] The attention lavished on the display windows had raised their profile as a distinctive New York attraction. The "window drama" of Fifth Avenue was seen "as a legitimate part of the Manhattan entertainment field" with the premieres of windows being reviewed "as seriously as the Broadway productions."[17] Fifth Avenue was also likened to "a huge, outdoor art museum"; its shop windows reproduced works of art in their displays, tying in with museum exhibitions and employing major artists such as Salvador Dalí as display designers.[18] Whether seen as a theatrical space or a gallery, as a district akin to Broadway or more like the Metropolitan Museum of Art, Fifth Avenue was "a continuous pageant" that presented "a series of 'still' pictures as typical of New York as Radio City or the Empire State Building."[19]

With the appearance of the bells at Lord & Taylor, the shop windows of Fifth Avenue were no longer "still pictures." These were "animated windows" bringing motion to the avenue.[20] They were designed to emphasize the movement of the bells, with a lowered floor "allowing a longer and more graceful sweep for the white bell ropes" and a carefully considered use of lighting to create "delightful moving shadows."[21] Lord & Taylor followed this display of motion with another striking window that premiered on November 12, 1938. Reminding Fifth Avenue shoppers that they should be getting ready for winter, the department store filled its windows with a blizzard.[22] Hundreds of pounds of artificial snow swirled in the frosted windows, accompanied by wintry sound effects on a record player. Crowds lined up on the street to gaze at the display, and on its first day, there was reportedly a 50% increase in winter clothing sales.[23] Like the moving bells, which were fabricated from "gold-leaf papier-mâché" and set in motion by a machine, the blizzard was artificial—its snow was made from "cornflakes treated with acid" and its motion generated by an enormous mechanical blower.[24] Tom Lee, the window designer for Bonwit Teller, joined this chorus of movement, creating "animated window displays" in which illuminated fashion bulletins "similar to those which run around newspaper buildings" revolved around the bottom of several miniature Eiffel Towers.[25]

Both Lee and Dana O'Clare, who designed Lord & Taylor's windows, were central figures in what was described as an "artists' revolution in display."[26] Lee's windows were particularly lauded for their artistry—the New York City arts tour of the Work Projects Administration (WPA) reportedly began at the Bonwit Teller shop windows.[27] Lee and O'Clare had started their careers with an interest in designing for theater, and their shop windows elaborated on this background through striking displays of motion. Creating dramatic moving images of tolling bells, winter weather and Parisian fashion bulletins, they introduced motion display to Fifth Avenue shop windows.

Motion had been an element of shop windows elsewhere in New York, the United States and internationally for decades. In the 1910s, Leonard S. Marcus writes of how "mechanical props included not only cracker box clocks and revolving turntables, but also flashing lights and at least one mannequin that rolled its eyes."[28] Astonishing motion devices were also being used in France, with "the Galeries Lafayette's window displays of miraculous mechanized dolls" in 1938 drawing crowds "so great that the queues, barricades, and police lines have stretched as far back as the Rue de

Provence."[29] Perhaps with such extravagant displays and crowded streets in mind, the Fifth Avenue Association (FAA)—which represented store owners—was deeply concerned about motion appearing in shop windows on the avenue.

Since 1920, there had been a policy that Fifth Avenue shop windows could not use any kind of motion in their displays. Although the FAA had no legal authority, they played a major role in regulating the activities on Fifth Avenue. Max Page describes the early formation of this retailing body: "The central idea behind the FAA's advocacy was to retain an exclusive retail and residential area, where immigrants would be scarce and beggars absent, where the more flamboyant popular culture growing on Broadway would be held in check, and where a genteel, controlled commercial culture would hold sway."[30] As an extension of this vision, the Association reaffirmed their policy against any motion in shop windows in a meeting that took place on April 24, 1938. Fearing a sudden upsurge of animation—with another department store just that week using "motion in a special World's Fair preview window"—the FAA justified their stance against moving displays "on the grounds that it is not in the best interest of the Fifth avenue shopping district, and all they do is invariably attract a large crowd of idlers who have nothing better to do than gaze at moving things, such as building construction, excavating, etc."[31] Acknowledging the popular and critical success of the animated windows at both Lord & Taylor and Bonwit Teller, "It was pointed out by an official of the association this morning that although motion has been used in good taste on occasions, the association's special committee has agreed that exceptions cannot make for a steadfast rule that will be adhered to."

Lee was defiant. Perhaps with the success of his Eiffel Tower windows in mind, he argued, "If the association tries to enforce such a ruling, it will not be successful, because motion is such a dynamic, news-making selling force, that stores will prefer to disregard such an edict, rather than forego valuable display ideas."[32] Backing up Lee's defense of motion, *Women's Wear Daily* went on to note, "It can be pointed out that the two outstanding Fifth avenue windows mentioned which used motion belong in the selected list of 'all-time greats' among displays. Not only did the Lord & Taylor and the Bonwit 'shows' play to capacity audiences, but the stores attributed actual increases in business to them." The FAA would not budge. Responding directly to Lee, the general manager of the Association acknowledged the success and quality of certain displays using motion at higher class department stores, but insisted that motion would degrade the avenue.[33]

When the animated blizzard appeared in the windows of Lord & Taylor later that year, the FAA acted. Deeming this use of motion "unethical," they lodged a protest with Walter Hoving, the president of the department store.[34] They were clear about their rationale: "The policy of the association opposes the use of motion, moving objects, live models, mechanical devices or other similar contrivances in window displays and was instituted in 1920 to make Fifth avenue outstanding as the world center of good taste, fine quality and high distinction in commercial display."[35] The presence of motion was seen to coarsen the more elegant spectacles of Fifth Avenue, which was especially worrisome considering the masses of tourists that were expected to visit New York for the World's Fair. With a sense of decorum firmly in mind, the FAA also restated their regulation against any use of sound accompanying displays on Fifth Avenue, such as the tolling of the bells and the howling winds of the blizzard. Despite these edicts and aware of the enormous success of those that had broken the rules, Fifth Avenue stores were "in a fighting mood."[36] In a "wave of bell-mindedness," they filled their windows with a "medley of sound and motion" for the 1938 Christmas season, which included more than a dozen revolving displays. Franklin Simon defiantly showcased "changing colored lights" accompanied by organ music and the "famed big, swinging golden bells with chime accompaniment" returned to Lord & Taylor.[37]

This rapid and dizzying intrusion of motion on Fifth Avenue continued to be met with repeated criticism by those representing the FAA. Responding to their conservatism, New York newspapers and magazines took up the cause for animated windows. An article in *Women's Wear Daily* began with a quote from Tennyson, "Ring out, wild bells, to the wild sky," to make it clear on which side of the debate they stood.[38] Phyllis McGinley wrote a poem for the *New Yorker* about the subject. Entitled "Still Life," the poem bemoaned the "Stale, flat, unprofitable view" of the "lords of commerce" at the FAA.[39] Beginning with a quote from the regulation against motion, the poem goes on to playfully capture its deadening effect: "No pinwheel, rocket, colored flare./No festive blizzard snowing paper." Weaving together references to the windows that were appearing at the time on Fifth Avenue with references to more long-standing practices of eye-catching motion display, McGinley highlights the charm and appeal of such visual enticements. The poem ends with an invocation to leave Fifth Avenue behind and join the crowds watching the construction work that was going on at Rockefeller Center instead—at least there, something dynamic was on view.

The FAA feared that motion would transform the avenue and, in doing so, make it like other commercial districts of New York that used motion as an attraction. An early justification for the rule against motion spelled this concern out: "If the Fifth avenue merchant wants to let down the bars to this type of mechanical display, it can be anticipated that living models and other appurtenances characteristic of 'cheaper' streets will make their appearance..."[40] Motion was simply too undignified for the FAA, who worried that it would turn Fifth Avenue into a less refined environment like "Grand Street" in Lower Manhattan or even "the Coney Island midway."[41] As well as worrisome connections to commercialism, the presence of motion had linked shop windows with other forms of art and spectacle. While static shop windows were appreciated for their connections to theater and the visual arts, the presence of motion was disruptively intermedial. Elles M. Derby, the general manager of the FAA, offered a dire warning: "if the use of motion in window displays persists, it will spell the doom of Fifth avenue because it would lead to the widespread and uncontrolled use of motion, which would transform our renowned windows into theatrical sets rather than a valuable means of presenting merchandise."[42] Motion threatened the established identity of shop windows. The FAA's concerns indicate the impact that motion was thought to have at the time—its presence was seen as a threat that could radically change the well-established form of the shop window. For those stores and display designers who were intent on using animation in their shop windows, a new approach was needed to allow for motion on the avenue, an approach which could rein in motion's disorderly power.

Artistic Motion and Commercial Motion

While the Fifth Avenue Association was resisting animation on the avenue, animation was becoming increasingly commonplace in other retail spaces throughout the city. One of the most important reasons for this popularity was the visual attraction of motion. For example, the window display designer for the New York Telephone Company would painstakingly record the number of spectators at his displays; he found that the visual allure of color or an interesting design lacked the magnetic effect of motion: "Simply to disconnect the electric socket on almost any moving display will cut down the number of lookers by sixty, seventy, and eighty per cent."[43] The attraction of motion was frequently linked to peripheral vision's sensitivity to movement. The idea that this had an instinctual basis was a recurring refrain, explained by Cochrane in *Motion Display Mechanics*:

> When Guz and Alley Oop were the Moguls of Moo, dinosaur dodging had become a deep-rooted instinct of the human race. During previous millennia the fear of fleet-footed monsters had naturally developed an instinctive ability to sense the presence of anything moving at an angle of 90° on either side of the prehistoric nose. Scientists tell us that instinct still survives, and the greater number of people who see a motion display, but never glimpse one that has no motion, corroborates the scientists.[44]

As well as catching the attention of passersby, motion could also transfix them. This was evident in the comparison between animated shop windows and the construction of Rockefeller Center noted earlier; both spectacles of movement were seen to attract crowds who gathered to gawk at motion and activity.

The FAA was concerned that the visual attraction of motion would detract from the prestigious aura of the avenue and at the same time draw in spectators who would block the street. Others were much more eager to embrace the tremendous potential for motion displays to act as both an attractive and magnetic force. An article on shop windows in *Vendre*, a French advertising magazine, described how "modern animated windows" correspond "precisely to the ideal conditions of the shop window" as they "physically impress the retina of the passerby" and offer a "second phase of attraction" that holds their gaze and leads them into the store.[45] For each of his *Display Animation* yearbooks, Cochrane expressed this sense of motion's power in an epigraph drawn from Shakespeare's *Troilus and Cressida*: "Things in Motion sooner catch than what not stir."[46] Slightly misquoting the original—where "things in motion sooner catch *the eye*"— Cochrane suggests that motion has an almost physical effect, pulling in a spectator who will stand and gaze at an animated display.

Designers created elaborate animated effects to ensure that their displays would hold the attention of onlookers. For example, a "parade of animated toys in a Macy show-window stage" used "seventy-six different and separate motions."[47] François Martin, the co-designer of this display, explained its ambitious aims: "We wanted the window gazer to have more than a bold outline in vivid color; we wanted him to always find a new surprise, something he didn't see the first time. To achieve this we worked again for variety, we worked again for animation and tempo, different speeds and directions, trying always for smooth natural motion." Such intricate uses of motion could create visually interesting displays which required time to take in, with audiences absorbed by the fascinating variations and life-like qualities of animation. Other displays used motion to create similarly enthralling effects, such as mechanically mimicking the erratic hopping of a lamb (Fig. 2.2) or using new display materials to depict falling rain.[48] Changing colors and moving lights could offer further aesthetic potentials—"special illumination" was described as "a fundamental element in the art of Animated Display," able to "accentuate mechanical Motion or in itself cause the animation."[49]

For Cochrane, once a viewer is drawn to a display through the effective use of motion, the animation can express further meanings. He explained that "mere motion for itself is quite meaningless. The moving display element or elements must naturally tie up with and emphasise the selling thought."[50] This could be done "by attraction value only, as a means of drawing attention to merchandise and copy, or in the shape of an emotional

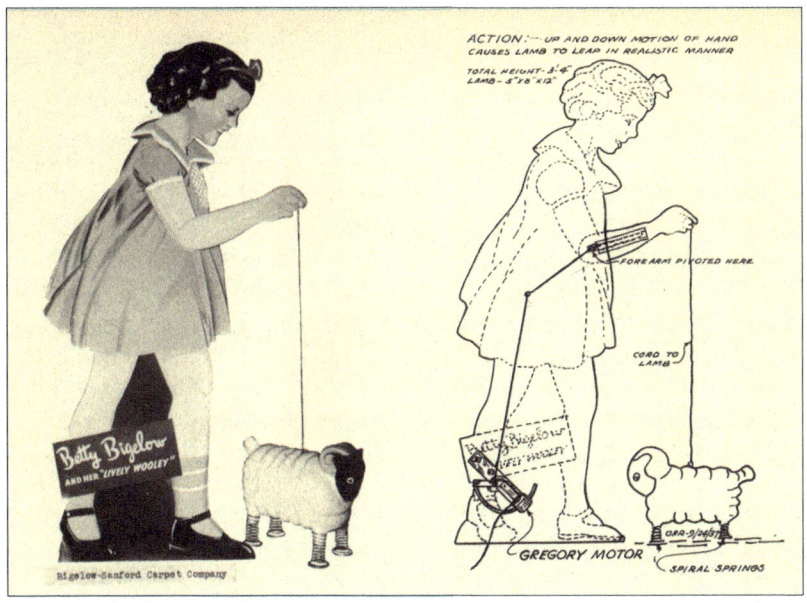

Fig. 2.2 Motion display for Bigelow-Sanford Carpet Company. *Display Animation, 1938: The Year Book of Motion Displays,* 171

human-interest appeal, a strongly dramatized sales message, or a demonstration of service value – a choice which depends upon the nature of the offering." These multifaceted possibilities of entwining motion with advertising relied upon a sense that motion could do much more than simply catch and hold attention—motion could also create powerful expressive and emotional affects within a cohesive overall design.

Rather than defending the attractive or magnetic appeals of motion in advertising, those who wanted to keep using animation in their Fifth Avenue windows drew upon this more artistic and dramatic idea of animation. They argued that motion could play a vital role in the composition of a window and therefore have an aesthetic value. Developing a notion of a new kind of visual advertising, Tom Lee gave a lecture at the Uptown Retail Guild in 1938 in which he explained, "Within the past two years window display has come of age and the public has been educated to expect the same good taste and dramatic arrangement in this form of publicity that they find in advertisements."[51] Linking the new art of window design to the trend in print advertising to create self-contained tableaux rather than directly solicit attention through eye-grabbing sales messages, motion could become artistic and dramatic. Walter Hoving, the president of Lord & Taylor, defended motion along these lines. He agreed with the FAA's opposition to "the use of any hurdy-gurdies, turnstiles or pinwheels and other attempts to attract the passer-by's attention to merchandise in the windows."[52] But he still saw a place for animated windows: "when motion is used as an integral part of an institutional display which is well and artistically executed, it should not be condemned." Hoving's view was an extension of Bel Geddes's approach to shop window design, in which "Merchandise and background should always tie up intimately, as actors and scenery are an integral part of the successful play on the stage."[53] In the case of animated displays, though, it is motion that can function as the "integral part"—not used to draw attention to merchandise or sales, but rather carefully woven into a shop window's overall composition.

With Lord & Taylor's blizzard and bell windows exemplifying this kind of integrated window display, even the FAA had to admit that Hoving had a point. Still, there was concern over motion in shop windows—given its novelty and unpredictable uses, it was feared that it could lead to "the degeneration of the artistic display into bizarre and fantastic interpretations."[54] These concerns were put to rest when Hoving took over as president of the FAA in 1939. Their policy was amended in light of "the advance made in the art of window display technique in the last few years" which "has resulted in utilizing motion in such ways as to achieve extremely artistic and attractive effects."[55] Motion would be allowed if "properly controlled" and not "used indiscriminately." In order to ensure the proper use of motion, a Department of Window Display Standards was established. Headed by Jean McLaren, the department investigated and approved window displays: "The Association now invites decorators to submit their plans for using motion; if they're really artistic, it's O. K. by the Association."[56] Describing the change of the policy on motion as "one of the important tasks of the Association" in 1940, the FAA's newsletter noted that "fifty-four plans involving the use of motion in window displays in our section were submitted to our Department of Window Display Standards. Of these, seventeen were granted approval and thirty-seven were disapproved."[57] The animated window could belong on Fifth Avenue as long as its dynamism was judged to be sufficiently artistic.

One of the more striking window displays to be approved was designed by James Gosling for Franklin Simon. This "animated showing" depicted scenes of live models promoting autumn fashions in an elegant setting (Fig. 2.3).[58] Framed and displayed behind convex glass disks that miniaturized the scenes to the size of just a few inches, the effect was described as "that of seeing a perfect performance of color television." Gosling, who had a background in mechanical engineering, filed a patent for the display device in which he described how "motion is utilized, yet in a shielded manner, so that its effect is confined to a relatively small number of passers-by who form an audience for the display. The dignity of the store window is maintained, yet its attraction powers are considerably increased."[59] Drawing a crowd whose attention was focused on a framed image of movement, the device offered the containment of motion that was valued on Fifth Avenue. Despite its display of live models and its emphasis on eye-catching appeals, the window was described by the FAA as having "an artistic effect in keeping with the character and dignity of Fifth Avenue."[60] The Association's ruling went on to note that motion would be allowed in shop windows "if it is properly controlled and used in such way as is not necessarily harmful to Fifth Avenue." By composing and aestheticizing motion, this shop window display offered a vision of controlled motion and an aura of artistic quality that accommodated the new regulations on the avenue.

For scholars of film, media and consumer culture, the significance of shop windows as a cultural form goes far beyond their role as an advertisement for goods and retailers. Shop windows were central to what William Leach describes as "the development of a new commercial aesthetic" in the

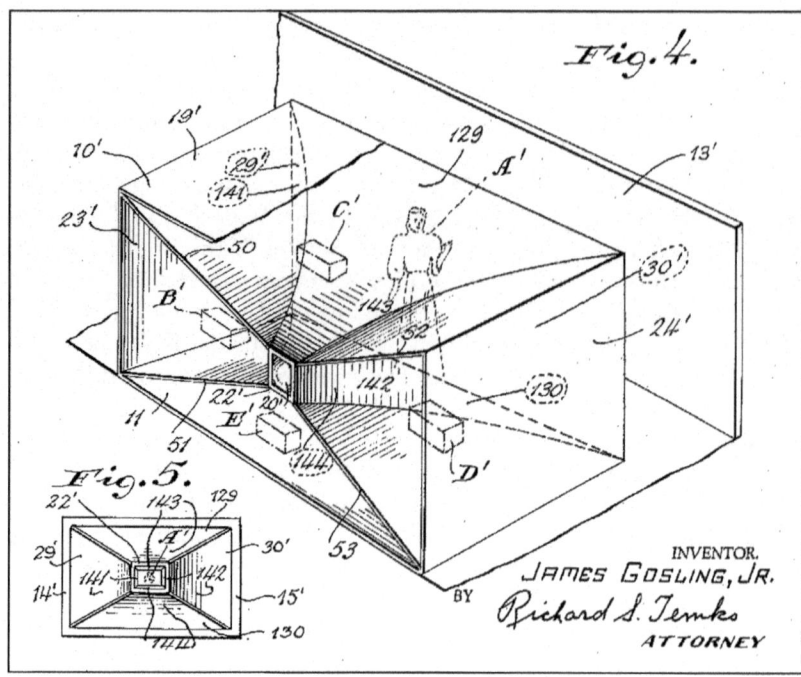

Fig. 2.3 Detail from James Gosling Jr., "Advertising Device." Patent 2,273,259, filed October 30, 1940

late nineteenth century and early twentieth century.[61] Leach explains how merchandisers and designers "helped create a remarkable landscape of glass, perhaps the most powerful field of desire yet to appear in American cities" (41). Aestheticizing the display of products by amplifying their beauty and separating them from spectators, shop windows "began to change the way people related to goods" (61). With the introduction of animation, shop windows were becoming even more distant from a simple collection of products—they were becoming miniature works of art, inviting a spectator's gaze.

In a similar vein, Anne Friedberg describes how film scholars and cultural historians—including Charles Eckert, Jeanne Allen, Mary Ann Doane and Jane Gaines—have drawn an "analogy between the shop window and the cinema screen."[62] Friedberg argues that shop windows, along with panoramas and other nineteenth-century spectacles, contributed to and prepared audiences for later forms of spectatorship, such as watching a film: "'Window-shopping' implies a mode of consumer contemplation; a speculative regard to the mise-en-scène of the display window without the commitment to enter the store or to make a purchase. Cinema spectatorship relies on an equally distanced contemplation: a tableau, framed and inaccessible, not behind glass, but on the screen" (66–68). By incorporating movement into their design, shop windows resonated with "an integral feature of both cinematic and televisual apparatuses: a *mobilized 'virtual' gaze*" (2). The relation between shop windows and cinema was a topic of interest at the time, with talks such as "Putting on a Better Show in the Show Window" pointing to "the stage and screen as the source of inspiration in making the window gain strength as a responsible sales medium."[63] Features of film aesthetics including close-ups, lighting effects, color, spatial depth and motion could all contribute to the impact of a shop window. And animation deepened this relationship between shop windows and motion pictures, an overlap between media that could lead to a display, such as the one designed by Gosling, being likened to moving images on a television set.

As well as extending existing links between consumer culture and motion pictures, animated shop windows were also creating new artistic practices and modes of representation by allowing viewers to peer into a newly vitalized world emerging before their eyes. In 1957, the FAA published a book about the history of Fifth Avenue which reflected on how the resolution of the debates over motion in shop windows had been a key event in maintaining the quality of the retailing area: "the happy means between 'artistic motion' and 'commercial motion' has been established and now golden bells may ring at Christmas time and a tasteful type of animation is permitted so that Fifth Avenue outdoes itself with its seasonal window displays."[64] Of course, the aims of "artistic motion" were much the same as "commercial motion"—they were both ultimately focused on selling products. But by distinguishing between commercial and artistic motion, animation was invested with aesthetic and compositional values. In one respect, this was a way to control animation. New forms and emergent media are often met with attempts to develop rules and protocols in order to define, circumscribe or standardize them. Animated displays were no different, with institutional bodies and regulatory procedures asserting control over their potentially disruptive and unpredictable effects. The elevation of motion to the status of art also suggested how animation could offer new forms of advertising, design and expression that transformed earlier practices. Both containing animation's transformative qualities and celebrating its aesthetic potentials, Fifth Avenue had become a central site of New York's animation culture.

Douglas Leigh on Broadway

At the same time that motion was transforming Fifth Avenue shop windows, Broadway's illuminated signs were attracting considerable attention through their new technologies and uses of animation. For decades, Broadway had offered dazzling signs that were "turning, wheeling, spinning, cavorting, flashing and blinking."[65] For many commentators, this landscape of motion in light reached its apex on November 1, 1940, when Douglas Leigh premiered his new sign for Wilson Whiskey (Fig. 2.4). In the outdoor advertising lexicon, as an article in the *New Yorker* explained, the sign was an "animated spectacular," a type of billboard which is a "larger-than-average sign that has unusual neon or bulb animated effects."[66] After several years of designing astonishing animated spectaculars on Broadway, this was the most complex and ambitious sign that Leigh had created. The article in the *New Yorker* recounted how, every couple of days, Leigh would take a tour of his signs, driving with his wife from their home in Beekman Place to Columbus Circle, up to the Upper West Side and down

Fig. 2.4   Wilson Whiskey sign at night. *Popular Science* (1940). Framepool

again into the area around Times Square. The itinerary took in animated signs of various types that he had created for Coca-Cola, Schenley whiskey, Gillette, Silex, Bromo-Seltzer and Four Roses. The tour ended at his Wilson Whiskey sign in Times Square, at Broadway and 46th Street. And Leigh would "look across Broadway with what amounts to worship" at his latest creation.

As the most high-profile designer of animated spectaculars—dubbed the "Sign King" in the mainstream press—Leigh aimed to extend and transform the existing milieu of motion on Broadway. One of the most vital qualities of Leigh's signs, as Kirsten Moana Thompson and others have explored, was their evocative use of animation.[67] In many respects, the Wilson Whiskey sign was the culmination of Leigh's work up to this point, fully realizing his underlying principles of designing signs by gathering together multiple forms of motion in a single animated spectacular.

Leigh's Wilson Whiskey sign was made up of three parts, each of which emphasized a different motion effect. At the top of the sign, on either side of a thirty-five-foot high sculpture of a whiskey bottle, eight enormous plastic tubes contained surging fountains of water "which spout into a mushroom effect."[68] Fifty-six floodlights beneath their base gave "a kaleidoscopic colour effect to the water patterns" so that "when the watery mushrooms break up, myriad multi-colored watery bubbles float in translucent tubes." This vivid spectacle evoked the illuminated fountains that had enchanted spectators at exhibitions and fairs for more than half a century, using the phenomenon of total internal reflection where light becomes encased in water to create the effect of streams and droplets which appeared as if they were colors in motion. Leigh's sign entwined this popular spectacle with advertising, suggesting luminous fountains of whiskey. The sign's left panel also symbolized its product, showing an "animated highball-pouring effect": "From a lighted bottle of whiskey and a lighted bottle of soda, whiskey and soda pour into a glass and mix, and give an effervescent action effect, a study in bubbles" (31). This action was shown in a loop through automated switches, called "flashers," that would turn the bulbs off and on, a technique of creating illuminated animation that had been in use for decades. The central panel of the sign used a new technology called Epok. An enormous screen containing thousands of light bulbs presented a three-part animated show: a short cartoon entitled "The Three Bears," (Fig. 2.5) a patriotic interlude "described as a kaleidoscopic montage of the history of the United States" and log-rolling as "the sport of the month."[69] Each section of the Wilson Whiskey sign used a different

Fig. 2.5   Central Epok panel for the Wilson Whiskey sign. *Popular Science* (1940). Framepool

technique to create spectacular motion, moving from the nineteenth century to the twentieth century to the contemporary moment, with Epok at its center.

Shortly after the sign premiered, on November 13, 1940, Leigh was a guest on the popular radio program, *Texaco Star Theater*, hosted by Fred Allen.[70] Leigh was asked how the "electric extravaganza" of the sign's central Epok panel was achieved. Leigh explained: "First a scenario is worked out, drawings are made and photographed, then the film is projected on a small screen made up of hundreds of photoelectric cells. Then the images are transmitted to the larger screen on the sign." Using this technique, the sign could present a changing program of animated shows—running several minutes in length—on the thousands of bulbs that made up its central panel. Fred Kerwer, Leigh's technical assistant, described the technology with breathless wonder: "This thing has infinite possibilities."[71] Unlike the "flashing" technology that was typically used for animated spectaculars, Epok used the photoelectric effect. "No moving parts, all done electronically," Kerwer explained proudly. "Compared with other signs, there's not enough flashing equipment in the world to operate this sign for a minute." Epok introduced a greater range of animations that could be displayed on signs, as well as providing the opportunity to change the animated show regularly. Leigh saw these as vital qualities, noting that "we realized that while cartoons are basic attention getters, the public after a while becomes accustomed to them as to anything else and the way to keep this type of sign from losing its attention value is to constantly develop fresh material into the cartoon stories. Therein lies the lure of the cartoon sign – its genuine flexibility in both picture and word."[72] Rather than designing a sign with a single animation in mind, Epok opened up a new field of possibility where the advertisement could be comparatively limitless.

Leigh's use of Epok was seen as a key reason for his pre-eminent position among sign designers at the time, with one account noting that his "real success dates from the day he got exclusive U. S. rights for 17 years on a moving picture-type of outdoor sign invented by Kurt Rosenberg of Austria – the electric animated cartoon."[73] Describing his first encounter with this new technology in 1936, Leigh explained how Rosenberg entered his office and "in his broken English, told us that he had developed an animated cartoon sign, and had it set up in a vacant office up the street. We went up to see it and realised that here, for the first time, was a new kind of action. Here were pictures that moved."[74] The technology was soon employed in a series of signs that went up on Broadway starting in 1937, including an earlier sign for Wilson Whiskey and one for Old Gold cigarettes. Plans were quickly developed to expand the presence of Epok in New York and to other American cities, and the following year an Epok sign—described as a "new kind of open-air cinema"—was put up in Trafalgar Square.[75]

Broadway and the area around Times Square were the central locations for Leigh's Epok output, with the technology's dramatic, cinematic and spectacular allures corresponding with the characteristic appeals of the area. The Broadway Association embraced extravagant displays of motion, unlike their counterparts at the Fifth Avenue Association who had banned electric signs decades earlier and were engaged in contested negotiations around movement of any sort in Fifth Avenue displays. Just a few months before the premiere of Leigh's latest Wilson Whiskey sign, plans for restricting the size and placement of billboards—including illuminated signs—were included in a major revision of New York's 1916 zoning laws by the City Planning Commission. The Broadway Association was defiant—well aware of the dynamic attraction of animated spectaculars on Broadway, they quickly registered a protest.[76] The Commission agreed. They held firm in their argument that a limit needed to be imposed upon "excessive outdoor advertising displays," while acknowledging that there were "certain areas where signs, far from being a draw-back, are among the City's principal and traditional attractions."[77] The Commission allowed for exceptions, particularly for areas around Broadway and Times Square. Following this decision, the Broadway Association issued a celebratory press release which reported on a survey conducted by the Association's Times Square Committee: "The marked increase in crowds along the Great White Way may be due to the attention drawn by animated signs, the Broadway Association reported today. A 33 minute 'free show' in electric lights is provided for an estimated 1,100,000 strolling sightseers every night by a dozen spectaculars in and around Times Square."[78] The press release went on to note the multitude of signs that showed animation in lights; although it was not yet finished, the first one mentioned was the "new Broadway landmark" of the Wilson Whiskey sign.

Leigh's sign wholeheartedly engaged with the wider context of Broadway. With its Epok panel set alongside other animation technologies, the sign combined novel and existing forms of spectacular display, encapsulating and going beyond the diverse spectacles of motion that surrounded it. This multifaceted quality extended to how the sign would be positioned in order to best take advantage of its particular location. Leigh explained that the idea behind a sign can often be "more of an adaptation and excellent use of space than a symbol of the product."[79] This approach was evident in the Wilson Whiskey sign, which used its place in a carefully considered manner. Pedestrians walking down Broadway would first glimpse the part of the sign angled toward them, showing Wilson Whiskey and soda being mixed. They would then see the sign's central sections as they arrived in Times Square. In this more pedestrianized area, there was less need to hurry along the street—spectators could pause to watch the sign's animated show. The sign's enormous bottle and tubes of surging water were also positioned to take advantage of their place in the urban scene—pointing (and gushing) upwards, they corresponded to the verticality of Manhattan's skyline rather than presenting a boxed-in image of movement separated from its environment. Each section of the sign related to its place within New York and on Broadway in a different way, generating multiple perspectives on the place of the spectacular (Fig. 2.6).

As well as embedding the sign in its urban location, Leigh consciously linked it to the entertainment culture of Broadway. For Wilson Whiskey's premiere, Joan Crawford switched on the sign, and celebrities including Al Jolson, Bert Lahr, Louella Parsons, Martha Raye, Eddie Cantor and Sabu joined her for this "free show for Broadway's sidewalk patrons."[80] At the

Fig. 2.6   Daytime view of the Wilson Whiskey sign. "No Better Whiskey in Any Bottle Wilson 'That's All,'" November 18, 1941, R. C. Maxwell Company Records. Duke University Libraries

premiere, Epok even projected live performances as Jolson, Cantor and Raye got in on the act: "By passing through the light beam of the display's projector and throwing their shadows onto the bank of photo cells, they appeared in lights on the display's screen."[81] In his interview with Fred Allen, Leigh explained how "creating a sign was something like putting on a spectacle. I thought a sign designer should approach his work as a showman."[82] Allen asked, "In other words a sign creator should be sort of a cross between Ziegfeld and Edison…" Leigh replied, "Exactly." Coupling new technologies of animation with established contexts of showmanship,

Leigh generated a fittingly Broadway ballyhoo around his latest animated spectacular.

This sense of a sign as akin to a Broadway show was further developed by Leigh in his reaction to the dimming of city lights that was necessitated during the Second World War. As a response to this darkening of Broadway at night, sign designers and corporations had to find innovative ways to continue their spectacular advertising. This included experiments with "ultra-violet or 'black light' to illuminate paints" and plans for "gigantic fabric awnings and metal shields which permit the scintillating displays, but prevent the lights from striking clouds and setting up a glow which silhouettes United Nations' ships, making them easy prey for Axis submarines lurking offshore."[83] In keeping with the animated appeal of signs, one idea for limiting the night-time illumination of Broadway involved "substituting motion for light, making the district a maze of mechanical devices – whirling windmills, waving arms, winking eyes, beckoning fingers, dancing feet" (9). This extraordinary vision of movement would have combined Broadway's animated spectaculars with a dreamlike use of motion displays. While not opposed to these suggestions, Leigh's preferred solution was to take "the huge signs on tour of the United States just as Broadway shows go on tour to smaller cities." Linking his animated spectaculars to theatrical shows, Leigh was developing the same kind of intermedial comparisons that circulated around the animated shop windows on Fifth Avenue.

Another way that Epok became entwined with other media was through its close relation to cinema. The idea of cinematic billboards had long been an interest of designers and advertisers, and by the late 1930s, this possibility was a topic of fascination in the United States and internationally. In an article from 1937 detailing the thoughts of leading French artists and advertisers on "the poster of the future," cinematic qualities were front and center; Henry Le Monnier, among others, described how signs will be "illuminated at night, sometimes moving, perhaps even cinematographic."[84] Epok was, in many respects, a realization of this cinematographic future for signs—its patent described it in cinematic terms as an "Incandescent Lamp Cinematographic Apparatus" and accounts in the popular press repeatedly compared it to cinema.[85] The link between Epok and cinema was quite direct: through its use of the photoelectric cell, the Epok technology offered the necessary efficiency, control and timing for a live-action 16 mm film to be shown on its bank of lights. And film screenings did appear on Epok signs, such as "a silhouette motion picture taken on a ski jump."[86]

But the effect of Epok was also quite distinct from cinema; Epok lacked sound, gradations of light and detailed resolution, with its images constructed from a limited number of bulbs that created pixelated images. Within these constraints, Leigh focused on producing animated films that foregrounded simple figures engaging in dynamic activities. For example, "Hop, Skip, and Jump," which premiered to "capacity street crowds," showed "a cat that jumps on a pogo stick, a cow that jumps over the moon, a pole vault, athletes jumping over hurdles, a ski jump, and a jumping husband motivated by his wife's foot."[87] More like early cinema than mainstream films at the time, Epok presented changing programs of loosely connected attractions in which motion was a primary appeal.

Epok shows were also closely connected to animated films. *Time* magazine characterized an early Epok sign as "an electric animated cartoon," noting how the sign for Old Gold (designed by the cartoonist Otto Soglow) "resembles a Walt Disney cinema short."[88] Leigh invited comparisons between Epok and animated film, describing how animated films offered lessons for his own productions—he had reportedly viewed "every Mickey Mouse short and he saw 'Snow White' fourteen times."[89] Animated films and Epok shows also had similar production methods, with an article noting how Leigh "is not averse to hearing himself described as the 'Cecil B. DeMille of advertising,' though his work is much more like that of Walt Disney, as he supervises every detail of his work at a studio in the Bronx, and has a downtown office where idea men, gag men, artists, photographers, laboratory experts, etc. collaborate with him."[90] Such close connections between animated film and Epok inspired the Hastings School of Animation, located in the Gaiety Building across the street from Leigh's Wilson Whiskey sign, to announce that "the actual construction and working of the sign would be included in their curriculum."[91] The Epok sign had become an exemplary site of animation within New York's animation culture. As one account explained, "Light has become a medium for painting pictures which move, and tell a story."[92] However, despite the evident similarities between animated films and Epok, they were quite distinct media. By this period, animated films had developed a complex aesthetic which entwined motion with sound, color and depth. The Epok animations, on the other hand, had to be less complex: "The films are made much the same way the Mickey Mouse films are, except the job is simpler, the sole medium being black and white squares."[93] As well as aesthetic differences, the production of Epok films was considerably less technically complex than the production methods used for mainstream animated films. Moreover, Epok was immersed in its own distinct network of values, functions and exhibition practices.

Rather than downplaying its distinctiveness in order to associate it with cinema and animated film, Leigh elaborated on further intermedial qualities of Epok in interviews and promotional material. One advertisement posed the question "What is Leigh-Epok?" before describing it as a combination of different media: "It's 1/3 electric sign, 1/3 television, 1/3 movie."[94] While clearly merging the electric sign and cinema, Epok's relationship to television was less immediately obvious—the connection between these two forms was addressed by Leigh in interviews where he would highlight the similarity of their technologies: "It is really so simple – very much like television. But where television operates by lines, our cartoons operate by dots or lines."[95] Epok was also linked to more well-established popular media. An advertisement for "the illuminated sign that stopped Broadway in its tracks" described how the "flexibility of the device, the almost infinite variety of potential uses, leads observers to believe that Epok overnight has revolutionized the entire electric sign business... and has introduced the greatest advertising invention since radio."[96] Recurring comparisons to radio drew attention to how both forms offered free entertainment to a mass audience and how Epok signs could integrate their shows with advertising messages in a manner much like radio programs at the time. The "Old Gold Parade," for example, was a "five-minute show, with thirty-one different characters, each doing a humorous stunt as it marches by," with commercials "woven in as part of the parade."[97] Another advertisement emphasized how the sign drew upon the immense popularity of comic strips, with the headline "America Loves Cartoons."[98] The connection with comic strips was made directly in "The Old Gold Funnies" Epok show, which presented "fifteen pages of funnies" with images of "a hand turning some of the pages" that would reveal new scenes of action and humor.[99]

Epok's intermediality was promoted in advertisements and within its shows, generating a sense that the illuminated sign had become mutable and multifaceted, with dynamic new potentials of mass appeal, advertising impact and aesthetic form. Unlike the wary response to animated shop windows on Fifth Avenue, the transformative potentials of motion and its association with different media were eagerly welcomed on Broadway.

ANIMATION, ART AND MEMORY VALUE

Early in his career, Leigh had developed a multifaceted approach for designing animated spectaculars which he summarized in an article from 1934: "The creating of spectaculars is a technique and art in itself. When one sets about to create a design or model for a spectacular display, he should aim at a design that will have memory value, day-time value, night-time value, and price value."[100] These different values were carefully woven into the design of the Wilson Whiskey sign. Its day-time value was evident particularly through its top section—with the massive bottle of whiskey—that promoted the product without relying on the effect of night-time illumination. At night, though, the sign would achieve its full brilliancy, becoming vividly illuminated in its animated sections. Leigh also had to balance the advertising potential of a sign with the financial outlay required to construct and exhibit it, which he termed the "price value." Animated spectaculars were, after all, very expensive forms of advertising. Although the expense would rise further with an Epok sign, an article in *News-Week* explained that this was well justified as it may cost the advertiser "about 50 per cent more than standard 'spectaculars,' but Leigh claims they draw 500 per cent more attention."[101]

While pragmatic considerations of day-time value, night-time value and price value were important, the value that most concerned Leigh was "memory value." For Leigh, signs had to be designed so that their advertising message would be remembered—this would allow for signs to achieve their aim. Since the 1910s, memory value had been a recurring topic of interest in studies of the psychological effect of different aspects of advertisements, such as their size or their use of color.[102] Animation offered a new means of creating memory value. Shortly after starting his own company, Leigh explained: "By memory value is meant the incorporation of an animated element that should be part of the spectacular to make it unique and individual – an element created solely for the one advertiser."[103] He offered several examples of such animations, including his sign for A&P coffee with steam rising from an enormous cup and his sign for Kool cigarettes which depicted their product's emblem, a penguin, who was automated to wink 100,000 times a day. For Leigh, the striking and original quality of these instances of motion would help make such advertisements "individual" and "long remembered."

When creating memory value, motion was not simply an added attraction; it was carefully integrated with the product being advertised. This related to a long-standing focus of advertising which T. Jackson Lears describes as "the effort to endow the commodity with life."[104] With animated spectaculars, this effort to invest products with a sense of liveliness was being realized through animation. Leigh wrote, "The animation of a sign should tie up intimately with the product advertised.... That is, it shouldn't be motion for the sake of motion, but should tell a story relating to the product."[105] While the winking penguin and rising steam hardly tell stories in a traditional sense, motion is used to endow the image of the animal with fantastic liveliness and create a microdrama from the everyday sight of a hot cup of coffee. Blown up to enormous proportions and emblazoned in light, motion holds the viewer's attention, expresses the product being advertised and presents a vivid and memorable image.

Leigh saw that increasing the scope of animation in signs could increase their effectiveness, as "the more animation in the display, the more memory value it contains."[106] This idea was reflected in the variety and intensity of motion effects that would appear in his signs. One account marveled at how one of Leigh's signs had "fourteen animations, more than any other sign in the world" and an advertisement heralded another as "the most animated sign on Broadway."[107] The animations in animated spectaculars could take many different forms. Leigh described how animation could be created through a "theatrical or stage effect" and "revolving stages, actual water flowing, actual smoke, wind machines, etc."[108] Articles from the time were also keen to emphasize the variety of animation effects that could be presented on signs; *Modern Mechanix*, for example, explained: "An animation is any individual bit of action – stars flickering, candles burning, words flashing on and off, etc."[109] The diverse forms that animation could take, and the possibility of combining different kinds of motion, offered rich opportunities for experimentation and creativity.

Rather than emphasizing a single animation effect, the Wilson Whiskey sign reflected Leigh's ambitious approach to the design of animated spectaculars by using animation in multiple ways. This contrasted with Broadway's largest sign at the time, advertising Wrigley's chewing gum, which took up a city block to show "multi-colored tropical fish slowly swimming in a sea-green sea."[110] Tama Starr and Edward Hayman describe how the sign's use of motion had a "meditative" and "hypnotic" quality, reflecting Wrigley's motto, "Steadies the Nerves."[111] This cohesive design was quite different from the multiplicity of motion in the Wilson Whiskey sign, and Leigh was keen to defend the unique quality of his work:

Although the sign is considerably smaller than the Wrigley animated-fish sign two blocks south, Leigh thinks it is the most spectacular spectacular in existence. He likes to point out that the Wrigley sign, which was put up by General Outdoor, is far less complicated than his. "That sign is merely fifteen small signs attached together," he says. "Wilson is the finickiest of them all."[112]

Instead of joining together multiple panels to create an overarching design and animation effect, Leigh used different kinds of animation in his Wilson Whiskey sign. Like the Wrigley's sign, there was an emphasis on advertising the product: images of flowing liquid in the top section, the mixing of whiskey and soda and the enormous whiskey bottle all evoked the product being sold. But the Wilson Whiskey sign was not unified in its form—as well as being separated spatially, the individual sections foregrounded different technologies and effects of motion.

Other Broadway signs were also experimenting with a diversity of animated effects. The Wondersign, which first appeared on Broadway in April 1939, showed a changing series of animations—an article in the trade journal *Signs of the Times* described it as "Thirty-Six Spectaculars in One!"[113] The article went on to describe how the sign would present a program of advertising in a repeated show, lasting twelve minutes, created by "electrically controlled relays which permit the gradual evolution of designs, lettering, packages and trademarks." Early advertisements on the sign were wide-ranging, including "messages from makers of Wonder bread, Piel beer, Enna Jettick shoes, La Palina cigars, Hamilton watches, and from the Sitroux Company, and William Jameson & Co." Images of their products and logos, as well as miniature scenes such as amber beer poured into an empty glass, would take shape in front of the spectator's eyes. While the Wondersign could not show the movement of these images, only their gradual appearance, it was still heralded as "the sign whose color and action make it one of Broadway's most startling attractions"—located next to one of Leigh's signs, it was claimed that the Wondersign would even "exceed it in novelty."[114]

Like Epok, the Wondersign was seen to combine different media. Advertising executives who had viewed a prototype version described the sign as a "new advertising medium combining numerous elements of all other mediums, plus 'fireworks' dramatization."[115] The Wondersign's dramatic qualities were often compared to the lightning sketch, a theatrical entertainment in which an artist would rapidly draw an elaborate cartoon or caricature in front of an audience. Donald Crafton describes how this would become "an archetypal formula for a multitude of films, out of which the first animated cartoons evolved."[116] Evoking this important early genre of film, the Wondersign was described as presenting "the illusion of an invisible hand tracing a design and lettering colored electric bulbs much as an artist draws a sketch."[117] The lightning sketch had been transposed to a Broadway billboard, now "drawn by an invisible pen dipped in electricity."[118]

This extraordinary form of artistic creation had long been associated with animated signs. Michael Cowan describes how the "invisible hand" that animates such advertisements entwined a sense of magical trickery with the animator's unseen "*control* over the image."[119] Reactions to the Wondersign resonated with these important themes of animation and advertising, highlighting the sign's wondrous qualities alongside its relation to automation and mechanization. One early demonstration of the technology was greeted by astonished spectators who declared that it was "absolute magic" akin to the letters of fire written on the wall during Belshazzar's feast in Babylon.[120] Another account described the sign in more mechanistic terms as a modern version of a Jacquard loom, and there were recurring comparisons between the sign's mechanism and the workings of a player piano.[121] These varied reactions indicate that rather than creating a unified effect, the Wondersign was seen as a mixture of existing media and forms, much like Epok and Leigh's Wilson Whiskey sign.

The Wondersign was an American version of a French sign, the Luminograph, which had made a prominent appearance at the International Exposition of Art and Technology in Modern Life in Paris in 1937. Located inside an enormous arrow directing spectators to the entrance of the exposition's advertising exhibit, the Palace of Publicity, the sign attracted enormous crowds and became a symbol for contemporary advertising.[122] This emblematic quality was further established by its association with Jean Carlu, a well-known advertising poster artist in France, who ran the Luminograph Company and was credited with the "improvements, and artistic and commercial adaptation" of the sign's patent.[123] With the Luminograph, Carlu's influential approach to poster design and advertising was extended to an electric sign. In his article "Should a Poster Be a Work of Art?" from 1931, Carlu outlined his vision of poster design. Responding to the article title's question resolutely in the affirmative, Carlu argued that a poster should be "conceived in accordance with primary laws of aesthetics which regulate works of art in general. Therefore, we insist that a poster, to achieve its purpose fully, and thereby being a *good poster*, must be considered as a work of art."[124]

Carlu approached art in instrumental terms, resonating with the machine age and its fascination with industrial art. He described how artists use "form and colour" like "a mechanism" to create an emotional response.[125] A poster operates in the same manner to create a desire for the product being advertised, functioning as "a machine for advertising" and "no less than a work of art, a machine for exciting emotion" (95). And a poster must also be memorable, an especially difficult challenge in a contemporary context filled with advertising images. In order to achieve these aims, a poster should use a "graphic symbol" of the product that has a "very great intensity of expression, for it addresses the emotions even before it speaks to reason" (101). Creating an emotional impact through artistry and a memorable advertisement through intensified imagery, Carlu hoped to develop a "graphic means – drawn from aesthetics and psychology – that will, when applied to the fundamental stratum of the individual, allow us to engrave on his mind what image we will, in such a manner that it will not be forgotten" (92). While posters might achieve this effect, the gradual emergence of trademarks and product symbols in the Luminograph was actively "engraving" images in light through the machinery of the sign and—by extension—in the spectator's memory.

Much like Carlu, Leigh's vision of advertising focused on intensified and symbolic expression. But rather than emphasizing the graphic presentation of an image, Leigh used motion as the key way to create a memorable impact. In doing so, he attached advertising to motion:

As for animation – anything that moves captures attention. All right; if we animate our display, let's animate the portion of it that ought to get the attention. Let's animate where the animation belongs. Let's animate the name, the selling phrase, the stage effect. Motion and design unrelated to the product being advertised convey no coherent meaning. Every effect should be directly symbolic.[126]

While this clearly served advertising purposes, it also indicated an approach to designing signs which used animation in a manner much like an artist deploys color or line—as a source of expressive and affective power. Like Carlu, Leigh envisioned advertising as an art suited to a contemporary age.

A 1941 profile on Leigh in the *New Yorker* described how he "has an almost religious feeling about the importance of lights in the modern scheme of things" and "thinks of his creations as works of art."[127] The profile offers a vivid picture of Leigh's engagement with his work, describing him sitting in the Automat on Broadway and 46th Street and gazing at several of his signs, including the recent Silex one with "bright-red neon lips, under which the words 'Yum Yum' appear from time to time. 'Look at that mouth!' Leigh says, with all the fervor of a Cézanne contemplating one of his apples" (25). Specific images and individual moments of animation could become artistic, offering instances of memorable, expressive and symbolic beauty. The Wilson Whiskey sign had assembled these elements in its different sections and through the shifting animations of its Epok panel. It is no wonder that Leigh thought of it as his "masterpiece" (26).

ROCKEFELLER CENTER AND THE HALL OF MOTION

Whereas animated spectaculars were a celebrated feature of the area around Times Square, animation in shop windows was a subject of debate and regulation on Fifth Avenue. Although the two locations were adjacent to one another, they reacted to animation in distinctly different ways. There was little, if any, direct overlap between the forms of animated advertising used in each location. Even the use of a "tiny electric signboard, like Douglas Leigh's Wilson Whiskey" in a Fifth Avenue shop was a step too far—"it was cute, but the Association persuaded them to take it out."[128] Despite these differences, the two districts were part of a shared animation culture in which the advertising potential of motion was a topic of considerable interest. Captivating a mass audience and drawing the attention of the popular press, animated shop windows and animated spectaculars were among New York's principal attractions. Introducing motion to static forms or expanding the scope of motion was seen to offer something much more than a minor adjustment to past practice. One of the most important reasons for this was that motion could have a second level of meaning or affect beyond its initial eye-catching attraction. Motion could become artistic, dramatic, symbolic and memorable—to name just a few of the qualities emphasized by its exponents during this period. Motion was also seen to destabilize existing forms. In some cases, this meant that it created a sense of intermediality, where displays became likened to dramas and moving billboards became akin to open-air television sets. Disrupting established categories, as well as the boundaries between art and advertising, motion was creating new media.

While the examples discussed in this chapter were the most prominent examples of such uses of animation, other animated displays within New York were also contributing to its animation culture. And these were not only wound up with commercial activities—educational displays offered a similarly multifaceted kineticism. Just off of Fifth Avenue, on the ground floor of Rockefeller Center's RCA Building, the New York Museum of Science and Industry was establishing itself as a leading site of dynamic display. Popularly called "The Hall of Motion," the Museum offered an abundance of moving sights: "thousands of models, replicas, dioramas, working demonstrations, and visitor-operated machines dramatize the scientific achievements and industrial development of the machine age."[129] Following its move to Rockefeller Center in 1936, the director of the Museum, Robert P. Shaw, saw the institution's future as based in the new realm of motion exhibits. These would foreground motion to such an extent that by 1941, the Museum's educational activities were seen to be done "principally through dynamic exhibits."[130]

As Karen A. Rader and Victoria E. M. Cain explain in *Life on Display*, the popularity of animated educational displays grew substantially over the course of the 1930s.[131] Major institutions such as the American Museum of Natural History in New York had joined this trend toward dynamic instruction, with an account of a motorized model of a snake in *Profitable Showmanship* marveling at its appeal: "With all the elaborate and expensive static displays in that museum to compete with – the little sand snake stole the show because it moved."[132] Going further, Waldemar Kaempffert, the director of the Museum of Science and Industry in Chicago, "aspired to install as many mechanized, visitor-operated exhibits as possible."[133] In 1933, Kaempffert described the effect of these kinds of displays: "Enter the main doorway and pass into the first court. You see – what? Animation everywhere."[134] In a similar vein, Shaw marveled at the potentials of animation, questioning the usefulness and appeal of static exhibits. One primary reason for this was that motion could demonstrate technological and scientific processes much more effectively than static displays, enlarging a viewer's perception and enriching their understanding.

Leigh's Wilson Whiskey sign was the subject of one of the Museum's temporary displays, combining a dynamic attraction with educational aims. The sign was shown in two ways. Like a typical cinema screening, there was "a preview showing in the little theater of the film for the new giant electric animated cartoon."[135] This was accompanied by "an exhibit of the mechanics of the photoelectric process which animates the cartoons so you may see how it works!" Presenting the Wilson Whiskey sign as both an animated film and an educational exhibit, the Museum display entwined entertainment with technology.

This was a recurring strategy that informed how Shaw would present dynamic exhibits, taking shape in his development of a Progressive Exhibit Method of Presentation which aimed to communicate knowledge about science and technology in narrative form. Designing exhibits according to this method, the planning would begin with a script and then develop individual sections that would show different aspects of the overall scientific area. As Shaw put it, in terms which recalled the integrated and dramatic presentation of merchandise in shop windows, this was "much like preparing a scenario for a play, the difference being that we cast science exhibits, instead of men and women, in the role of actors."[136] Shaw explained the development of this display strategy, with the first attempt at creating an exhibit of this kind presenting the subject of electrotechnology with "lively and intriguing action." Motion was pivotal to the overall effect:

> Standing in the entrance, the visitor catches a glimpse here of a ring spinning mysteriously and continuously on a glass plate, and there of a steel band spontaneously leaping from one side to the other of a metal arch, both without any apparent motivating force. A sudden blue flash of electricity, like a small streak of jagged lightning, catches his eye in one corner, while almost immediately his attention is arrested by a crackle and buzz from another direction.

Seeing "objects… moving miraculously" (167), the visitor is curious and fascinated. Drawn further into the exhibit, they then engage with its educational and dramatic values as the source of motion and its relation to electrotechnology is explained. Within this narrativized exhibit, motion further attracts the visitor's attention through exhibits that can be activated by pushing a button or pulling a lever so that they "spring into dynamic action." Motion's mysterious and enticing qualities give it a power over spectators, engaging their faculties and piquing their interest. Underlying the power of movement to engage visitors, Shaw writes of a "motive instinct" which he describes as a "natural urge to see or set things in motion" (165).

Unlike the animations behind glass on Fifth Avenue or elevated above the street on Broadway, the New York Museum of Science and Industry brought motion into the hands of the spectator. Although Shaw had adapted motion display to the requirements and practices of educational exhibition, his approach was part of a wider understanding of animation at the time which foregrounded its attractive force, its capacity to hold attention and its dramatic potentials. While the ideas of "artistic motion," "memory value" and the "motive instinct" gave different inflections to the value of animation, there was a shared sense that motion could transform existing practices and ways of perceiving in New York's animation culture. As the next chapter explores in its account of animation at the New York World's Fair, this served the purposes not only of advertising and instruction, but also to draw spectators further into the dynamism of industry and modernity.

NOTES

1. "Trinity Diorama," *Time*, March 15, 1937, 41.
2. Edward Heckler Burdick, "Lilliput Outgrows Gulliver," *Popular Mechanics*, May 1939, 661.
3. Advertisement for Andrews and Perillo, *Display Animation, 1937: The Year Book of Motion Displays*, ed. I. L. Cochrane (New York: Reeder-Morton Publications, 1937), 232.
4. Advertisement for Stevenson Animotor, *Display Animation, 1936: The Year Book of Motion Displays*, ed. I. L. Cochrane (New York: Reeder-Morton Publications, 1936), 222–223.
5. *Display Animation, 1936*, 117.
6. *Display Animation, 1936*, 7.
7. *Display Animation, 1937*, 7–8. Cochrane discusses the influence of the Century of Progress Exposition on page 55.
8. I. L. Cochrane, *Motion Display Mechanics* (New York: Reeder-Morton Publications, 1939), 8.
9. A. L. Sugar, "Animated Displays," *Co-operative Review*, September 1938, 282.
10. See especially André Gaudreault and Philippe Marion, "A medium is always born twice...," *Early Popular Visual Culture* 3, no. 1 (May 1995): 3–15.
11. See "Lord & Taylor's Fifth Avenue Windows are Dressed in the Cellar," *Life*, March 28, 1938, 28; Henry Lee, "It's in the Window," *American Artist*, June 1941, 14; *Display Animation, 1938: The Year Book of Motion Displays*, ed. I. L. Cochrane (New York: Reeder-Morton Publications, 1938), 27. For an account of the different trends in shop window

design in the 1930s, see Leonard S. Marcus, *The American Store Window* (New York: Whitney Library of Design, 1978), 28–40. Marcus also discusses individual window designers, including Tom Lee (on pages 62–64) and Dana O'Clare (on pages 65–67).

12. "Lord & Taylor Bells Keep Ringing – By Request," *Women's Wear Daily*, December 6, 1937.

13. "Avenue Art," *Time*, December 5, 1938, 37.

14. Norman Bel Geddes, *Horizons* (Boston: Little, Brown, and Company, 1932), 259.

15. "Find Window Displays, Ads Gain in Favor," *Women's Wear Daily*, July 7, 1939.

16. "Avenue Art," *Time*, 37.

17. Munn Peters, "Free Show," *Cue*, March 19, 1938, 11.

18. "Avenue Art," *Time*, 38.

19. Margaret Hess, "Our Show Window Pageant," *New York Times*, April 30, 1939.

20. *Display Animation, 1938*, 27.

21. *Display Animation, 1938*, 27; Cochrane, *Motion Display Mechanics*, 178.

22. "Snowstorm in Store," *New York Times*, November 13, 1938.

23. "Fifth Ave. 'Blizzard' Spurs Winter Trade," *New York Times*, November 15, 1938.

24. The construction of the bells with gold leaf and papier mâché is noted in Lee, "It's in the Window," 14; the motorized mechanism for the bells is noted in Peters, "Free Show," 11; the device used for the blizzard display is mentioned in "Fifth Ave. 'Blizzard' Spurs Winter Trade."

25. "Revolving Bulletins Flash Paris Opening News in Bonwit Teller Windows," *Women's Wear Daily*, February 10, 1938.

26. Lee, "It's in the Window," 14.

27. "Plate Glass Preview," *Cue*, July 8, 1939, 13.

28. Marcus, *The American Store Window*, 20.

29. Genêt, "Letter from Paris," *New Yorker*, January 1, 1938, 51.

30. Max Page, *The Creative Destruction of Manhattan, 1900–1940* (Chicago: University of Chicago Press, 1999), 54.

31. "Oppose Motion in Windows of 5th Ave. Stores: Recommended by Committee on Standards of Window Decoration Is Adopted by Fifth Ave. Assn. Board," *Women's Wear Daily*, April 25, 1938.

32. "5th Ave. Stores Seen Not Foregoing Motion Windows," *Women's Wear Daily*, April 26, 1938.

33. "5th Ave. Assn. Trying to Set Example in Stand on Windows," *Women's Wear Daily*, April 27, 1938.

34. "'Blizzard' in Window of Store to Halt," *New York Times*, November 16, 1938.

35. "Lord & Taylor Snow Displays Out Tonight, But Not Because of Protest," *Women's Wear Daily*, November 16, 1938.
36. "Wails of Complaints Heard Above Din of Fifth Ave. Christmas Bells," *Women's Wear Daily*, December 1, 1938.
37. "Avenue Art," *Time*, 37.
38. "Wails of Complaints Heard Above Din of Fifth Ave. Christmas Bells," *Women's Wear Daily*.
39. Phyllis McGinley, "Still Life," *New Yorker*, December 3, 1938, 114.
40. "5th Ave. Assn. Trying to Set Example in Stand on Windows," *Women's Wear Daily*.
41. "Wails of Complaints Heard Above Din of Fifth Ave. Christmas Bells," *Women's Wear Daily*.
42. "Lord & Taylor Snow Displays Out Tonight, But Not Because of Protest," *Women's Wear Daily*. Marcus discusses how the use of motion in windows was seen to be problematic as it "offered a kind of amenity or entertainment" that went against the "highly exclusive airs" associated with Fifth Avenue shop windows (*The American Store Window*, 65).
43. Kenneth Goode and Zenn Kaufman, *Profitable Showmanship* (New York: Prentice-Hall, 1939), 160.
44. Cochrane, *Motion Display Mechanics*, 10.
45. Jack Roberts, "L'Étalage et la vente," *Vendre*, September 1938, 434.
46. *Display Animation, 1937*, 3.
47. *Display Animation, 1937*, 91–93.
48. Cochrane, *Motion Display Mechanics*, 93 and 101.
49. Fred M. Wolff, "Lighting Animated Displays," in *Display Animation, 1937: The Year Book of Motion Displays*, ed. I. L. Cochrane (New York: Reeder-Morton Publications, 1937), 215.
50. I. L. Cochrane, "American Motion Displays Part 2: Cardboard and Other Small Units," *Display*, April 1938, 46.
51. "High Window Display Quality Standard Urged," *Women's Wear Daily*, March 1, 1938. For a detailed discussion of trends in the wider field of advertising in the period, see Roland Marchand, *Making Way for Modernity, 1920–1940* (Berkeley: University of California Press, 1985).
52. "Lord & Taylor Seek New Window Ruling," *New York Times*, November 19, 1938.
53. Bel Geddes, *Horizons*, 271.
54. Donald L. Pratt, "Tempest of Controversy Follows Blizzard in Window," *Women's Wear Daily*, November 17, 1938.
55. "Fifth Avenue Assn. Amends Policy on Motion in Windows," *Women's Wear Daily*, October 12, 1939.
56. "Liberal Regime," Talk of the Town, *New Yorker*, February 3, 1940, 16.
57. "Motion," *Members' Bulletin*, Fifth Avenue Association, Inc., January 1941, 7, New York Historical Society.

58. Virginia Pope, "'Tiny' Style Show Based on Illusion," *New York Times*, September 10, 1940.

59. J. Gosling Jr., "Advertising Device," US patent 2,273,259, filed October 30, 1940, and issued February 17, 1942, 1.

60. "5th Avenue Group Backs Franklin Simon Display," *New York Herald Tribune*, September 12, 1940.

61. William Leach, *Land of Desire: Merchants, Power, and the Rise of a New American Culture* (New York: Vintage, 1993), 9.

62. Anne Friedberg, *Window Shopping: Cinema and the Postmodern* (Berkeley: University of California Press, 1993), 66.

63. "Adopt Principle of Stage and Screen to Window Displays Is Advice to Fashion Group: Cosmetic Section Hears Francis D. Gonda at Women's City Club Yesterday – Elements of Good Showmanship in Displays Pointed Out as Light, Motion, Architectural Quality, Creation of Personality," *Women's Wear Daily*, July 21, 1938.

64. *Fifty Years of Fifth* (New York: International Press, 1957), 37.

65. Meyer Berger, "New Constellations on the Old White Way," *New York Times*, March 29, 1936.

66. E. J. Kahn Jr., "Lights, Lights, Lights," *New Yorker*, June 7, 1941, 23.

67. Kirsten Moana Thompson, "Rainbow Ravine: Colour and Animated Advertising in Times Square," in *The Colour Fantastic*, eds. Giovanna Fossati, Victoria Jackson, Bregt Lameris, Elif Rongen-Kaynakçi, Sarah Street and Joshua Yumibe (Amsterdam: Amsterdam University Press, 2018), 163–177. See also Tama Starr and Edward Hayman, *Signs and Wonders* (New York: Doubleday, 1998).

68. "Premiere Wilson Spectacular," *Signs of the Times*, December 1940, 30.

69. Thomas M. Pryor, "Noting the Week's Screen Events," *New York Times*, September 29, 1940.

70. Douglas Leigh, interview by Fred Allen, *Texaco Star Theater*, November 13, 1940, http://www.oldtimeradiodownloads.com/comedy/fred-allen-texaco-star-theater/fred-allen-texaco-star-theater-40-10-16-03-death-takes-a-boniface.

71. Henry Lee, "Very Latest Broadway Spectacular Employs New Principle Called Epok," *New York World-Telegram*, October 12, 1940.

72. Douglas Leigh, "What's the Idea?," *National Sign Journal*, October 1940, 22.

73. "Spectacular," clipping, *Time*, July 18, 1938, Douglas Leigh Collection, Archives of American Art, Washington, DC. The magazine *Shelf Appeal* provided an account of Epok's invention, explaining how Kurt Rosenberg and his brother Hans Rosenberg (a successful producer of animated advertising in Germany who was described as "the Walt Disney of Europe") had worked together for several years "in conjunction with A. E.G., German electrical trust" to develop the technology and, after relocating to Sweden,

"its development for commercial purposes was carried by Reklamaktiebolaget 'Epok,' the Swedish firm the Rosenbergs set up" ("Sign Cinemas for Five Cities," *Shelf Appeal*, February 1938, 60).

74. Leigh, "What's the Idea?," 15.

75. "New Kind of Open-Air Cinema," *The Times*, March 9, 1938.

76. "Proposed Curb on City Billboards Modified by Plan Board After a Flurry of Protests," *New York Times*, June 28, 1939.

77. "Minutes of Meeting of the City Planning Commission," City Planning Commission, May 29, 1940, 344. http://www1.nyc.gov/assets/planning/download/pdf/about/cpc/19400529.pdf.

78. "Animated Signs Attract Visitors, Association Finds," press release, The Broadway Association, September 23, 1940, Douglas Leigh Collection, Archives of American Art, Washington, DC.

79. Leigh, "What's the Idea?," 14.

80. "Premiere Wilson Spectacular," 28. For an account of the theatrical nature of the premieres of signs, see also Thompson, "Rainbow Ravine," 175.

81. "Premiere Wilson Spectacular," 31.

82. Leigh, interview by Fred Allen.

83. "Broadway Blackout," *Popular Mechanics*, August 1942, 8.

84. E. Courchinoux, "L'Affiche de l'avenir," *Vendre*, April 1937, 202.

85. Kurt Rosenberg, "Incandescent Lamp Cinematographic Apparatus," US patent 2,069,851, filed October 9, 1933, and issued February 9, 1937. For comparisons between Epok signs and cinema see, for example, "New Kind of Open-Air Cinema," *The Times*.

86. Meyer Berger, "About New York," *New York Times*, December 8, 1939.

87. "New 'Shows' Presented on Leigh's Cartoon Displays," *Signs of the Times*, March 1940, 114.

88. "Spectacular," *Time*.

89. Kahn Jr., "Lights, Lights, Lights," 26.

90. Danton Walker, "Broadway Cavalcade: The Great White Way," *Daily News*, October 4, 1940.

91. "School of Animation to Study Broadway Sign," *New York Post*, October 5, 1940. An earlier article in the *New York Post* noted the school's location in the Gaiety Building: "School Post Box," *New York Post*, February 25, 1939.

92. Donald G. Cooley, "Creating the Spectaculars," *Modern Mechanix*, June 1937, 59.

93. "Leigh's Biggest," Talk of the Town, *New Yorker*, August 7, 1937, 10.

94. Advertisement, Douglas Leigh Collection, Archives of American Art, Washington, DC.

95. Douglas Leigh, interview by Adelaide Hawley, *Woman's Page of the Air*, transcript, WABC, October 29, 1940, Douglas Leigh Collection, Archives of American Art, Washington, DC.

96. Advertisement, Douglas Leigh Collection, Archives of American Art, Washington, DC.
97. "New Cartoon Shows Opening on Broadway," *Signs of the Times*, January 1939, 60.
98. Advertisement, Douglas Leigh Collection, Archives of American Art, Washington, DC.
99. "New 'Shows' Presented on Leigh's Cartoon Displays," *Signs of the Times*, 114. While animated films were closely linked to comic strips, especially in their early years as a popular form, the serial form of comic strips was also influencing print advertisements in their use of "continuity copy." See T. Jackson Lears, *Fables of Abundance* (New York: Basic Books, 1995), 330.
100. Douglas Leigh, "This Business of Selling Big Spectaculars," offprint from *Signs of the Times*, December 1934, Douglas Leigh Collection, Archives of American Art, Washington, DC.
101. Clipping, *News-Week*, July 31, 1937, 31, Douglas Leigh Collection, Archives of American Art, Washington, DC.
102. See, for example, Henry F. Adams, "The Relative Importance of Size and Frequency in Forming Associations," *The Journal of Philosophy, Psychology and Scientific Methods* 12, no. 18 (September 1915): 477-491.
103. Leigh, "This Business of Selling Big Spectaculars."
104. Lears, *Fables of Abundance*, 292.
105. Cooley, "Creating the Spectaculars," 60.
106. Leigh, "This Business of Selling Big Spectaculars."
107. Cooley, "Creating the Spectaculars," 142; Advertisement, *Signs of the Times*, August 1936. Douglas Leigh Collection, Archives of American Art, Washington, DC.
108. Leigh, "This Business of Selling Big Spectaculars."
109. Cooley, "Creating the Spectaculars," 142.
110. Cooley, "Creating the Spectaculars," 60.
111. Starr and Hayman, *Signs and Wonders*, 130.
112. Kahn Jr., "Lights, Lights, Lights," 26.
113. "Thirty-Six Spectaculars in One!," *Signs of the Times*, May 1939, 18.
114. Cliff Taylor, "Big City Sign," *Mechanix Illustrated*, October 1939, 74; "RKO Times Sq. Electric Sign for Fair Ballyhoo," *Variety*, March 1, 1939, 8.
115. "Thirty-Six Spectaculars in One!"
116. Donald Crafton, *Before Mickey: The Animated Film, 1898–1928* (Chicago: University of Chicago Press, 1993), 48.
117. "Advertising News: To Show a New-Type Sign," *New York Times*, January 20, 1939.
118. Taylor, "Big City Sign," 75.

119. Michael Cowan, "Advertising and Animation: From the Invisible Hand to Attention Management," in *Films That Sell: Moving Pictures and Advertising*, eds. Bo Florin, Nico de Klerk and Patrick Vonderau (London: BFI, 2016), 95.
120. Gaston Varenne, "L'Exposition de l'union des artistes modernes au salon de la lumière," *Art et Décoration*, 1935, 415.
121. Pierre Argence, "A l'exposition de 1937. – Le Palais de la publicité et l'exposition du groupe de la publicité," *Vendre*, October 1937, 523; Taylor, "Big City Sign," 130.
122. Argence, "A l'exposition de 1937," 523.
123. Taylor, "Big City Sign," 76.
124. Jean Carlu, "Should a Poster be a Work of Art?," *Commercial Art*, March 1931, 95.
125. Carlu, "Should a Poster be a Work of Art?," 92.
126. Leigh, "This Business of Selling Big Spectaculars."
127. E. J. Kahn, Jr., "Lights, Lights, Lights," 23 and 24.
128. "Motion in the Avenue," Talk of the Town, *The New Yorker*, January 7, 1939, 14. The article is referring to an Epok sign for Wilson Whiskey that Leigh created before his 1940 sign for Wilson Whiskey.
129. Guilds' Committee for Federal Writers' Publications, Inc., *New York City Guide* (New York: Random House, 1939), 342.
130. Frank B. Jewett to Frederic B. Pratt, memorandum, July 2, 1941, p. 1, box 20, folder 196, Office of the Messrs. Rockefeller records, Cultural Interests, Series E, Museums – Museum of Science and Industry 1925-1949, Rockefeller Archive Center, Sleepy Hollow.
131. Karen A. Rader and Victoria E. M. Cain, *Life on Display: Revolutionizing U. S. Museums of Science and Natural History in the Twentieth Century* (Chicago: University of Chicago Press, 2014).
132. Goode and Kaufman, *Profitable Showmanship*, 161. In their book, Goode and Kaufman discuss other ways that motion was a dynamic attraction, particularly for advertisers.
133. Rader and Cain, *Life on Display*, 115.
134. Rader and Cain, *Life on Display*, 116.
135. Irving Hoffman to Douglas Leigh, n.d., Douglas Leigh Collection, Archives of American Art, Washington, DC.
136. Robert P. Shaw, "The Progressive Exhibit Method," *The American Physics Teacher* 7 (June 1939): 166.

62   K. MOEN

REFERENCES

"5th Ave. Assn. Trying to Set Example in Stand on Windows." *Women's Wear Daily*, April 27, 1938.
"5th Ave. Stores Seen Not Foregoing Motion Windows." *Women's Wear Daily*, April 26, 1938.
"5th Avenue Group Backs Franklin Simon Display." *New York Herald Tribune*, September 12, 1940.
Adams, Henry F. "The Relative Importance of Size and Frequency in Forming Associations." *The Journal of Philosophy, Psychology and Scientific Methods* 12, no. 18 (September 1915): 477–491.
"Adopt Principle of Stage and Screen to Window Displays Is Advice to Fashion Group: Cosmetic Section Hears Francis D. Gonda at Women's City Club Yesterday – Elements of Good Showmanship in Displays Pointed Out as Light, Motion, Architectural Quality, Creation of Personality." *Women's Wear Daily*, July 21, 1938.
"Advertising News: To Show a New-Type Sign." *New York Times*, January 20, 1939.
Argence, Pierre. "A l'exposition de 1937. – Le Palais de la publicité et l'exposition du groupe de la publicité." *Vendre*, October 1937.
"Avenue Art." *Time*, December 5, 1938.
Bel Geddes, Norman. *Horizons.* Boston: Little, Brown, and Company, 1932.
Berger, Meyer. "About New York." *New York Times*, December 8, 1939.
Berger, Meyer. "New Constellations on the Old White Way." *New York Times*, March 29, 1936.
"'Blizzard' in Window of Store to Halt." *New York Times*, November 16, 1938.
"Broadway Blackout." *Popular Mechanics*, August 1942.
Burdick, Edward Heckler. "Lilliput Outgrows Gulliver." *Popular Mechanics*, May 1939.
Carlu, Jean. "Should a Poster be a Work of Art?" *Commercial Art*, March 1931.
Cochrane, I. L. "American Motion Displays Part 2: Cardboard and Other Small Units." *Display*, April 1938.
Cochrane, I. L. *Motion Display Mechanics.* New York: Reeder-Morton Publications, 1939.
Cochrane, I. L., ed. *Display Animation, 1937: The Year Book of Motion Displays.* New York: Reeder-Morton Publications, 1937.
Cochrane, I. L., ed. *Display Animation, 1938: The Year Book of Motion Displays.* New York: Reeder-Morton Publications, 1938.
Cooley, Donald G. "Creating the Spectaculars." *Modern Mechanix*, June 1937.
Courchinoux, E. "L'Affiche de l'avenir." *Vendre*, April 1937.
Cowan, Michael. "Advertising and Animation: From the Invisible Hand to Attention Management." In *Films That Sell: Moving Pictures and Advertising*, edited by Bo Florin, Nico de Klerk and Patrick Vonderau, 93–113. London: BFI, 2016.

Crafton, Donald. *Before Mickey: The Animated Film, 1898–1928.* Chicago: University of Chicago Press, 1993.

"Fifth Ave. 'Blizzard' Spurs Winter Trade." *New York Times,* November 15, 1938.

"Fifth Avenue Assn. Amends Policy on Motion in Windows." *Women's Wear Daily,* October 12, 1939.

Fifty Years of Fifth. New York: International Press, 1957.

"Find Window Displays, Ads Gain in Favor." *Women's Wear Daily,* July 7, 1939.

Friedberg, Anne. *Window Shopping: Cinema and the Postmodern.* Berkeley: University of California Press, 1993.

Gaudreault, André and Philippe Marion. "A Medium is Always Born Twice…" *Early Popular Visual Culture* 3, no. 1 (May 1995): 3–15.

Genêt. "Letter from Paris." *New Yorker,* January 1, 1938.

Goode, Kenneth and Zenn Kaufman. *Profitable Showmanship.* New York: Prentice-Hall, 1939.

Gosling, James, Jr. "Advertising Device." US patent 2,273,259, filed October 30, 1940, and issued February 17, 1942.

Guilds' Committee for Federal Writers' Publications, Inc. *New York City Guide.* New York: Random House, 1939.

Hess, Margaret. "Our Show Window Pageant." *New York Times,* April 30, 1939.

"High Window Display Quality Standard Urged." *Women's Wear Daily,* March 1, 1938.

Kahn, E. J., Jr. "Lights, Lights, Lights." *New Yorker,* June 7, 1941.

Leach, William. *Land of Desire: Merchants, Power, and the Rise of a New American Culture.* New York: Vintage, 1993.

Lears, T. Jackson. *Fables of Abundance.* New York: Basic Books, 1995.

Lee, Henry. "It's in the Window." *American Artist,* June 1941.

Lee, Henry. "Very Latest Broadway Spectacular Employs New Principle Called Epok." *New York World-Telegram,* October 12, 1940.

Leigh, Douglas. "This Business of Selling Big Spectaculars." *Signs of the Times,* December 1934.

Leigh, Douglas. "What's the Idea?" *National Sign Journal,* October 1940.

Leigh, Douglas. Collection. Archives of American Art, Washington, DC.

Leigh, Douglas. Interview by Fred Allen. *Texaco Star Theater,* November 13, 1940. http://www.oldtimeradiodownloads.com/comedy/fred-allen-texaco-star-theater/fred-allen-texaco-star-theater-40-10-16-03-death-takes-a-boniface.

"Leigh's Biggest." Talk of the Town. *New Yorker,* August 7, 1937.

"Liberal Regime." Talk of the Town. *New Yorker,* February 3, 1940.

"Lord & Taylor Bells Keep Ringing – By Request." *Women's Wear Daily,* December 6, 1937.

"Lord & Taylor Seek New Window Ruling." *New York Times,* November 19, 1938.

"Lord & Taylor Snow Displays Out Tonight, But Not Because of Protest." *Women's Wear Daily*, November 16, 1938.

"Lord & Taylor's Fifth Avenue Windows are Dressed in the Cellar." *Life*, March 28, 1938.

Marchand, Roland. *Making Way for Modernity, 1920–1940*. Berkeley: University of California Press, 1985.

Marcus, Leonard S. *The American Store Window*. New York: Whitney Library of Design, 1978.

McGinley, Phyllis. "Still Life." *New Yorker*, December 3, 1938.

"Minutes of Meeting of the City Planning Commission." City Planning Commission, May 29, 1940. http://www1.nyc.gov/assets/planning/download/pdf/about/cpc/19400529.pdf.

"Motion in the Avenue." Talk of the Town. *The New Yorker*, January 7, 1939.

"Motion." *Members' Bulletin*. Fifth Avenue Association, Inc., January 1941, 7.

"New 'Shows' Presented on Leigh's Cartoon Displays." *Signs of the Times*, March 1940.

"New Cartoon Shows Opening on Broadway." *Signs of the Times*, January 1939.

"New Kind of Open-Air Cinema." *The Times*, March 9, 1938.

"Oppose Motion in Windows of 5th Ave. Stores: Recommended by Committee on Standards of Window Decoration Is Adopted by Fifth Ave. Assn. Board." *Women's Wear Daily*, April 25, 1938.

Page, Max. *The Creative Destruction of Manhattan, 1900–1940*. Chicago: University of Chicago Press, 1999.

Peters, Munn. "Free Show." *Cue*, March 19, 1938.

"Plate Glass Preview." *Cue*, July 8, 1939.

Pope, Virginia. "'Tiny' Style Show Based on Illusion." *New York Times*, September 10, 1940.

Pratt, Donald L. "Tempest of Controversy Follows Blizzard in Window." *Women's Wear Daily*, November 17, 1938.

"Premiere Wilson Spectacular." *Signs of the Times*, December 1940.

"Proposed Curb on City Billboards Modified by Plan Board After a Flurry of Protests." *New York Times*, June 28, 1939.

Pryor, Thomas M. "Noting the Week's Screen Events." *New York Times*, September 29, 1940.

Rader, Karen A. and Victoria E. M. Cain. *Life on Display: Revolutionizing U. S. Museums of Science and Natural History in the Twentieth Century*. Chicago: University of Chicago Press, 2014.

"Revolving Bulletins Flash Paris Opening News in Bonwit Teller Windows." *Women's Wear Daily*, February 10, 1938.

"RKO Times Sq. Electric Sign for Fair Ballyhoo." *Variety*, March 1, 1939.

Roberts, Jack. "L'Étalage et la Vente." *Vendre*, September 1938.

Rockefeller, Office of the Messrs. Records. Rockefeller Archive Center, Sleepy Hollow.

Rosenberg, Kurt. "Incandescent Lamp Cinematographic Apparatus." US patent 2,069,851, filed October 9, 1933, and issued February 9, 1937.

"School of Animation to Study Broadway Sign." *New York Post*, October 5, 1940.

"School Post Box." *New York Post*, February 25, 1939.

Shaw, Robert P. "The Progressive Exhibit Method." *The American Physics Teacher* 7 (June 1939): 165–172.

"Sign Cinemas for Five Cities." *Shelf Appeal*, February 1938.

"Snowstorm in Store." *New York Times*, November 13, 1938.

"Spectacular." *Time*, July 18, 1938.

Starr, Tama and Edward Hayman. *Signs and Wonders*. New York: Doubleday, 1998.

Sugar, A. L. "Animated Displays." *The Co-Operative Review*, September 1938.

Taylor, Cliff. "Big City Sign." *Mechanix Illustrated*, October 1939.

"Thirty-Six Spectaculars in One!" *Signs of the Times*, May 1939.

Thompson, Kirsten Moana. "Rainbow Ravine: Colour and Animated Advertising in Times Square." In *The Colour Fantastic*, edited by Giovanna Fossati, Victoria Jackson, Bregt Lameris, Elif Rongen-Kaynakçi, Sarah Street and Joshua Yumibe, 163–177. Amsterdam: Amsterdam University Press, 2018.

"Trinity Diorama." *Time*, March 15, 1937.

Varenne, Gaston. "L'Exposition de l'union des artistes modernes au salon de la lumière." *Art et Décoration*, 1935.

"Wails of Complaints Heard Above Din of Fifth Ave. Christmas Bells." *Women's Wear Daily*, December 1, 1938.

Walker, Danton. "Broadway Cavalcade: The Great White Way." *Daily News*, October 4, 1940.

Wolff, Fred M. "Lighting Animated Displays." In *Display Animation, 1937: The Year Book of Motion Displays*, edited by I. L. Cochrane, 215. New York: Reeder-Morton Publications, 1937.

CHAPTER 3

The World's Fair

When the New York World's Fair opened on April 30, 1939, visitors found themselves amid a world of motion and dynamism. Surging crowds moved through the site and its countless exhibition spaces, with more than 40 million people attending the Fair over its two seasons from April to October in 1939 and from May to October in 1940. Hundreds of live performances, exhibits of industry in action, and advertising and instructional films were on show throughout the exhibition site, spread across 1000 acres in Flushing Meadows, Queens (Fig. 3.1). Even the two massive buildings that made up the Fair's iconic "Theme Center," the circular Perisphere and the triangular Trylon, were put into motion. Nightly light shows made it seem as if the Perisphere had come alive: "by the magic of a battery of projectors the illusion of movement is created. It seems to revolve, seems to swim round and round" like a "living, moving sphere."[1] The dynamism on show helped create a vitalized world that fit neatly into the wider aims of the Fair's planners. Responding to the hardships of the Depression and the threat of impending war with a technocratic approach to modern life, the Fair highlighted themes of technology, industry and international cooperation as signs of progress. Grover Whalen, the president of the Fair, described how important it was for the exhibits to communicate a sense of promise and optimism: "The talents and genius of many men and women – architects, designers, artists, engineers, industrialists, businessmen, civic leaders, and educators – have been assembled to give graphic demonstration to the dream of a better 'World of Tomorrow.'"[2] Modern techniques

© The Author(s) 2019
K. Moen, *New York's Animation Culture*, Palgrave Animation,
https://doi.org/10.1007/978-3-030-27931-8_3

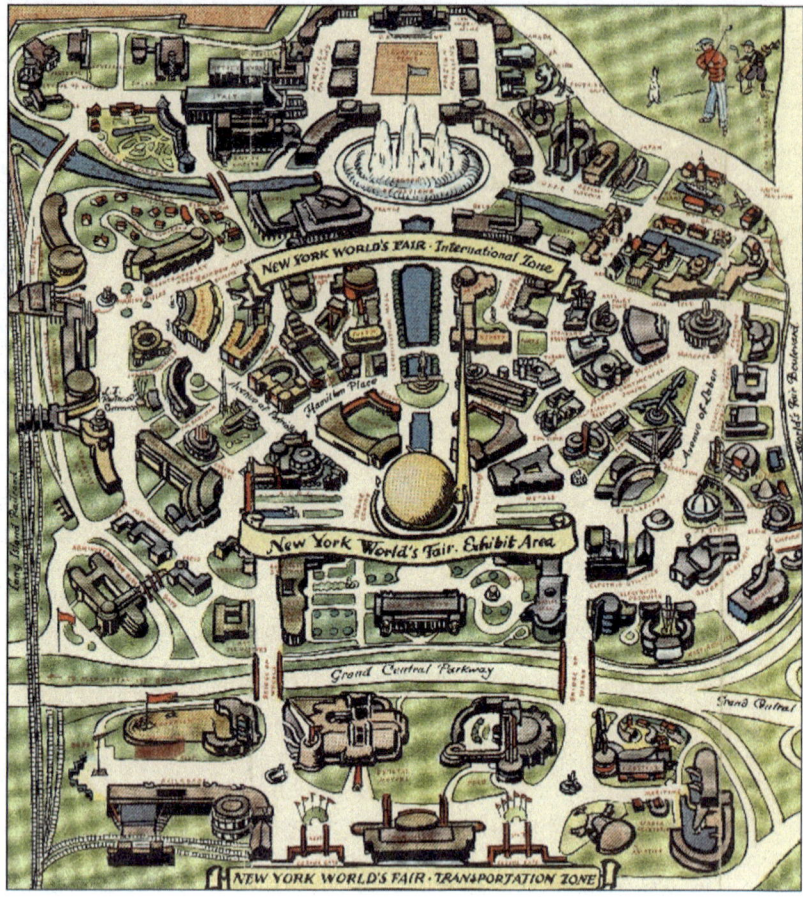

Fig. 3.1 Detail from Tony Sarg, "New York 1939 Official World's Fair Pictorial Map." Tony Sarg Publications, 1939. David Rumsey Historical Map Collection

of animated display helped turn this vision of the future into "a pulsing reality" that "will delight you and instruct you."

The Fair was filled with different exhibits that used animation to create spectacular attractions, novel mixtures of media, dramatic shows and educational illustrations. The uses of motion went from the ridiculous to the sublime, from Mr. Shavemaster and other "talking and animated robots" at the Chicago Flexible Shaft Company's exhibit to "an animated diorama" of Niagara Falls with "an effect of moving water" at the New York State exhibit.[3] I. L. Cochrane, whose work describing and promoting motion display was discussed in the previous chapter, was thrilled by the extraordinary uses of animation, with most of his 1939 *Display Animation* yearbook documenting examples from the Fair. He wrote that the Fair and San Francisco's smaller Golden Gate International Exposition "have set the future pace" for the "merchandising showman."[4] Robert P. Shaw was also astounded by the wealth of display ideas on show, studying the Fair's exhibition techniques in order to develop new ideas for his own methods of instructional display at the Museum of Science and Industry. Funded by The Rockefeller Foundation, the volume that resulted from this research detailed hundreds of different examples of display at the Fair, with frequent reference to their uses of animation. Shaw explained, "With the development and construction of the New York World's Fair 1939 it was evident that it would be the greatest spectacle of its kind and that in this gigantic presentation all of the best exhibition techniques of the past, and probably new ones especially developed for this exposition, would be utilized."[5] Shaw was right. Among these exhibition techniques, animation was at the forefront, used to vibrantly display the wonders of contemporary industry, new technologies and scientific developments.

Picking up on the buzz that was being generated around the Fair, designers and advertisers began to tie their work in with the spectacles on view at the Fair: "Creators of window displays in New York have been quick to grasp the inspirations and ideas employed by those responsible for the displays at the World's Fair. During the past month many of the big stores have filled their windows with displays which have used some material or some idea from the Fair."[6] Among these displays, a miniaturized version of the Perisphere that "simulates all the color and action of the real thing" offered a striking spectacle of motion for retailers.[7] Further integrating advertising in the city with the Fair, the major department store Gimbels planned to showcase their "animated window displays" at a special "Displalounge" in the Communications Building.[8] Douglas Leigh was also drawn into the orbit of the Fair—the illuminated tubes of flowing liquid in the Wilson Whiskey sign were reportedly "modelled on the World's Fair Lagoon of Nations."[9] Such examples indicate how the Fair was using animation in ways that overlapped with the animated windows and displays that were becoming increasingly central to New York's visual culture. But the Fair's exhibits served another purpose than just advertising—they were a means to express the lofty vision of a "World of Tomorrow" through spectacles and new media of motion that represented the dynamism of modern life.

Although the scope of animation at the Fair was unprecedented, the use of motion in Fair exhibits was not new. Chicago's Century of Progress Exposition, which ran from 1933 to 1934, was a major event in the turn from static to moving displays. Charles G. Dawes—the brother of the chairman of the exposition's board as well as vice-president for Calvin Coolidge and a recipient of the Nobel Peace Prize—was a major proponent of movement at the Fair: "Everybody loves to watch a moving mechanism. Put motion into your Fair. Make the wheels turn."[10] As well as providing a visual attraction, motion could also be used to educate. Writing for *Commercial Art* in 1936, Jacquelene Abbott Keyes explained that motion displays responded to "the need on the part of the public to gain an intimate knowledge of these machines which were fashioning their lives. Thus the static display gave way to a display of processes. Action which led to production became the first law of fair and exhibition technique."[11] Just a few years later, at the New York World's Fair, these ideas of motion as a visual delight and educational tool had taken on new life.

Drawing on the same kind of ideas as the advertising designers working in New York, exhibits used motion as a visual attraction, as a means of holding the spectator's attention and as an opportunity to invest existing media with animated qualities. For example, the World's Fair Corporation sponsored a series of "focal exhibits" about modern technologies and scientific discoveries. These exhibits were filled with motion, combining animation with a range of media including "motion pictures, magic, circus, cartoon, comic strips, diorama, puppets, etc." in order "to dramatize the exhibit material."[12] In the Medicine and Public Health show, for instance, motion was used for educational purposes: "Descriptive matter will be minimized. The use of dioramas, animation, puppets, gigantic, mobile enlargements of the human body and its organs, and motion pictures, will vivify lessons in the structure of the human body and its various functions."[13] Others turned toward more artistic emphases to express their subject matter, such as the Food exhibit's "surrealistic extravaganza" that "dramatizes the important part that food plays in life" through "colorful, animated three dimensional displays."[14]

Some of the focal exhibits used animation metaphorically, as a means of suggesting speed, dynamism and other features of modernity. The Communications show used an "animated presentation" involving polarized light and moving models to visualize "man's annihilation of time and space by efficient means of communications."[15] The "annihilation of time and space" was a recurring phrase in nineteenth-century accounts of the effect of modern technologies and modes of transportation, referencing—as Lynne Kirby explains—"a temporal and spatial shrinkage and a perceptual disorientation" in "a new world of speed, velocity, and diminishing intervals between geographical points."[16] The exhibit expressed this idea in terms of communication technologies through "animated dioramas" that were "designed to impart a sensation of the electrical speeds by which thoughts are flung across continents as quickly as a boy throws a ball across a room."[17] Giving visual form to an abstract idea, motion became a metaphor to express the speed of modern communication.

The focal exhibit for Production and Distribution also used motion to express a dynamic quality of modern life: "the vast complex of activity set in motion all over the country by every act of consumption."[18] The exhibit's centerpiece was an "animated mural" that depicted interconnected activities of commerce and production projected on a massive curved screen. Drawing on the form of the nineteenth-century cyclorama, which encircled spectators in a huge painting on a curved canvas, the exhibit was publicized as a "vast animated cyclorama" that offered "an entirely new four-dimensional art form."[19] The aim was to show how "every human activity creates waves of activity far away from the original source of motion, just as a stone dropped into a quiet pond sets up ripples at the farthest shore" (1–2). By exhibiting financial and industrial activities through animated effects, underlying processes of modernity were revealed. Much like the advertising strategies in New York's animation culture, exhibits were transforming existing media forms through motion, creating novel spectacular, dramatic and artistic effects. In these and many other examples, motion was also being used to vividly demonstrate the workings of a dynamic modern world.

The expanded role of animation was nowhere more pronounced than in the exhibitions hosted by the major automobile corporations, Ford and General Motors. Ford's centerpiece, "The Cycle of Production," presented an array of animated figures in a giant revolving display; not to be outdone by their competitor, GM's "Futurama" presented an expansive display of new approaches to highway design, filling its panorama of a futuristic American landscape with miniature moving cars and other animated sights. Entwining spectacles of motion with their visions of the modern age, these were massive undertakings that drew upon a vast range of expertise—from sculpting to engineering—with resources and budgets that matched the most opulent Hollywood production. They were greeted with extended commentaries in both the popular press and specialist journals on topics such as art, design and architecture; they also attracted huge audiences, becoming the most popular exhibits at the Fair.[20] These displays were created by two of the most important industrial designers of the twentieth century, Walter Dorwin Teague and Norman Bel Geddes.

Jeffrey L. Meikle describes how "The profession known as industrial design emerged during the Great Depression of the 1930s."[21] Unlike the more exclusive design products of earlier in the century, "the economic collapse and the ongoing democratization of consumption worked together to give designers for mass production greater influence and status than they had have ever enjoyed before." In light of the Depression, "Desperate competition forced manufacturers to rely on anyone who persuasively claimed an ability to endow everyday products with distinctive modern qualities that would attract a dwindling public of active consumers. Those who offered this essential service became known as 'industrial designers'— a phrase evoking businesslike practicality rather than the pre-industrial aura surrounding the various 'applied arts' or 'arts in industry'" (106). While Teague and Bel Geddes, working out of their offices in midtown Manhattan, were two of the most prominent figures to draw upon industrial design for exhibits at the Fair, others were also involved in such activities—this included Egmont Arens, who designed the Production and Distribution exhibit, and Donald Deskey, who designed the Communications exhibit (as well as the interiors at Radio City Music Hall).

The Fair offered an unprecedented opportunity for industrial designers. Teague described how an "experimental field" had been opened up

> because the carnival spirit does not demand that every flight of invention be justified by utilitarian logic.... Hence world's fairs have always provided a field-day for designers to try out, in form and building technique, all sorts of ideas that would not be tolerated if their permanent acceptability had to be guaranteed in advance.[22]

Teague and Bel Geddes took advantage of this freedom. Not only did they expand the scope of their design practice, they also extended their design ideas to include animation. Tracing how their approach to design and their innovative uses of animation were interwoven with the Fair's wider themes, this chapter explores how Teague and Bel Geddes contributed to New York's animation culture by creating exhibits that displayed modernity in motion. More than simply exhibits with the added attraction of animation, the Cycle of Production and Futurama were designs of motion.

WALTER DORWIN TEAGUE AND THE CYCLE OF PRODUCTION

After working in the field of advertising, Teague turned to design in the late 1920s. Over the course of the following decade, his functional and sleek designs ranged from cameras to gas stations. While prioritising simplicity, unity and order, Teague also foregrounded a dynamic quality in his work. This was particularly evident in his streamlined designs, for which he was an influential advocate. A. Joan Saab writes of how streamlining "dominated the design world during the 1930s," rising to particular prominence at the New York World's Fair as "a metaphor and a mantra for those who wanted to combine notions of technological progress with aesthetics. As a style, streamlining simultaneously embodied the pared-down zeitgeist of the Depression years while suggesting futuristic vitality, movement, and change."[23] Streamlining was initially developed as a design principle that used smooth, curved and parabolic shapes for cars, ships and trains so that they would be faster and more efficient in their movements, encountering less resistance from air or water. It then expanded beyond these functional aims to include designs for things that do not move. Meikle writes, "Within a few years streamlining spread from planes, cars and trains to non-moving artefacts at every scale – from radios and vacuum cleaners to store fronts and restaurant interiors. Streamlining swept past other expressions of modernity with an irresistible metaphoric power."[24] New streamlined designs emerged at a rapid pace in the 1930s.

Streamlining had a range of different appeals and values at the time. Meikle explains that streamlining's success was partly due to its evocation of "a common assumption that society's larger processes had to be rendered smother, less complex, more frictionless in operation. The streamlining of appliances, vehicles, and even the interiors of government buildings visually expressed this desire."[25] Streamlining was also tied in with "technological progress" due to its basis in science and engineering; at the same time, "its rounded, enclosing forms, particularly when applied to architecture, suggested a need for protection and stability" that resonated with "an obsession with control." Streamlining's associations with smoothness, progress and control were all evident in Teague's designs. But Teague expressed a particular fascination with the idea of dynamism:

one reason why we are streamlining so many things today, things which will never move and have no excuse for being streamlined in the sense that they need to be adapted to the flow of air currents, is simply because of the dynamic quality of this line which occurs in streamline forms, and it is characteristic of our age – this line that starts with a parabolic curve and ends in a long backward sweep.[26]

For Teague, streamlined forms were deeply interconnected with modern taste: "We are a primitive age, a dynamic people, and we respond only to the expressions of tensions, of vigor, of energy." Both design and display could become strikingly effective by aligning themselves with this wider cultural sensibility.

Teague was at the forefront of new approaches to exhibition design, developing innovative ways of displaying the modern world through motion. Roland Marchand explains how Teague had "reaped widespread publicity for his role in bringing drama and coherence to the Ford exhibit" at Chicago's Century of Progress Exposition.[27] Corporations began "seeking that optimal blend of motion, simplicity, spectacularity, and visitor participation" that designers were particularly adept at creating. Teague's success resulted in later commissions for Ford, leading up to his design of the Ford exhibition at the New York World's Fair. His earlier work designing exhibitions used motion in multifaceted ways. At the Century of Progress Exposition, moving machines that demonstrated production processes were set alongside revolving displays, such as moving globes that showed different activities of Ford throughout the world. This attention to the movement of displays extended to how Teague planned for the movement of visitors as they walked through the exhibition space. Aiming to "control the movement of people," he wrote, "People must *flow* in an exhibit. Audiences follow the line of least resistance just as water does, and it is much easier to take them around a slow curve than to make them turn an abrupt corner. We bore that in mind in laying out our plan."[28] A sensitivity to the importance of motion also shaped the outward form of buildings. Cheryl R. Ganz describes how Albert Kahn's circular Ford building at the Century of Progress Exposition resembled "cogs on a gear wheel," and Teague used a similar effect for the Ford building at the California Pacific International Exposition, which ran from 1935 to 1936.[29] For the New York World's Fair, Teague—in his role as an advisor to the Board of Design—used "asymmetric forms" in his design of the Transport section to imbue it with a "dynamic quality" that "suggested movement."[30]

This was seen as a "startling contrast" to earlier architectural plans, which were "altogether static." Whether contributing to the design of exterior or interior architecture, Teague carefully considered the effects of motion.

Teague's interest in dynamism as a feature of design found its most sustained expression in the Ford exhibit for the 1939 Fair, which incorporated many different elements that evoked and presented motion. In one of its most striking architectural features, the "Road of Tomorrow," visitors drove on a spiral ramp that wound around the Ford building; this was a "dynamic exhibit, visible to crowds nearly everywhere on the grounds."[31] In his study of exhibition techniques at the Fair, Shaw wrote of the "color and motion" of this sight, describing how it "gave a note of animation to the building which added much to its attraction."[32] The aesthetic effect of motion was "heightened after dark when floodlighting illuminates the cars and projects their moving shadows on the white walls."[33] Constructing a curved ramp that both displayed and channeled the movement of a stream of automobiles, Teague was developing his earlier approach to movement in exhibition design. Inside the Ford building, this emphasis on movement was further expanded in a plethora of moving displays. Setting the tone for the exhibit, visitors were greeted outside by a sculpture perched atop the Entrance Hall: a twenty-five foot high statue of Mercury. Aestheticizing the values of speed and industry, the statue was described in a press release as a "symphony of line and motion" that had transformed Mercury into "a god of the machine age."[34]

The centerpiece for the Ford exhibit, the Cycle of Production, drew together different strands of Teague's interest in motion as a feature of design. Located in the Industrial Hall, the Cycle of Production was a massive rotating display, weighing over 150 tons and spanning more than 100 feet across (Fig. 3.2). Likened to "a wedding cake" and "a revolving mountain," its circular tiered platform displayed eighty-seven animated figures who were engaged in various activities related to car manufacturing.[35] Around the base of the platform, these figures were shown mining, gathering and otherwise extracting twenty-seven different materials used in making a car. Moving upwards to the top of the platform, the materials were shown in various phases of processing, refinement and transportation until they reached three Ford automobiles at the summit. With lines of moving figures operating in an animated assembly line, the display presented a lively vision of production that resonated with Teague's interest in designing with motion. Moreover, much like the architectural design of the earlier Ford exhibition building, the overall shape of the display evoked

Fig. 3.2 "150-Ton Turntable at Ford Exposition, New York World's Fair, 1939." From the Collections of The Henry Ford. Gift of Ford Motor Company

the wheel of a car: the lines of materials in different stages of production were like spokes radiating from a central hub, continuously revolving.

The Cycle of Production was an elaborate development of a display that Teague had showcased at the Chicago exposition entitled "Out of the Earth," which also slowly revolved to reveal how materials used in car manufacturing were obtained from nature. On top of this hemispherical display, a half-section of a Ford V8 car illustrated how twelve different materials were used in the manufacturing of a car—arrows jutted out and ran along the contours of the display, connecting each material with a diorama that depicted how that material was obtained from nature. Not only sharing the same industrial theme as the Cycle of Production, this display also suggested the form of a wheel with a car as its hub and the arrows to different materials visually suggesting spokes. While the overall design of the Cycle

of Production was quite similar to this display, it also offered a striking innovation: the static figures in the dioramas had been freed from their cases
and put into motion. With dozens of animated figures, working alongside
animated models of machinery, transportation and industry, production
came alive. By showing the different stages of the production process, an
impression of animated life was intensified and expanded—rather than relying on demonstrations and displays scattered throughout the exhibition to
show the range of processes involved in production, they were gathered
together into a single vision of industry in motion.

Within the display itself, individual scenes of motion were highly varied.
There were delightful details, such as a moving model of a cat playing with
a ball of yarn, alongside more elaborate depictions of industry in sequences
displaying how the manufacturing process used materials such as aluminum
and copper (Fig. 3.3). The "iron sequence," for example, used animated
displays that began with "an open pit iron mining scene" and led upwards
to animated models of "a blast furnace," a "steel rolling mill," a "forging
press" and "a stamping scene where Ford V-8 frames are manufactured."[36]
Each scene used striking instances of animation, such as a "fiery flow of
molten metal" (3), to simulate activities and processes. In order to lend
levity to the display's industrial subject matter, the appearance of figures
sometimes drew upon the iconography of toys and comic strips. As *Exhibition Techniques* pointed out, "Done in broad caricature they illuminated
the dry facts with their humor, contributed an air of simplicity and gave
the exhibit novelty, color and animation. It is hard to see how the long
list of industries, products and processes could have been made acceptable
without this charming device."[37] The design of the figures, however, was
not entirely benign—there were a number of racial stereotypes. Largely
relegated to the lower tiers of the display, these figures reflected the distribution of labor in Ford's corporation. Greg Grandin describes how "Ford
imagined himself a friend of African Americans, hiring them in large numbers – more than his competitors were – and paying them the same as he
did whites. Yet most of his African American employees were confined to
the [River Rouge plant's] worst work, in its foundry, rolling mill, or paint
shop, with little opportunity for advancement...."[38] In a similar manner,
ethnic caricatures were also shown predominantly along the lower tiers of
the display, evoking Ford's internationalism and unwittingly indicating its
exploitations.

Throughout the display, figures were heavily stylized, almost as if they
were smoothly articulated forms designed for motion. The curved forms

Fig. 3.3   "Copper Display, Ford Exposition, New York World's Fair, 1939." From the Collections of The Henry Ford. Gift of Ford Motor Company

of figures suggested fluid and efficient movement. Other aspects of the display, such as models of nature and machinery, also relied upon rounded edges and curved lines, evoking the streamlined shapes of waves, eggs and raindrops. This flowing visual design was integrated with more linear forms that suggested order: the lines of production which culminated at the cars and the steps leading up to different levels of the display. While the figures and their animated movements were highly varied, the overall impression was of continuously repeated cycles of motion working together in a highly structured and unified whole. There were instances of play and leisure, but the overall emphasis was on figures that were visually entwined with their labor. Perpetually bent over machinery with torsos and limbs designed for work, figures evoked the streamlined quality that Teague saw as present "constantly throughout our bodies."[39] Like the control of people's movement that was so vital to assembly lines and that Teague had planned for in his design of exhibition spaces, the movements of the figures were integrated into a functional design. Streamlining, motion display, dynamic architecture and the control of human motion all coalesced in the Cycle of Production. Teague was designing motion to balance a vision of industrialized labor with the allure of modern dynamism.

This vision of labor in motion also related to the larger scope of Ford's manufacturing process. Terry Smith explains how, with the development of the new River Rouge plant in the 1920s, Ford had sought "to expand and liberate the 'organic flow' of Highland Park, and to join it to a system of transportation which brought raw materials from sites owned by the company to the Rouge and then distributed the processed product to selling/consumption points."[40] In this vision, "The 'purity' of mass production... was projected as sheer movement, both within the plant, now broken up into separated functional sites joined by rail lines, and within the system as a whole, also broken up into sites of extraction, loading, transport, unloading, then redistribution, which were joined by railways and shipping." Mirroring these activities, the Cycle of Production interconnected models of different production processes with a supply chain that spanned the globe, depicting each instance of animated labor as part of a much larger dynamic whole.[41]

The spectacle of international co-operation reflected Ford's multinational corporate strategy, as well as the emphasis on internationalism in the Fair's "World of Tomorrow."[42] This was an important issue for Teague as well. He wrote of the "increasing interdependence" of people throughout the world, "knitting the whole human race into one social and economic organism, so that a strike in Detroit is felt on a rubber plantation of Brazil and a frost in Florida affects the breakfast tables of Chicago and London."[43] Teague linked the issue of global interdependence to contemporary world events, writing of how the "wave of nationalism" that "is at the moment fighting a vicious but a hopeless counter-action... is doomed to collapse because men can no longer live apart from other men, even in national groups." Through its dynamic depiction of an interconnected hive of activity that crossed national boundaries, the Cycle of Production celebrated the unifying powers of industry—eliding its underlying hardships, disparities and exploitations. Industrial activities, human labor and global capitalism were working together in a vision of productive and harmonious motion.

Rhythm and Design

As well as presenting a streamlined vision of labor and production, the Cycle of Production reflected Teague's visionary approach to the potentials of design. Teague outlined his design philosophy in *Design This Day: The Technique of Order in the Machine Age* (1940), explaining how products should be designed so that they are both functional and beautiful. Such ideas were commonplace at the time; for example, publicity for Ford explained how, in the "partnership" between engineers and artists in the design of cars, "The engineer makes use of the artist's talent to give his ideas beauty and grace; the artist uses the engineer's skill to give his ideas practical substance."[44] For Teague, the close relationship between function and beauty had a deeper significance, underpinning the immense potential of design. Expressing deep concerns about the state of war engulfing the world, as well as the suffering wrought by the industrial revolution, Teague saw a desperate need for a "rational reorganization of our world" based on the values of "a perfectly functioning order" and "the beauty of rightness."[45] Well aware that designing "better household equipment and better mechanical devices" might seem to have a rather limited effect in achieving this, he argued that such products of design

> are of no real value unless they are easy first essays in the fundamental redesign of our world: harbingers of a wholesale reorganization of our chaotic scene. The world is in too dire need of redesign, in its broad aspects as a place where human life can flourish and develop, for us to be satisfied to stop at better gadgets. (1–2)

Making beautiful and functional objects resonated with a far-reaching reorganization of contemporary life.

In order to redesign the world along the lines he envisaged, one of the most important principles to be employed was rhythm. Three chapters of *Design This Day* were devoted to the subject of rhythm, exploring its different implications and potentials. Teague drew analogies between design and music, suggesting that they shared a common structure based in rhythms that "are the binding force creating unity, and the evidence of sound construction and complete effectiveness of the organic whole."[46] While visual rhythms are "less readily perceptible" than musical rhythms, design nevertheless has its own rhythmic basis "expressed in lines, areas, forms, textures, colors, light and shade" (131). Designing products—or exhibitions—with such rhythmic qualities helps create cohesiveness, aesthetic beauty and compositional variety. Design needed to be rhythmic in order to "give us a satisfying sense of order, unity, rightness – beauty" (127).

The Cycle of Production carefully used rhythm to create a sense of both order and beauty for its industrial subject matter. The use of color, for example, was integrated with the overall design: "The color combination of each display had not only to be harmonious within itself but it had to fit in with the general color scheme of the adjacent displays."[47] While such considerations were important for creating the visual rhythms in the Cycle of Production, it was animation that most immediately and powerfully conveyed rhythm. The animation of the figures in the Cycle of Production was geared toward this effect, with "more than 100 motors on the turntable activating" the "133,600 moving parts" that worked together to create rhythmic patterns of motion.[48] The head animator explained how they used "every known fundamental mechanical principle" to animate the figures, each of which "presented a distinct problem for the animation varied in each – from a movement of an arm to a perfect golf swing pivot on a figure chopping at a tree with an axe."[49] The subtleties and variations of animated activities created a panoply of rhythmic cycles. For example, for the "figure of a man carrying two baskets of tung nuts" (Fig. 3.4) the animators aimed "to get those baskets to swing in correct rhythm with the figure's body movements as he simulated walking" (2). Creating this particular movement was particularly challenging, as the animators discovered that when the figure was moved to another floor of the building in which they were working, "the difference in the height above sea level would absolutely destroy the proper rhythm." As well as being carefully planned for in the animation of individual figures, rhythms were integrated into the

Fig. 3.4 "Men at Tung Trees Display, 'Ford Cycle of Production,' Ford Exposition, New York World's Fair, 1939." From the Collections of The Henry Ford. Gift of Ford Motor Company

overall composition—the animated scenes were a part of a recurring cycle of well-ordered movements.

For Teague, the significance of rhythm extended far beyond design. He argued that rhythm is a fundamental basis for life, "from the beating of our hearts and the breathing of our lungs to our life-cycle itself."[50] Teague explained that design could correspond with rhythm's fundamental role in life so that "by integrating our own work rhythmically we are repeating the structural scheme of the universe in which we live. Rhythm is the principle of order in the world and in ourselves" (127). One of the main influences for Teague's understanding of rhythm was the writing of John Dewey, whose 1934 book *Art as Experience* is cited multiple times in *Design This Day*. For Dewey, the role of rhythm is vast. He describes how rhythms underpin the processes of nature, writing that "every uniformity and regularity of change in nature is a rhythm."[51] This is exemplified by "the ebb and flow of tides, the cycle of lunar changes, the pulses in the flow of blood, the anabolism and katabolism of all living processes" (149). Design could both draw upon and express this principle of rhythmic order.

As an extension of its role in nature, rhythm was essential to both art and science. In a quote cited by Teague, Dewey writes, "The first characteristic of the environing world that makes possible the existence of artistic form is rhythm."[52] The central role of rhythm in art is evident in a range of forms, from musical rhythms to poetic prosody to painterly composition. In relation to science, Dewey connects rhythm to a similarly wide range of areas: "Astronomy, geology, dynamics, and kinematics record various rhythms that are the orders of different kinds of change. The very conceptions of molecule, atom, and electron arise out of the need of formulating lesser and subtler rhythms that are discovered" (149). Drawing upon such ideas, Teague saw rhythm in design as something much more than an aesthetic choice. Rhythmic design created order and beauty from a fundamental principle of art, science and nature.

In the Cycle of Production, production processes were invested with order and beauty through their animated rhythms. This cast industrial production in the light of natural processes; the production cycle was shown to have the same rhythmic force as the life cycle or the lunar cycle. Dewey wrote of how rhythm was ever-present in human labor: "With the working of wood, metal, fibers, clay, the change of raw materials into consummated result, through technically controlled means, is objectively manifest. In working the matter, there are the recurrent beats of patting, chipping, molding, cutting, pounding, that mark off the work in measures."[53] Presenting the rhythm of labor and extending it to include a shared rhythm between people, technologies and the overall production process, the Cycle of Production showed modern industry as harmonious with the same rhythmic motions that form the basis of creative and natural processes.

Teague used motion to represent modern industrial processes in a way that was closely entwined with his own design philosophy. Others also incorporated motion into their representations of industrial processes, although with sometimes less fully realized results. The initial plans for the Production and Distribution exhibit, for example, reveal the challenges that designers faced in using motion to express ideas of modernity. Planners for this exhibit had focused on developing a vivid illustration of the technical and rather abstract subject of the economics of production and distribution. This proved to be difficult. One of the most obvious ways to show economic processes in a dynamic manner was through film, but doubts about this approach were summarized in an early planning memorandum:

> It takes time to view a movie. We are dealing with material that is hard to present interestingly anyway; people are not likely to go into a movie unless it is very well sold outside. Undoubtedly an animated cartoon of the Mickey Mouse type could be prepared which would be a wonderfully gilded pill of economic information but I think it would take several years of experiment to develop it and more money than we have.[54]

Moreover, the point was raised in one of the planning meetings that "the thing should be dramatized with as few movies as possible, as there will be too many movies at the Fair."[55] In order to make the exhibit stand out—while at the same being visually absorbing and educationally sound—planning turned toward how it could communicate its message through a motion display.

Since early in the century, the idea of flow had been a way of representing the transformation of materials into products, as well as their distribution; "flow sheets," "flow diagrams" and "flow charts" had become standard graphic visualizations of this process.[56] For the Production and Distribution exhibition, plans were developed to make these conceptual diagrams come alive by using motion displays to show how "the flow of goods and money" was a foundation for modern society.[57] The Cycle of Production was seen in a similar light, described as a "lesson in the intricate economy of mass production" and a "flow sheet of the automobile industry."[58]

While the Production and Distribution exhibit had a similar aim to the Cycle of Production, its designers explored different animated approaches to present the flow of goods and finances. One idea involved a large mechanized display case that spectators could walk around and peer into from both sides. At one end, it would show "the flow of money" between homes, stores, warehouses, factories and banks.[59] At the other end, "parallel with the flow and counterflow of purchasing power," it would show "the flow of goods and, if possible, services" (3). Symbols of finance and products would move back and forth, from one end to the other, so that the viewer would "see that there is a real connection between the flow of money and the flow of goods. A very considerable amount of economic theory could be presented in an extremely understandable way by such a machine." And, by "containing as much motion as possible," it would hopefully attract and hold the interest of spectators (2).

Another more ambitious idea for the exhibit was "setting up in three dimensions a sort of glorified 'flow-chart'" using "glass tubes combined with symbols of some sort for the various stages of the distribution process."[60] These tubes could be vacuum-powered, showing different materials represented by paper or other objects moving through the system. Short films could even be projected at different intervals on the device, showing stages of distribution in "small motion picture frames." Rather than an old-fashioned "chart on a piece of paper," this would be a "dramatization of a chart" (2). One concern was that this depiction of flow offered only a partial view of production and distribution: "From the point of view of economic theory it lacks the ability to represent the concept of time. It could show quite clearly the relationships that exist in a logical sense between different parts of the economic system, but the time relations and the place relations could not be shown." Another concern about this approach related to its entertainment value—if different iterations of the process were shown only as short movies, the "dramatic possibilities seem rather small" (1). As much as representing flow offered a potentially novel way of educating the public about production and distribution, it raised issues of aesthetics and form that proved to be challenging for the planners of the exhibit. With such considerations in mind, these initial ideas were abandoned.

The Cycle of Production presented something quite different through its more elaborate and carefully considered use of animation. Rather than presenting a steady flow of movement, the Cycle of Production used a combination of different animated rhythms to create a sense of multiple kinds of motion. For Dewey, "When there is a uniformly even flow, with no variations of intensity or speed, there is no rhythm. There is stagnation even though it be the stagnation of unvarying motion… There is no rhythm of any kind, no matter how delicate and no matter how extensive, where variation of pulse and rest do not occur."[61] Presenting varied pulses of human and industrial activity, the Cycle of Production used animated rhythms to create a much richer sense of liveliness than was evident in the plans for the Production and Distribution exhibit. This was not the same as the "illusion of life" that Disney studios and other animators at the time were working toward in order to fabricate natural motion.[62] Instead, live-liness was a more abstract quality that Teague saw as necessary for design: "we must introduce a certain vitality and inspiration that gives a thing life and gives it that changing aspect that we require in anything that is wholly satisfying."[63] In the Cycle of Production, Teague was designing motion— making it rhythmic and investing it with beauty. Much like the animated spectacles of advertising that were taking place in shop windows and bill-boards, motion was being drawn into wider considerations of aesthetics and cultural value. But rather than expressing an advertising message, motion was used to express modernity. Contemporary industry was depicted as part of a well-ordered and dynamic modern age, alive with the rhythms of nature and life.

As well as his major commission for Ford, Teague designed exhibits for other corporations at the Fair, including "United States Steel, Eastman Kodak, National Cash Register, and Consolidated Edison."[64] Teague's design of the Consolidated Edison exhibit extended his approach to anima-tion from industrial subjects to the life of a city, transforming New York itself into a motion display: "an animated, lighted, colored architectural model of the metropolitan area, from skyline to 6-car subway trains speeding under the streets."[65] Named "The City of Light," this animated diorama spanned almost a city block (Fig. 3.5). It presented the life of New York over the course of a day in a twelve-minute animated show, with climactic scenes of a massive storm and the city's resilience, thanks to the power company. This vision of the city in action included details such as moving elevators and changing traffic lights; further animated effects were added in its second season, including new illuminated signs in Times Square, to create an even more vivid impression of New York coming alive.[66] These animations were synchronized with the show's musical score, poetic narration and lighting effects by "a robot machine" that "operates a standard motion picture film, with all sounds recorded on the voice-track, and notches which control the mechanical changes."[67] Filmic effects were created when, at certain points in the show, "a panel in the face of the diorama would slide out of the way" to reveal "a close-up of some phase of the city's life" such as a hospital or baseball field.[68]

The vitalized vision of New York in the City of Light was advertised as presenting not "merely a spectacle" but also "a city of light and movement and sound so that you could see it live and breathe and see what *makes* it live and breathe."[69] Of course, what makes New York live and breathe—as far as

Fig. 3.5 "Consolidated Edison—City of Light Diorama—Model." The New York Public Library

the display's corporate sponsors were concerned—was the energy supplier, Consolidated Edison, whose power over light and motion was shown in dynamic fashion. Dramatizing how "the allied services of electricity, gas, and steam supply the heat and energy which are the lifeblood of the city," the City of Light aimed to demonstrate just how fundamental industry was to our daily lives.[70] Much like the rhythms of industry depicted in the Cycle of Production, seamless and vibrant motion was the outward sign of a smoothly functioning, pulsing, lively modern age.

NORMAN BEL GEDDES AND FUTURAMA

Norman Bel Geddes aimed to present motions of modernity in his design of the Futurama exhibit for General Motors. Like Teague, Bel Geddes was a well-established and influential industrial designer. Gregory Votolato

writes, "Among the first generation of industrial designers to establish con-
sultancies in the late 1920s, Norman Bel Geddes became the most closely
identified with the first popular machine-based styling innovation, Streamlining, which he applied to everything from small kitchen gadgets to major
building designs. Bel Geddes discovered that streamlining lent objects of
utility a drama which was entirely metaphorical."[71] This sense of drama was
central to the reputation of Bel Geddes, extending to his work in a range
of creative and industrial fields. Christopher Innes argues that "the start of
industrial design in a modern sense… came out of theater," with Bel Geddes (alongside Joseph Urban) exemplifying a changing approach to design
that incorporated dramatic and immersive qualities.[72] These qualities were
evident not only in Bel Geddes's innovative staging of plays, such as *The
Miracle* in 1924, but also in his design work outside of the theater, which
included dramatic shop windows where "the merchandise is presented as
the actors."[73]

In his theater work, Bel Geddes saw motion as a vital dramatic quality
that could work alongside light and sound to create "emotional beauty."[74]
For example, in his "staging manuscript" for the *Divine Comedy* in 1923,
Bel Geddes drew up a detailed table—"more along the lines of a composer's orchestration than a literary play"—that indicated how "various
major elements such as the dialogue, movement of the principal actors,
movement of the chorus, lighting and music" would be coordinated for
maximum dramatic effect in every fifteen seconds of the play.[75] When Bel
Geddes turned from theater design to industrial design in the 1920s, he
continued to explore the potentials of motion. In his 1932 book *Horizons*,
he detailed how his work designing cars, airplanes, trains and steamships
foregrounded streamlining as a functional and aesthetic principle based on
speed and movement. Other ideas that drew upon motion included designing a factory assembly line with "concentric rings of manufacturing space"
for the more efficient movement of production and an Aerial Restaurant
in which "the entire structure slowly revolves" so that patrons get a constantly changing view from their elevated vantage point.[76] Turning from a
dramatic focus, Bel Geddes was drawing motion into design considerations
for new modes of travel, work and leisure.

This background in designing with motion shaped the creation of Futurama, the centerpiece of the General Motors exhibition. In the early planning stages, General Motors executives thought that it was vital for Bel
Geddes to "find out what Teague is doing for Ford, because if it in any way
conflicts, GM will not be interested."[77] Given that the General Motors

building would be adjacent to the Ford building, and Teague had been a trailblazer with his innovative approaches to exhibition, executives were understandably wary of being upstaged by their competitor. But there was no reason to worry. While Futurama shared an interest in using motion to demonstrate the workings of modernity, Bel Geddes was planning something quite different from the Cycle of Production. While the Cycle of Production envisioned the modern production process as a harmonious world of rhythmic motion, Futurama showcased how a new system of highways could enable free-flowing traffic. Both exhibits had turned away from long-standing practices of showing actual motors or machines in action, instead presenting a more imaginative vision of how motion and modern life were entwined.

The Futurama exhibit would go on to overshadow the Ford exhibit in its scale, popularity and influence. Visualizing how new approaches to highway planning might transform America's cities and countryside in the next two decades, Futurama was described in the Fair's *Official Guide Book* as presenting a huge "continuous animated panorama."[78] The scope of the exhibit was extraordinary. Spread over 35,738 square feet, the *Guide Book* noted that Futurama was "the largest and most realistic scale-model ever constructed," reportedly containing "approximately 500,000 individually designed houses; more than a million trees of eighteen species; and 50,000 scale-model automobiles, of which 10,000 are in actual operation over super-highways, speed lanes and multi-decked bridges." The route that spectators took in order to view this enormous display was carefully planned—they were carried along a viewing track above the scenery on moving chairs which were located on a conveyor belt. Through a speaker in the chairs, a voice-over narration provided detailed information about the sights below; each chair was also equipped with a mechanism that would restrict the spectator's vision—like blinders for a horse—and focus their attention on certain details. Gazing upon an incredible expanse of natural landscapes, roads, towns, cities and highways, visitors "experience the sensation of traveling hundreds of miles and viewing the scenes from a low-flying airplane." As well as creating a vivid sense of realism, Futurama also gave an impression of fantastic possibilities: "This magic Aladdin-like flight through time and space is Norman Bel Geddes' conception of the many wonders that may develop in the not-too-distant future."[79]

The exhibit told a story of sorts. Beginning with a sedate rural scene, the viewer followed the first sign of animated movement that came into view as a truck emerged, moving along a side road and then turning off to join a highway. As the journey continued, more and more details of the highway system come to light, such as carefully planned feeder roads, dual motorways, multilevel roads and innovations in traffic control. Other aspects of the American landscape are also shown, including modern industrial projects and a changing terrain. After ascending the heights of a mountain range, in the distance a large city came into view—based on St. Louis, but modernized and expanded for twenty years in the future.[80] The spectator is brought closer and closer to the city, with its modern urban planning, futuristic buildings and bustling activity (Fig. 3.6). In the tour's climactic moments, an enlarged view of the city is transformed when "Suddenly the spectator, in his chair, is swung about! He can scarcely believe his eyes. He is confronted with the full-size street intersection he was just looking on."[81] Entering a life-sized model of a city block, the visitor effectively enters the future.

Fig. 3.6 "General Motors—Futurama—Models of High-Rise Buildings." The New York Public Library

Futurama coalesced with the themes of the Fair and its "world of tomorrow" in stunning fashion. With more than 20 million visitors, the exhibit was a huge success; it was covered ecstatically in the popular press and a Gallup poll found it to be the favorite exhibit at the Fair.[82] Futurama also had a lasting impact. Although it is difficult to measure its precise influence, Innes describes how many elements of the traffic planning it displayed so spectacularly—"barriers separating traffic moving in opposite directions," "gently curving access ramps, interchanges, and overpasses allowing vehicles to maintain speed" and "multiple feeder lanes on expressways in high-density areas, separating local from through traffic"—became integral to highway design in 1950s and 1960s America (Fig. 3.7).[83] Cliff Ellis describes the enormous impact that this had:

> While one cannot demonstrate direct connections between Futurama and subsequent government policies, it clearly projected vivid images of an

Fig. 3.7 "General Motors—Futurama—Model of Highways Intersecting." The New York Public Library

appealing automotive future to a large popular audience. Bel Geddes' urban visions and industrial designs were dramatic, compelling and immediately understandable by the untrained observer. Futurama stocked the social consciousness with images of an auto-dominated future, precisely at the time when politicians, highway engineers and planners were forging the diverse strands of urban freeway planning thought into funded public policy.... By the mid-1950s, opportunities for a more balanced urban transportation system in the USA had been lost, as extensive urban freeway construction began and the alternatives faded away.[84]

Futurama dramatically visualized a redevelopment of the American landscape, making it enticing, fascinating and thrilling. While Bel Geddes followed up with a book, *Magic Motorways* (1940), that explained the ideas and research behind this redesign of the highway system in more detail, it was Futurama that most powerfully presented the planning ideas for millions of spectators. The drama of motion was the driving force behind its enormous impact.

Futurama drew upon a range of established practices from theater and other forms of popular spectacle. For example, visitors began their journey in a darkened room, a long-standing practice in panoramas which would often place spectators in a transitional space before they entered to view enormous painted depictions of landscapes and historical events. Futurama's mobile view from above also related to those nineteenth-century panoramas which offered an aerial perspective so that viewers would peer down on huge landscape paintings moving by; as Erkki Huhtamo explains, "spectators were placed in the position of the aeronauts, and the world below was depicted as the balloonists had purportedly experienced it."[85] More modern dramatic techniques were also incorporated into Futurama. Drawing on his own work with dramatic display, Bel Geddes wanted Futurama to use "the simplest kind of lighting – the kind used for window display."[86] Furthering this contemporary feel, cinematic qualities were integrated into descriptions and plans for the exhibit, with the overall movement of the spectators around and through the exhibit likened to "a movie camera panning a set."[87] Borrowing from theatrical techniques and other media, Futurama was a massive assemblage of dramatic forms.

The overall dramatic qualities of the exhibit—the showmanship of entering the darkened room at the beginning and seeing a model city at the conclusion, the aerial viewpoint from moving chairs and the extraordinary scale and detail—were closely linked to Bel Geddes's background as a theater designer. And motion was integral to Futurama's dramatic unfolding. The plethora of animated details and the intricate circulation of traffic on the highway system were essential to its operation, effects and aims. These moving parts were tied together with dramatic qualities of narration, lighting effects and the overall structure of the spectator's journey from an illustrative map to a city of the future. Further integrating its aesthetic elements, Futurama interconnected sound with movement: it used a mechanism that projected sound by using photoelectric cells in a manner "similar to sound motion pictures" and, at the same time, controlled "the speed of the cars so that the 'guide' always speaks each word at the correct moment."[88] Not content with just integrating motion with sound, Bel Geddes drew the spectator into this moving world. Much as Teague carefully considered the movement of people in an exhibition space, the spectators in Futurama followed the highway system and vehicles in their automatically moving chairs.[89]

Futurama was itself a design with motion as its primary concern. In *Horizons*, Bel Geddes defined a design as "a mental conception of something to be done."[90] In this respect, "A visual design is the organism of an idea of a visual nature so that it may be executed. It is the practice of organizing various elements to produce a desired result. Design deals exclusively with organization and arrangement of form." The highway system depicted in Futurama was such a design, with Bel Geddes describing it as "a visual dramatization of a solution to the complex tangle of American roadways."[91] Expanding his earlier approach, in which design was "concerned with form, space, color; with the proportioning of solids and voids and the rhythmic spacing of these elements," Bel Geddes was now thinking in terms of designing motion.[92] Further articulating his approach to visual design, Bel Geddes wrote, "The governing factor as to what is pleasing to the eye is the *idea*, which is of an emotional nature – an emotion of pleasure, satisfaction, excitement, exhilaration, stimulation." This approach was an extension of his earlier approach to theatrical design; he had described his work on the *Divine Comedy* as "altogether the result of an idea" that was designed "to express emotional beauty."[93] Turning to industrial design, he continued to emphasize an emotional and dramatic impact. In order to express the *idea* of the visionary highway system in such a way, animation was vital. Without it, the design of the highway system would be inert and lifeless. Being able to see the movement of automobiles—the "visual dramatization" of the design idea—created the emotional power that Bel Geddes sought in his design work.

Futurama combined Bel Geddes's interest in drama, design and motion. These were central aspects of his company's work at the time. In 1937, before the contract to make Futurama was finalized, Benjamin L. Webster wrote a letter on behalf of Bel Geddes to the Fair's Chairman of Committee on Theme, Robert D. Kohn.[94] In the letter, Webster outlined some initial ideas of how the Bel Geddes company might approach designing the Production and Distribution focal exhibit. As discussed earlier, this exhibit went through different forms in its planning stages—such as using animated flow charts—to depict its subject matter in a dynamic manner. Webster also suggested incorporating motion into the display, "which will make it very arresting and create an interest which a static display would lack." He further explained: "In all display work for the World's Fair we are attempting to introduce motion in the display wherever possible, believing that this is the best way to dramatize an idea in the most arresting manner." While Bel Geddes did not receive the contract for the Production and Distribution exhibit, the idea of motion's dramatic display potentials played out on a much grander scale in Futurama. With the backing of GM, the expense of the exhibit became a secondary concern; the emphasis on motion and drama as a means to express a design idea took on expansive form.

Animating Design

The movement of vehicles along Bel Geddes's highway presented the central dramatic idea of the Futurama exhibit. This swarm of activity circulating through the panoramic expanse was logistically challenging to create, involving hundreds of miniature cars, as well as trucks and buses, coursing through the highways. The animation used a "continuous running chain for each lane of traffic" with cars "attached to the chains by connecting rods passing through the roadbed at a point invisible to the spectator."[95] At certain points, this required a flap that would lift up so that the rod could pass through and close up again when the car had gone by. While the basic mechanism was rather straightforward, the animation itself was quite complex and required extensive planning. The movement of the cars had to be varied, especially in the more intricate sections of the highway system. Not only would it look unrealistic if they all moved at the same speed, it would also be visually uninteresting. So, blueprints were drawn up that detailed how different cars should move. Diagrams for animation, such as "Animation for Super Highways Model Sequence Intersection" and "Animation for Superhighways Model Sequence from Farm to Super-Highway," provided precise calculations of timing, with cars of a certain color traveling at particular speeds, switching lanes and changing speeds at set intervals.[96] Much as Teague took into account variations of movement to create a sense of rhythm through animation, Bel Geddes needed to employ ordered variations to illustrate movement as something more complex than a simple steady flow in order to give motion qualities of realism, vitality and visual appeal.

This elaborate depiction of vehicles moving across the American landscape was, in part, an extension of Bel Geddes's abiding interest in military maneuvers. Around the time of the First World War, he had created an elaborate game that modeled war scenarios; friends and colleagues would gather around a game board that was "28 feet long and four feet wide," spending "four days in arranging the several thousand units on its surface."[97] *The New York Sun* reported on one season of the game in 1932: "There were fourteen players on a side, seated on either side of an enormous relief map – which was the game board. This map, complete to scale, with mountains, valleys, rivers, cities, railroads, motor roads, coal mines – every principle resource and facility of a modern nation shown in minute proportions."[98] With weekly sessions that took place over the course of months, the article explained how the players would mobilize an enormous number of "military and naval units" which were "represented by pins – red and yellow pins – pins by the hundreds and thousands – pins in amazing clusters and depositions." The movement of these military units was regulated by a voluminous collection of rules and notes, based on detailed calculations and extensive historical research.

Bel Geddes developed this interest in war games in the mid-1930s with an idea for an "Animated Battle Map" that would "record the important battles of the world by means of slow motion color photography with narrative sound track."[99] Rather than taking the more familiar form of illustrations or written accounts, the historical reconstruction would be created by filming models in a manner "somewhat similar to that of the animated motion picture." Showing the "continuous simultaneous motion" of trains, ships, planes and other military activities, the animated battle map "will assist in the full comprehension of relationships and will insure proper emphasis of all movements." In his description of the project's aims, Bel Geddes wrote, "The element of movement is the outstanding contribution of this process."[100] Planning the motion for these animated battle films included detailed calculations of movement, much like the blueprints of automobile travel on the Futurama highways, so that "troop or ship movement will be represented with mathematical accuracy at their various ratios of speed, and will appear to be moving of their own accord." As well as presenting carefully ordered movements and varied instances of animation in a manner similar to Futurama, scenes would be shown from the same vantage point, with the camera viewing the scene "as from an airplane" (2).

The ideas behind these war reconstructions, with their miniaturized worlds and coordinated mobile units, influenced the development of Futurama. While its highway system looked toward a peaceful future, it nevertheless resonated with the same militaristic concerns. Bel Geddes explained how Futurama's redesigned highway system "will supplement American defense. Mobility has always been the keynote of warfare from the beginning of time, and today with the highly mechanized transport developments in military machines this factor reaches its highest importance."[101] Moving from reconstructing the past to designing the future, Futurama expanded the significance of motion that was being explored through the War Games and Animated Battle Maps. Rather than a means to represent history and conflict, motion was used to project the infrastructure of a new American landscape.

Motion was also integral to Futurama's aesthetic and dramatic effects. The animation designer for Futurama sought a dramatic expression of motion by requesting "a *story* of the model animation" while at the same time seeking out further potential avenues of motion by asking "what objects will be seen in each model which can be animated."[102] In a planning meeting from 1938, Bel Geddes and his colleagues explored various potential uses of animation, "all of the things that might mean increased human interest and additional liveliness in the model" as "there is nothing deader than looking at a landscape from an airplane." For a vision of the future so deeply entwined with motion, stasis was to be avoided at all costs. With these concerns in mind, designers agreed "that in order to give the model life it would be wise to forget naturalism and increase the speed of everything so that motion which would not, under actual circumstances, be visible, will be definitely apparent." There were further considerations of how "to make action noticeable and show it up more clearly by reversing the motion – having animated objects off the road move in an opposite direction from that in which the spectators are moving, rather than moving in the same direction."

In order to add more life to the scene, many details of Futurama were planned with motion in mind. For example, there was a discussion of different ways of "getting action into the water," with Bel Geddes wanting "to have some animation in the nature of waterfalls and rapids."[103] One suggestion was "that waterfalls could be made to seem animated by building them of glass and placing behind them some twisted spiral shiny-surfaced wire which the light would hit." However, Bel Geddes wanted to avoid lighting tricks and thought that simply having real water flowing through some of the models would be a workable solution. While details of the landscape incorporated animation in innovative ways, the most elaborate animations took place in the final section of the exhibit, the "City of the Future." As well as showing everyday activities, such as people walking in the streets and cars parking, the plans for animation foregrounded spectacles of movement that captured the energy of the modern city, including animated spectaculars such as neon signs and revolving signs, "a building in the process of construction" and "show windows with lights blinking." Some of the suggested ideas were quite ambitious: "Buildings could also be shown with autogyros landing on their roofs delivering mail. Banners and flags could be waving in the wind." While not all of this detail was incorporated in the final version, the potential uses of animation were integral to the planning of Futurama's moving design; as the animation designer pointed out, "there definitely must be enough action outside of the streets, or it would look as if the automobiles were moving on highways running through a cemetery."

Futurama's lively city stood in stark contrast to an earlier design for urban planning that Bel Geddes had developed for a Shell advertising campaign in 1937. The miniature models developed for this campaign were similarly detailed and realistic to those in Futurama, but as they were made for print advertising and photography, they were static. Attempting to overcome this limitation, planning notes emphasized how motion could be suggested. Models of intersections, for example, should include "Some means of indicating variations of traffic speeds" and the "Smooth flow of traffic must be indicated by positions of vehicles."[104] While motion could only be suggested in a still photograph, Futurama showed actual movement. Rather than a static model, it presented an animated model. Like the transformation of static dioramas into animated figures in Teague's Cycle of Production, Bel Geddes was transforming existing media through animation.

Even though the Futurama on display in 1939 was described as "crowded with hundreds of delights of animation," the scale of animation was increased for the second season of the Fair in 1940, as its designers further realized the impact and appeal of motion.[105] A press release explained:

> Perhaps the most striking and popular new feature of the Futurama this year... is the greatly increased amount of animation. More than 16,000 miniature motorcars will be seen in actual operation over the express motorways... streamlined trains will speed through the countryside and at various other points motion will be in evidence. The problem of successfully animating the extensive area covered by the Futurama represents one of the most difficult technical jobs of its kind ever accomplished, it was said.[106]

An article in the *New Yorker* about these changes discussed the added animation in light-hearted fashion, describing how Futurama, "which played to capacity audiences all last year, has been air-cooled, repainted, and livened up with a great number of animated objects – tiny trains, more cars on the express highways, tiny clothes in a back yard fluttering in a Norman Bel Geddes breeze."[107] The sight of this Bel Geddes breeze and other charming details offered a respite from the larger world of animation coursing through this meticulously planned and carefully engineered exhibit.

Before Futurama, Bel Geddes was working with motion in diverse ways: designing with it, creating with it, researching it and even playing with it. Futurama drew upon all these different uses of motion for its dramatic, aesthetic, representational and educational qualities. It is no coincidence that Bel Geddes's diverse interests in movement as a principle of design coalesced at the World's Fair. This was a site of experimentation and dynamism that invited innovative displays. Moreover, in his New York office, Bel Geddes was located in the midst of a burgeoning landscape of animated display and spectacle that was itself crossing between art, drama, education, industry and design. Reflecting this context, shortly after the Fair had ended, sections of Futurama were installed in the New York Museum of Science and Industry. Frank B. Jewett, president of the museum, was thrilled:

> The principal aim of the museum is to present to the public in a graphic and dramatic manner, through modern exhibit techniques, the outstanding discoveries and developments of science and industry, and at the same time indicate to visitors the social and economic significance of these scientific

accomplishments. I know of no display in history which does this so effectively as the Futurama.[108]

For a site heavily invested in new modes of dynamic display, the Museum was particularly well-suited for an exhibition of Futurama, perhaps the most prominent work of New York's vibrant animation culture.

The Art of Motion at the Fair

The displays at the Fair were deeply embedded in New York's animation culture. Not only were they drawing enormous crowds and feeding into a wider use of motion display throughout the city, they were also engaging with the same approaches to animation as others in New York who were using animation for the purposes of advertising and education. Like motion displays in the city, the industrial exhibits at the Fair embraced the transformative potentials of motion—creating new forms of drama, spectacle and education. And like their counterparts who were designing shop windows, motion displays and animated spectaculars, designers at the Fair were deeply engaged with the aesthetics of motion, exploring its effects, potentials, and expressive power. Of course, there were differences. The Fair was a temporary site and designers had greater leeway to develop new kinds of animated displays, often with considerable financial resources. While this offered opportunities to develop animation in novel ways, the Fair's corporate and technocratic values guided the uses of movement, tying it in with displays of industry, infrastructure and science. The Focal Exhibits, General Motors, Ford and Consolidated Edison all used animation to show the dynamic motions of modernity: the flow of goods and commerce, the mobility offered by automobiles and highway systems, the rhythms of labor and global trade, and the energy that coursed through New York itself. However experimental and multifaceted these exhibits may have been, again and again they presented motion as something that could be controlled, ordered and harnessed. These displays sculpted motion like clay, shaping movement to accord with an idea of the smooth functioning of modern technology, industry and life.

Not all displays were quite so regimented in their uses of motion. There were, of course, the carnivalesque attractions of the midway and the fairgrounds. But even within the context of major corporate exhibits, there were displays which used motion in disruptive and playful ways. One example of this was the mobile mural created by the artist Henry Billings, who entwined motion with industry to create one of the Fair's most acclaimed works of art (Fig. 3.8). This enormous assemblage of oversized car parts and scientific imagery was the climax of the Ford exhibit's Entrance Hall, towering over spectators at a height of 30 feet. The mural aimed to express a hugely ambitious theme: "Man can change the form of energy, but he can neither create nor destroy it. The sun pours energy upon the earth, where it is stored in many forms. By controlling the channels through which it

Fig. 3.8 "Industrial Mural at Ford's Exhibit Hall, New York World's Fair, 1939." From the Collections of The Henry Ford. Gift of Ford Motor Company

flows, as it changes from one form to another, industry harnesses this energy for the benefit of man."[109] Different parts of the mural were arranged to express this central idea. At the base of the mural, six oversized gears framed images which showed "steps in the cycle whereby energy coming from the sun as heat is transformed into motor car power and how this is changed to other forms of energy"; in the center of the mural was a "huge V-8 engine cross-section" that demonstrated engineering prowess; and on its periphery, there were images of machines and conveyors, symbols of technologies and measuring devices, and scientific formulae.[110] Through its curious juxtapositions of machinery, manufacturing and science—coupled with its "activated" quality—the mural presented a striking collage of contemporary industry freed from its typical functioning and transposed into an abstract vision of controlled energy in motion.

With its dense arrangement of imagery, skewed perspectives and surrealist overtones, this was hardly a straightforward demonstration of technology and science. Described in *Life* magazine as the Fair's "most original and exciting work of art," the mural was chosen as the public's favorite indoor mural at the Fair in a poll conducted by the Mural Artist Guild.[111] Accounts also drew attention to an almost religious or mystical value of the mural, describing it as a "miracle of movement" and noting how it stood "against a curved wall, which resembles the apse of a church" so that "the mural itself suggests a gigantic altar piece."[112] Ecstatic effects were created when the mural was set in motion during its three-minute animated show:

> At the start music is heard and gears, pistons, sprockets turn slowly. Lights shining behind them throw their moving shadows on the wall and ceiling. The gears pick up speed, the shadows whirl faster and faster until the walls dance madly with them. The animated mural begins to slow down, pauses for a few seconds. Then the gears begin to slowly turn again.[113]

It is fitting that the mural was seen at the juncture between art, dance, religion and mysticism—it invested industrial manufacture with aesthetic appeals and esoteric meanings through an imposing array of symbols, designs and moving forms.

Unlike the vision of industry in the mobile mural, Isamu Noguchi's "Chassis Fountain," located in the Garden Court of the Ford exhibition, presented its industrial themes in a meditative and subtly unsettling manner (Fig. 3.9). The sculpture was made up of interconnected parts of a car's

Fig. 3.9   "Chassis Fountain, Ford Exposition Garden Court, New York World's Fair, 1939." From the Collections of The Henry Ford. Gift of Ford Motor Company

chassis which were set in the ground at a slight angle. Dynamism was created by the flow of water: "A spiral gear, eighteen feet tall, accents the action of the connecting rod. Water flowing down this gear will tend to show it in motion and the water spouting from the wheel will impart a dynamic quality to the whole fountain."[114] Displacing the power of an engine with a stream of water to create movement, the sculpture gestured toward natural processes rather than industrial ones. The fountain's dynamism was accentuated by its placement in the midst of Ford's "Road of Tomorrow," encircled by moving cars. In contrast to the cars driving by on the spiral ramp, the sculpture suggested a thwarted purpose; with its car stripped of its surface and stuck in the ground, functional qualities were made secondary to sculptural form. While publicity described this as a work that "expresses abstractly the power of the automobile," the sculpture also visually suggested, as David Gelernter notes, a car crashing into the ground.[115]

Noguchi's sculpture offered a potentially ironic counterpoint to the Ford exhibit's paean to the power of the automobile.

Alexander Calder—another major artist and sculptor working in New York at the time—designed a "Water Ballet" for Consolidated Edison that also used water to create a sense of dynamism. The exterior of the Consolidated Edison building, which housed the City of Light, was covered by "a curtain of dancing fountains" that evoked the theme of energy and hydro-electric power on display inside; these fountains were created by huge jets of water shooting upwards that "gave the building an air of spirited anima-tion in keeping with the subject matter of the exhibit it housed."[116] Calder planned to use the water basin adjacent to these fountains for the perfor-mance of his "Water Ballet." Although it is unlikely that it was actually performed, the idea was that the ballet would be a five minute show made up of several sections, including "plumes" of water that would shoot forth (suggesting dancers) and "bombshell jets" that would explode out of the basin (suggesting the "leap of a ballerina").[117] This liquid choreography would use "jets of water" as its "acting elements," projected "from 14 noz-zles which are designed to spurt, oscillate or rotate in fixed manners and at times as carefully predetermined as the movements of living dancers."[118] While carefully choreographed, this transformation of a ballet into liquid form celebrated the fluid potentials of movement. In contrast to the flow-ing sheets of water along the walls of the building and the robot-controlled animation in the City of Light inside, this vision of dancing water suggested a spectacle of expressive and explosive movement, a vigorous transposition of human bodies into moving water.

Billings, Noguchi and Calder were three of the most prominent artists to create mobile works at the Fair. While incorporating the mechanized movements and industrial motifs circulating around them, their works also suggested new arts of motion that drew upon—and transformed—the art of murals, sculpture and dance. In doing so, they offered alternative approaches to the well-ordered and functional designs that dominated the Fair's dynamic "World of Tomorrow." As the next chapter will explore further, using animation as a form of art allowed for alternative visions of motion, ones that were less constrained by the strictures of order and more open to expressive freedom.

NOTES

1. Edmund Gilligan, "The Report of a Subway Explorer of His Trip to a Magic City," *New York Sun*, April 29, 1939; *Display Animation, 1937: The Year Book of Motion Displays*, ed. I. L. Cochrane (New York: Reeder-Morton Publications, 1937), 55.
2. Grover A. Whalen, "We Welcome the World," *Official Guide Book of the New York World's Fair* (New York: Exposition Publications Inc., 1939), 5.
3. *Display Animation, 1939–40: The Year Book of Motion Displays*, ed. I. L. Cochrane (New York: Reeder-Morton Publications, 1939), 103; *Exhibition Techniques* (New York: New York Museum of Science and Industry, 1940), 120.
4. *Display Animation, 1939–40*, 7.
5. *Exhibition Techniques*, 7.
6. K. M. Reed, "World's Fair Influences New York Windows," *Display*, August 1939, 227.
7. I. L. Cochrane, *Motion Display Mechanics* (New York: Reeder-Morton Publications, 1939), 143.
8. "Report Gimbel 'Displalounge' for N. Y. Fair," *Women's Wear Daily*, March 22, 1940.
9. "Douglas Leigh Is B'way's Top Producer; His 17 Hit Shows Play to Standees Only," *New York Telegraph*, October 3, 1940.
10. "Eight Acres of Marvels in Fair Travel Building," *Chicago Tribune*, August 6, 1933.
11. Jacquelene Abbott Keyes, "The Fair—Demonstration of Modern Methods of Living," *Commercial Art*, December 1, 1936, 233.
12. "Production and Distribution Focal Exhibit," press release, n.d., box 184, folder 6, New York World's Fair 1939 and 1940 Incorporated Records, C1.02, Production and Distribution—Arens, E., New York Public Library.
13. "World of Tomorrow Focal Shows," press release, January 1, 1939, p. 11, box 182, folder 1, New York World's Fair 1939 and 1940 Incorporated Records, C1.02 Focal Exhibits, Department Store Focal Exhibits (1939), New York Public Library.
14. "Excerpt from 'Food Industries'—May 1939," n.d., box 475, folder 2, New York World's Fair 1939 and 1940 Incorporated Records, P1.531 Beverages, Coca Cola Co. (1939), 4 of 4, New York Public Library.
15. "World of Tomorrow Focal Shows," press release, 12.
16. Lynne Kirby, *Parallel Tracks: The Railroad and Silent Cinema* (Durham: Duke University Press, 1997), 44–45.
17. "World of Tomorrow Focal Shows," press release, 12.
18. *Official Guide Book of the New York World's Fair 1939* (New York: Exposition Publications Inc., 1939), 175.

19. "Production and Distribution Focal Show at the New York World's Fair," press release, n.d., pp. 1 and 2, box 184, folder 3, New York World's Fair 1939 and 1940 Incorporated Records, C1.02, Production and Distribution (1939), New York Public Library.
20. See Roland Marchand, "The Designers Go to the Fair II: Norman Bel Geddes, The General Motors 'Futurama,' and the Visit to the Factory Transformed," *Design Issues* 8, no. 2 (Spring 1992): 24.
21. Jeffrey L. Meikle, *Design in the USA* (Oxford: Oxford University Press, 2005), 105.
22. Walter Dorwin Teague, *Design This Day: The Technique of Order in the Machine Age* (New York: Harcourt, Brace and Company, 1940), 170.
23. A. Joan Saab, *For the Millions: American Art and Culture Between the Wars* (Philadelphia: University of Pennsylvania Press, 2004), 134.
24. Meikle, *Design in the USA*, 113.
25. Meikle, *Design in the USA*, 125.
26. Walter Dorwin Teague, "Plastics and Design," *The Architectural Forum*, February 1940, 94.
27. Roland Marchand, "The Designers Go to the Fair: Walter Dorwin Teague and the Professionalization of Corporate Industrial Exhibits, 1933–1940," *Design Issues* 8, no. 1 (Autumn 1991): 5.
28. Walter Dorwin Teague, "*Exhibition Technique*," *American Architect and Architecture*, September 1937, 33.
29. Cheryl R. Ganz, *The 1933 Chicago World's Fair: A Century of Progress* (Urbana: University of Illinois Press, 2008), 82.
30. Kenneth Reid, "Walter Dorwin Teague, Master of Design," *Pencil Points Magazine*, September 1937, 569.
31. "N. Y. Fair Exhibits Picture Ford Role in American Life," press release, n.d., p. 1, box 381, folder 7, New York World's Fair 1939 and 1940 Incorporated Records, P1.200 Passenger Cars, Ford Motor Co. (1939), November 1–December 31, 1 of 2, New York Public Library.
32. *Exhibition Techniques*, 35.
33. "N. Y. Fair Exhibits Picture Ford Role in American Life," press release, 1–2.
34. "World's Largest Sculpture of 'Mercury' Done in Steel Adorns Ford Fair Building," press release, n.d., p. 1, box 381, folder 7, New York World's Fair 1939 and 1940 Incorporated Records, P1.200 Passenger Cars, Ford Motor Co. (1939), November 1–December 31, 1 of 2, New York Public Library.
35. "Huge Ford Exhibit to Show Processing of Raw Materials," press release, n.d., p. 2. box 381, folder 8, New York World's Fair 1939 and 1940 Incorporated Records, P1.200 Passenger Cars, Ford Motor Co. (1939), November 1–December 31, 2 of 2, New York Public Library; Gilligan, "The Report of a Subway Explorer of His Trip to a Magic City."

36. "Huge Ford Exhibit to Show Processing of Raw Materials," press release, 2–4.
37. *Exhibition Techniques*, 55.
38. Greg Grandin, *Fordlandia: The Rise and Fall of Henry Ford's Forgotten Jungle City* (New York: Metropolitan Books, 2009), 242.
39. Teague, "Plastics and Design," 94.
40. Terry Smith, *Making the Modern: Industry, Art, and Design in America* (Chicago: University of Chicago Press, 1993), 35.
41. For a related discussion of how Ford's media strategies embraced "the orchestration of circulation" (316), see Lee Grieveson, *Cinema and the Wealth of Nations: Media, Capital, and the Liberal World System* (Berkeley: University of California Press, 2018).
42. Greg Grandin offers an insightful exploration of Ford's multinational strategies in *Fordlandia*.
43. Teague, *Design This Day*, 249.
44. "The Artist in Industry," press release, February 7, 1939, p. 1, box 381, folder 7, New York World's Fair 1939 and 1940 Incorporated Records, P1.200 Passenger Cars, Ford Motor Co. (1939), November 1–December 31, 1 of 2, New York Public Library.
45. Teague, *Design This Day*, 15–19.
46. Teague, *Design This Day*, 43.
47. "Ford Cycle of Production Scale Model," press release, n.d., p. 2, box 381, folder 7, New York World's Fair 1939 and 1940 Incorporated Records, P1.200 Passenger Cars, Ford Motor Co. (1939), November 1–December 31, 1 of 2, New York Public Library.
48. "Ford Fair Exhibit Provides Fun for the Men Who Built It," press release, n.d., p. 2, box 381, folder 7, New York World's Fair 1939 and 1940 Incorporated Records, P1.200 Passenger Cars, Ford Motor Co. (1939), November 1–December 31, 1 of 2, New York Public Library; "Ford's Titanic Animation," *Display*, August 1939, 229.
49. "Ford Fair Exhibit Provides Fun for the Men Who Built It," 1–2.
50. Teague, *Design This Day*, 128.
51. John Dewey, *Art as Experience* (New York: Minton, Balch & Company, 1934), 149.
52. Dewey, *Art as Experience*, 147.
53. Dewey, *Art as Experience*, 148.
54. "Focal Exhibit in Production and Distribution," memorandum, n.d., p. 3, box 184, folder 3, New York World's Fair 1939 and 1940 Incorporated Records, C1.02, Production and Distribution (1939), New York Public Library.
55. "Distribution Luncheon Meeting," meeting notes, n.d., p. 4, box 184, folder 3, New York World's Fair 1939 and 1940 Incorporated Records, C1.02, Production and Distribution (1939), New York Public Library.

56. S. J. Morris and O. C. Z. Gotel, "Flow Diagrams: Rise and Fall of the First Software Notation," *Diagrams* (2006): 132.

57. "Focal Exhibit in Production and Distribution," memorandum, 2.

58. Gilligan, "The Report of a Subway Explorer of His Trip to a Magic City"; Gerald Wendt, "Ford Motor Company," n.d., p. 2, box 381, folder 7, New York World's Fair 1939 and 1940 Incorporated Records, P1.200 Passenger Cars, Ford Motor Co. (1939), November 1–December 31, 1 of 2, New York Public Library.

59. "Summary of Ideas That Have Been Considered as the Basis of an Exhibit on Distribution," memorandum, n.d., p. 2, box 184, folder 3, New York World's Fair 1939 and 1940 Incorporated Records, C1.02, Production and Distribution (1939), New York Public Library.

60. "Summary of Ideas That Have Been Considered as the Basis of an Exhibit on Distribution," memorandum, 1.

61. Dewey, *Art as Experience*, 154.

62. See Frank Thomas and Ollie Johnston, *The Illusion of Life: Disney Animation* (New York: Hyperion, 1995). For a summary of the principles involved with this approach to animation, see Giannalberto Bendazzi, *Animation: A World History*, vol. 1 (New York: Routledge, 2017), 107–109.

63. Teague, "Plastics and Design," 93.

64. Marchand, "The Designers go to the Fair," 12.

65. Advertisement, *New York Sun*, April 29, 1939.

66. Leo Casey, "News Release No. 285," n.d., p. 2, box 418, folder 7, New York World's Fair 1939 and 1940 Incorporated Records, P1.501 Housing, Consolidated Edison Company of New York (1940), New York Public Library.

67. *The City of Light on the Plaza of Light at the New York World's Fair 1940*, programme, n.d., box 1841, folder 13, New York World's Fair 1939 and 1940 Incorporated Records, VII.E1.c. Participant Literature, Consolidated Edison Co., New York Public Library.

68. *Exhibition Techniques*, 119.

69. Advertisement, *New York Sun*.

70. Advertisement, *New York Sun*.

71. Gregory Votolato, *American Design in the Twentieth Century* (Manchester: Manchester University Press, 1998), 42–43.

72. Christopher Innes, *Designing Modern America: Broadway to Main Street* (New Haven: Yale University Press, 2005), 2.

73. Norman Bel Geddes, *Horizons* (Boston: Little, Brown, and Company, 1932), 259.

74. Norman Bel Geddes, *A Project for a Theatrical Presentation of the Divine Comedy of Dante Aligheri* (New York: Theatre Arts, 1924), 20.

75. "The Divine Comedy Project," manuscript, n.d., box 83, folder n4, Norman Bel Geddes Theater and Industrial Design Papers, Divine Comedy, Harry Ransom Center, University of Texas at Austin.

76. Bel Geddes, *Horizons*, 197 and 212.
77. Minutes of Promotional Meeting, January 27, 1938, p. 3, box 19a, folder 381.4, Norman Bel Geddes Theater and Industrial Design Papers, Meeting Minutes, Harry Ransom Center, University of Texas at Austin.
78. *Official Guide Book of the New York World's Fair 1939*, 208.
79. Futurama, programme, n.d., box 1851, folder 10, New York World's Fair 1939 and 1940 Incorporated Records, VII.E.1.c. Participant Literature, General Motors, New York Public Library.
80. "Success of Futurama, Which 2,000,000 Have Visited, Is Tribute to Bel Geddes," *New York Herald Tribune*, July 18, 1939.
81. Norman Bel Geddes, "Description of the General Motors Building and Exhibit for the New York World's Fair," n.d., p. 31, box 19b, folder 381.27, Norman Bel Geddes Theater and Industrial Design Papers, Description of Building and Exhibit, Harry Ransom Center, University of Texas at Austin.
82. In an office memo, the attendance for Futurama was listed as 24,000,000 visitors, or 66,000 per day. This was compared to the attendance at the World's Fair (44,929,000 total or 124,000 per day) and seasonal attendance at Yankee Stadium of approximately 1,000,000 (Mr. Hunt, memorandum, September 25, 1942, box 19a, folder 381.1, Norman Bel Geddes Theater and Industrial Design Papers, Client Correspondence [April 1938–June 1940], Harry Ransom Center, University of Texas at Austin).
83. Innes, *Designing Modern America*, 146.
84. Cliff Ellis, "Lewis Mumford and Norman Bel Geddes: The Highway, the City and the Future," *Planning Perspectives* 20, no. 1 (January 2005): 60.
85. Erkki Huhtamo, *Illusions in Motion: Media Archaeology of the Moving Panorama and Related Spectacles* (Cambridge, MA: MIT Press, 2013), 113.
86. Minutes of Promotional Meeting, April 2, 1938, p. 2, box 19a, folder 381.4, Norman Bel Geddes Theater and Industrial Design Papers, Meeting Minutes, Harry Ransom Center, University of Texas at Austin.
87. Minutes of Promotional Meeting, February 14, 1938, p. 7, box 19a, folder 381.4, Norman Bel Geddes Theater and Industrial Design Papers, Meeting, Minutes, Harry Ransom Center, University of Texas at Austin.
88. "Facts, Figures and Information on the General Motors Highways and Horizons Exhibit at the New York World's Fair," press guide, n.d., p. 7, box 1851, folder 10, New York World's Fair 1939 and 1940 Incorporated Records, VII.E.1.c. Participant Literature, General Motors, New York Public Library.
89. An early plan had the movement of spectators "synchronized with the car movement" ("Spectator's Transportation System," n.d., box 19a, folder 381.30, Norman Bel Geddes Theater and Industrial Design Papers, Spectator Conveyor System, Harry Ransom Center, University of Texas at Austin).

90. Bel Geddes, *Horizons*, 17.
91. Norman Bel Geddes, *Magic Motorways* (New York: Random House, 1940), 4. Lewis Mumford also saw Futurama as akin to a design idea, describing it as an "essay in modern urban and regional design." (Lewis Mumford, "The Sky Line in Flushing," *New Yorker*, July 29, 1939, 38.)
92. Bel Geddes, *Horizons*, 18.
93. Bel Geddes, *A Project for a Theatrical Presentation of the Divine Comedy*, 20.
94. Benjamin L. Webster to Robert D. Kohn, October 27, 1937, box 184, folder 4, New York World's Fair 1939 and 1940 Incorporated Records, C1.02 Focal Exhibits, Production and Distribution (1939), New York Public Library.
95. "Technical Supplement," April 7, 1938, pp. 4–5, folders 381.5a-b, Norman Bel Geddes Theater and Industrial Design Papers, Drawings, Harry Ransom Center, University of Texas at Austin.
96. See Norman Bel Geddes Theater and Industrial Design Papers, box 19a, folder 381.7, Production Specifications, Harry Ransom Center, University of Texas at Austin.
97. Norman Bel Geddes to C. D. Jackson, May 4, 1942, box 5, folder 56.1, Norman Bel Geddes Theater and Industrial Design Papers, War Games, Harry Ransom Center, University of Texas at Austin.
98. Edwin C. Hill, "In Spite of Kellogg Treaty, War Again Rages on Wide Front," *New York Sun*, January 12, 1932.
99. "A Project for Recording the World's Great Battles," n.d., p. 1, box 10, folder 179.1, Norman Bel Geddes Theater and Industrial Design Papers, Animated Battle Map, Harry Ransom Center, University of Texas at Austin.
100. Norman Bel Geddes, "Brief Outline of a Project for Recording the World's Greatest Battles in Motion Picture Map Form," n.d., p. 3, box 10, folder 179.1, Norman Bel Geddes Theater and Industrial Design Papers, Animated Battle Map, Harry Ransom Center, University of Texas at Austin.
101. Bel Geddes, *Magic Motorways*, 295–296.
102. "Notes on Meeting," November 1, 1938, pp. 2–3, box 19a, folder 381.7, Norman Bel Geddes Theater and Industrial Design Papers, Production Specifications, Harry Ransom Center, University of Texas at Austin.
103. "Notes on Meeting," 2.
104. "Model Series for J. W. T.—Shell Advertising," May 24, 1937, p. 1, box 55, folder 672.9, Norman Bel Geddes Theater and Industrial Design Papers, Model Photography to 1951, Harry Ransom Center, University of Texas at Austin.
105. "Prepared for Illustrated London News by General Motors Corporation," press release, n.d., p. 1, box 979, folder 2, New York World's Fair 1939 and 1940 Incorporated Records, PR1.5 Advertising, General Motors Corp., New York Public Library.

106. Press release, n.d., p. 3, box 1851, folder 10, New York World's Fair 1939 and 1940 Incorporated Records, VII.E.1.c. Participant Literature, General Motors, New York Public Library.
107. Russell Maloney and Eugene Kinkead, "Trylon, Trylon Again," *New Yorker*, May 11, 1940, 42.
108. "Futurama Is Kept as Museum Piece," *New York Times*, December 16, 1940.
109. Ruth Green Harris, "Public Taste in Murals," *New York Times*, July 28, 1940.
110. "Ford at the Fair," *Ford News*, April 1939, 78.
111. "Mobile Mural," *Life*, March 13, 1939, 42; "Mural on WPA Building Judged Best Outdoor Art," *New York Times*, August 7, 1939.
112. "Ford's Titanic Animation," 228; "Mobile Mural," 42.
113. "Mobile Mural," 42.
114. "Ford at the Fair," 81.
115. "Ford at the Fair," 81; David Gelernter, *1939, the Lost World of the Fair* (New York: Avon, 1995), 165.
116. *Exhibition Techniques*, 32.
117. "'Water Ballet' at Fair," *New York Times*, October 16, 1938.
118. Alexander Calder, "A Water Ballet," *Theatre Arts Monthly*, August 1939, 578.

References

Bel Geddes, Norman. *A Project for a Theatrical Presentation of the Divine Comedy of Dante Aligheri*. New York: Theatre Arts, 1924.
Bel Geddes, Norman. *Horizons*. Boston: Little, Brown, and Company, 1932.
Bel Geddes, Norman. *Magic Motorways*. New York: Random House, 1940.
Bel Geddes, Norman. Theater and Industrial Design Papers. Harry Ransom Center, University of Texas at Austin.
Bendazzi, Giannalberto. *Animation: A World History*, vol. 1. New York: Routledge, 2017.
Calder, Alexander. "A Water Ballet." *Theatre Arts Monthly*, August 1939.
Cochrane, I. L., ed. *Display Animation, 1937: The Year Book of Motion Displays*. New York: Reeder-Morton Publications, 1937.
Cochrane, I. L., ed. *Display Animation, 1939–40: The Year Book of Motion Displays*. New York: Reeder-Morton Publications, 1939.
Cochrane, I. L. *Motion Display Mechanics*. New York: Reeder-Morton Publications, 1939.
Dewey, John. *Art as Experience*. New York: Minton, Balch & Company, 1934.
"Douglas Leigh Is B'way's Top Producer; His 17 Hit Shows Play to Standees Only." *New York Telegraph*, October 3, 1940.

"Eight Acres of Marvels in Fair Travel Building." *Chicago Tribune*, August 6, 1933.

Ellis, Cliff. "Lewis Mumford and Norman Bel Geddes: The Highway, the City and the Future." *Planning Perspectives* 20, no. 1 (January 2005): 51–68.

Exhibition Techniques. New York: New York Museum of Science and Industry, 1940.

"Ford at the Fair." *Ford News*, April 1939.

"Ford's Titanic Animation." *Display*, August 1939.

"Futurama Is Kept as Museum Piece." *New York Times*, December 16, 1940.

Ganz, Cheryl R. *The 1933 Chicago World's Fair: A Century of Progress*. Urbana: University of Illinois Press, 2008.

Gelernter, David. *1939, the Lost World of the Fair*. New York: Avon, 1995.

Gilligan, Edmund. "The Report of a Subway Explorer of His Trip to a Magic City." *New York Sun*, April 29, 1939.

Grandin, Greg. *Fordlandia: The Rise and Fall of Henry Ford's Forgotten Jungle City*. New York: Metropolitan Books, 2009.

Grieveson, Lee. *Cinema and the Wealth of Nations: Media, Capital, and the Liberal World System*. Berkeley: University of California Press, 2018.

Harris, Ruth Green. "Public Taste in Murals." *New York Times*, July 28, 1940.

Hill, Edwin C. "In Spite of Kellogg Treaty, War Again Rages on Wide Front." *New York Sun*, January 12, 1932.

Huhtamo, Erkki. *Illusions in Motion: Media Archaeology of the Moving Panorama and Related Spectacles*. Cambridge, MA: MIT Press, 2013.

Innes, Christopher. *Designing Modern America: Broadway to Main Street*. New Haven: Yale University Press, 2005.

Keyes, Jacquelene Abbott. "The Fair—Demonstration of Modern Methods of Living." *Commercial Art*, December 1, 1936.

Kirby, Lynne. *Parallel Tracks: The Railroad and Silent Cinema*. Durham: Duke University Press, 1997.

Maloney, Russell and Eugene Kinkead. "Trylon, Trylon Again." *New Yorker*, May 11, 1940.

Marchand, Roland. "The Designers Go to the Fair: Walter Dorwin Teague and the Professionalization of Corporate Industrial Exhibits, 1933–1940." *Design Issues* 8, no. 1 (Autumn 1991): 4–17.

Marchand, Roland. "The Designers Go to the Fair II: Norman Bel Geddes, the General Motors 'Futurama,' and the Visit to the Factory Transformed." *Design Issues* 8, no. 2 (Spring 1992): 22–40.

Meikle, Jeffrey L. *Design in the USA*. Oxford: Oxford University Press, 2005.

"Mobile Mural." *Life*, March 13, 1939.

Morris, S. J. and O. C. Z. Gotel. "Flow Diagrams: Rise and Fall of the First Software Notation." *Diagrams* (2006): 130–144.

Mumford, Lewis. "The Sky Line in Flushing." *New Yorker*, July 29, 1939.

"Mural on WPA Building Judged Best Outdoor Art." *New York Times*, August 7, 1939.

New York World's Fair 1939 and 1940 Incorporated Records, New York Public Library.

Official Guide Book of the New York World's Fair 1939. New York: Exposition Publications Inc., 1939.

Reed, K. M. "World's Fair Influences New York Windows." *Display*, August 1939.

Reid, Kenneth. "Walter Dorwin Teague, Master of Design." *Pencil Points Magazine*, September 1937.

"Report Gimbel 'Displalounge' for N. Y. Fair." *Women's Wear Daily*, March 22, 1940.

Saab, A. Joan. *For the Millions: American Art and Culture Between the Wars*. Philadelphia: University of Pennsylvania Press, 2004.

Smith, Terry. *Making the Modern: Industry, Art, and Design in America*. Chicago: University of Chicago Press, 1993.

"Success of Futurama, Which 2,000,000 Have Visited, Is Tribute to Bel Geddes." *New York Herald Tribune*, July 18, 1939.

Teague, Walter Dorwin. "*Exhibition Technique*." *American Architect and Architecture*, September 1937.

Teague, Walter Dorwin. "Plastics and Design." *The Architectural Forum*, February 1940.

Teague, Walter Dorwin. *Design This Day: The Technique of Order in the Machine Age*. New York: Harcourt, Brace and Company, 1940.

Thomas, Frank and Ollie Johnston. *The Illusion of Life: Disney Animation*. New York: Hyperion, 1995.

Votolato, Gregory. *American Design in the Twentieth Century*. Manchester: Manchester University Press, 1998.

"'Water Ballet' at Fair." *New York Times*, October 16, 1938.

Whalen, Grover A. "We Welcome the World." *Official Guide Book of the New York World's Fair*. New York: Exposition Publications Inc., 1939.

CHAPTER 4

The Gallery

One month after the opening of the World's Fair, with its grandiose vision of a "World of Tomorrow," the Museum of Non-Objective Painting held an exhibition entitled "Art of Tomorrow" to inaugurate its midtown Manhattan gallery.[1] Amid plush surroundings, with the music of Beethoven and Bach wafting through the gallery, visitors were invited to gaze upon paintings by artists including Rudolf Bauer and Wassily Kandinsky. Funded by the Solomon R. Guggenheim Foundation and relocated to the Upper East Side in the 1950s, the Museum (now usually known as the Guggenheim) had a deep and lasting influence on New York art and culture. This first exhibition in 1939 displayed what the Museum's director, Hilla Rebay, saw as masterful examples of non-objective painting. Rebay passionately promulgated the values of this type of art in her work as the director of the Museum, as well as in public lectures, essays and correspondence with artists.[2] By moving beyond abstractions or representations of reality, and instead using geometric forms, colors and the space of the canvas as primary aesthetic qualities, non-objective paintings generated a powerful sense of compositional and rhythmic order. This could have a tremendous impact: "Outstanding is their power to uplift and influence the onlooker and their mysterious faculty to improve those who live with them, by creating or strengthening in them the sense for order to acquire a rhythmic balance in life."[3]

© The Author(s) 2019
K. Moen, *New York's Animation Culture*, Palgrave Animation,
https://doi.org/10.1007/978-3-030-27931-8_4

The similarity between the name of the Museum's exhibition, "Art of Tomorrow," and the Fair's "World of Tomorrow" was not a coincidence—in their respective spheres of art and design, they were both promoting ideas of a new world of order and progress. At the Fair, individual exhibits showcased these values in diverse ways, often incorporating—as the previous chapter discussed—animation and motion displays. The Fair's exhibits were set within a larger scheme which foregrounded a sense of order, with the Theme Center of the Trylon and Perisphere positioned "Like the hub of a wheel" that would connect "the zones that radiated out from it into one cohesive design."[4] The composition of the Theme Center and its reliance on the basic geometric shapes of the triangle and circle were related to non-objective painting. This connection was made in the frontispiece for the "Art of Tomorrow" catalog, which reproduced a painting entitled "The Holy One" (Bauer, 1937) that also foregrounded a large triangle and circle in its composition. A caption in the catalog claimed, "The theme center of the New York World's Fair owes its inspiration to this creation of Rudolf Bauer."[5]

For Rebay, the Theme Center at the Fair was just one of a host of examples in which the aesthetic of non-objective painting was extending beyond the canvas to wider contexts of modern life, "With architects, engineers and designers using motifs from Non-objective paintings for buildings, engines, advertisements, window-displays and so on."[6] Even industrial films would draw upon a non-objective style. *To New Horizons* (1940), a film that documented and promoted the Futurama exhibit, used tropes of non-objective art for its climactic finale. Accompanied by a voice-over narration that spoke of "the constantly greater possibilities of the world of tomorrow" and the "new horizons in the spirit of individual enterprise in the great American way," the last sequence of the film showed a series of geometric forms animatedly appearing onscreen: luminous spirals and twisting lines encircle linear forms which cut across the frame pointing upward. In a direct reference to the Trylon and Perisphere, the film's final image shows a triangle and circle emerging from the bottom of the frame, pointing toward the sky. This animated gesture toward progress and aspiration relied upon basic forms in motion to communicate a sense of uplifting potentials for the future. *To New Horizons* was hardly an exemplary non-objective work as its visual forms were abstractions of actual objects: roads, pillars and the Theme Center. Nevertheless, by coupling an overt depiction of progress with non-objective visual elements, the film entwined the values of the Fair and the Museum. This was just one example of how images and designs at the Fair shared qualities with non-objectivity. Presenting rhythm and well-ordered compositions, visual culture could vividly show what Rebay described as the "intense dynamic impetus of our time, from which great progress results."[7]

Many of the same ideas and values that had shaped Rebay's ideals of non-objective painting were also shaping contemporary trends in design. Paul Greenhalgh describes "two phases" of the "Modern Movement in design": the Pioneer phase, which emerged around the time of the First World War and ended in the late 1920s and early 1930s and the International Style, beginning in the early 1930s and lasting for decades.[8] Greenhalgh outlines how the first phase, a "set of ideas, a vision of how the designed world could transform human consciousness and improve material conditions," was supplanted by the second phase which was "less of an idea than a style and a technology; a discourse concerned principally with the appearance of things and their manufacture" (3). Taking shape and achieving "official respectability" in the 1930s, the International Style had emerged out of earlier ideas from the Pioneer phase. Greenhalgh writes that its "single most important ideal" was "to break down barriers between aesthetics, technics and society, in order that an appropriate design of the highest visual and practical quality could be produced for the mass of the population" (8). Rebay was suggesting a similar ideal in her desire for the forms of non-objective painting to become interwoven with the modern age. While art and design might lose some of their more visionary, spiritual and moral aspirations in the process, Rebay saw things differently—she eagerly embraced the sense that values of non-objective painting were being drawn into a wider sphere of modern life that included contemporary commercial and design activities.

One of the most important features of this expanding sense of non-objective painting was rhythm. Much like Teague's visionary approach to the rhythms of design, Rebay wrote of how non-objective paintings, if composed with sufficient intuitive genius, could become "alive with spiritual rhythm and organic with the cosmic order which rules the universe."[9] The potential of non-objective works to take rhythm beyond the confines of the canvas was thrilling for Rebay. In particular, she had long held an interest in film's capacity to vividly present rhythm by entwining images with motion and sound—soon after the Foundation and Museum were formed, they began to support animators.[10] Rebay was particularly drawn to the abstract animations of Oskar Fischinger, who had created an innovative body of work in Germany in the late 1920s and the early 1930s before relocating in 1936 to Los Angeles—which offered a very different animation culture than the one in New York—where he worked for studios including Paramount, MGM and Disney.[11] Rebay also had an affinity for other European animators who had begun making dynamic films based on the rhythmic motion of geometric forms in the 1920s, such as Hans Richter and Viking Eggeling.

Closer to home, animators in New York who were working outside of narrative and commercial filmmaking were drawn into the orbit of the Museum in the late 1930s and early 1940s. An extraordinary group of animated short films made during this period were linked to the Museum's artistic milieu, including Norman McLaren's *Dots* (1940) and *Loops* (1941), Dwinell Grant's *Themis* (1940) and Mary Ellen Bute's *Spook Sport* (1940) and *Tarantella* (1940), both of which included animation by McLaren. These works resonated with the wider aims of the Museum of Non-Objective Painting, exploring the aesthetics of rhythm, composition and non-representational art through animated film. At the same time, as this chapter will explore, these animators did not necessarily share Rebay's more rarefied sense of non-objective painting, sometimes creating playful animated alternatives to her artistic vision and sometimes disrupting or challenging its emphasis on ordered composition.

With films made by Bute, McLaren and Grant shown at the Museum or partially funded by the Foundation, Rebay was actively engaging with and helping shape New York's animation culture. However, the Museum of Non-Objective Painting was certainly not the only gallery in New York that approached animation as a form of art. A few blocks down, the Museum of Modern Art was collecting, distributing and showing animated films through its film library, under Iris Barry's directorship. These activities included developing "A Short History of Animation" program in 1938, with archival films ranging from Emile Cohl's *Fantasmagorie* (1908) to *Steamboat Willie* (1928); Bill Mikulak describes how Barry's accompanying program notes "accorded animation status as its own branch of film with its own technological and aesthetic innovations."[12]

The Museum also exhibited animation in ways similar to paintings with the "American Designs for Abstract Films" exhibition in April 1940. Curated by Barry, the exhibition foregrounded abstract animation, showing "rough work-drawings or collages" by Bute alongside work by Douglass Crockwell, Howard Lester and Horace Pierce.[13] The press release described how these artists "had turned spontaneously, separately and from various impulses, to the making of abstract films in color" (1–2). The exhibition was accompanied by a "continuous projection" of a "short abstract film in color by Douglass Crockwell" and a supplementary screening of mostly animated abstract films, including works by Bute, Richter, Fernand Léger, Marcel Duchamp and Len Lye (2–3). Even in its major "Art in Our Time" show from a year earlier, animation was prominent, with "a series of designs for abstract films by Léopold Survage... who in 1913 was first in this field" exhibited in the foyer (2). The press release used a quote from Survage to emphasize the artistic potential of animation: "an immobile abstract form does not say much... it is only when it is set in motion, when it is transformed and meets other forms, that it becomes capable of evoking a feeling." Through exhibitions, library activities and screenings, the Museum of Modern Art was offering a similar artistic vision of animated film as the Museum of Non-Objective Painting, though with a less prescriptive approach to its aesthetic potentials.

Also down the street from the Museum of Non-Objective Painting, the Art Institute of Light—located in Grand Central Palace adjacent to Grand Central Station—was continuing its lumia shows. These were created by the clavilux, an instrument invented by Thomas Wilfred, which projected compositions of light, form and color in motion.[14] Wilfred had established the Art Institute of Light in 1930 in order to create an institutional space for lumia: "To gather a Group of inspired Workers and to provide a Recital Hall, surrounded by Studios and Laboratories in which they may experiment, teach and demonstrate the results of their work on the use of LIGHT as an independent medium of Esthetic Expression."[15] As well as providing support, exhibition opportunities and educational materials for those interested in working with this medium of light, the Institute aimed to collect and preserve documents in a library, establish a museum, refine technologies of light projection and ultimately "bring about a general recognition of LUMIA – the Art of Light – which is opening a Gate to a new World of Beauty and appealing to the awakening Spirituality in Man."

Much like how the Museum of Non-Objective Painting was creating an institution around a particular form of spiritually uplifting art, Wilfred was developing an institution around lumia. By doing so, he was drawing motion into a sphere of art. While lumia was distinct from animated film—as it composed moving light by means of the clavilux rather than through film—an animated quality underpinned its artistic potentials: Wilfred wrote that lumia's most important elements were "Form and Motion."[16] Wilfred's work was well-known and much-admired. Grant was aware of it before he began making animated films and Bute had briefly worked with Wilfred before she began making films in the mid-1930s, deeply influenced by the creative and conceptual potentials of projected light in motion.[17]

The institutions of the Museum of Non-Objective Painting, the Museum of Modern Art and the Art Institute of Light shared, to varying degrees, a fascination with the artistic potentials of motion. At the time, animation was also becoming entwined with notions of art outside of the gallery—this was evident, as we have seen, in commercial and industrial contexts, from the artistry of animated shop windows to the industry-themed mobile sculptures at the World's Fair. This was by no means unprecedented—influential artists such as Survage, Marcel Duchamp and Naum Gabo had been evoking motion on the canvas and in sculptures going back decades. Animators such as Richter, Fischinger and Lye had also been opening up an emerging field of artistic expression based on film as an art of motion.[18] But here, in midtown Manhattan, animated film was becoming firmly embedded within the artistic establishment.

William Moritz describes the challenges of writing about non-objective animation, noting "the difficulty in establishing a viable verbal language to describe the multitude of colour, forms and textures, juxtapositions, movements and gestures which make up the very essence of these films."[19] While he writes that one might be "tempted" to focus on a historical genealogy in order to "impose some order or shape" on non-objective film, he cautions against such an approach. Too much of an emphasis on the earliest non-objective animated films can mistakenly give a sense of "primacy" to these works, implying that later films were derivations of them. Doing so "suggests and maintains connections or influences where none may have existed historically"; moreover, "it tends to confuse rather than clarify some essential aesthetic issues by supplying a similar rationale or structure to what may be only superficially similar visual effects." Moritz's insightful discussion informs my approach to the animators working in the field of non-objective animation in New York at the time. Rather than emphasizing historical lineages, I focus on the dynamism of their creative practice in the context of New York's animation culture.

This context helped enable the exploration of animation as art, while at the same time opening up new possibilities and expressive avenues. McLaren, Bute and Grant were all absorbed by the idea of animation as an artistic form. Grant described it as "a new medium" and "an entirely new art form"; Bute saw it as "a new medium of expression" that allows for "a seemingly endless source of new possibilities and means of expression."[20] In the Museum of Non-Objective Painting, this artistic turn toward motion coalesced around rhythmic design and ordered composition, providing a distinctive set of values that could be transposed to animated film. Tracing how the work of McLaren, Bute and Grant intersected with and also went beyond the institutional space and artistic values of the Museum of Non-Objective Painting, this chapter explores how animated film became a new form of art in New York's cultural scene.

NORMAN MCLAREN AND MOTION ITSELF

Arriving in New York in October 1939, Norman McLaren quickly set about finding work as a filmmaker and animator. While studying at the Glasgow School of Art in the early 1930s, McLaren had begun making films—one of these drew the attention of John Grierson, who hired him to work on advertising films at the General Post Office Film Unit in London. There, McLaren worked in various filmmaking capacities, eventually making *Mony a Pickle* (1938), which used stop motion animation, and *Love on the Wing* (1938), which showcased McLaren's distinctive practice of animating by drawing directly on film. Following his time in London, McLaren lived and worked in New York for two years before heading up to Canada, where he set up the animation department of the National Film Board (NFB) at Grierson's invitation. At the NFB, McLaren would refine and expand his creative work, becoming a globally influential and celebrated animator with films such as *Begone Dull Care* (1949) and *Neighbours* (1952), for which he won an Academy Award. In his relatively brief stay in New York, McLaren engaged with a multifaceted animation culture—and particularly the Museum of Non-Objective Painting—in diverse ways, generating ideas that he would develop in his later work, exploring new potentials of animated motion and engaging with the network of values that circulated around animation as a form of art.[21]

In New York, McLaren first found work as an animator in a context with little concern for art: NBC's experimental television station W2XBS, which had only recently begun broadcasting. Thomas H. Hutchinson, the station's director of programming, contracted McLaren to make a short Christmas-themed film for television broadcast after seeing some of his earlier work. McLaren described the resulting film as a "sort of moving 'Xmas card'" in which Christmas images, such as "stars, bells, xmas trees, stockings, holly, plum puddings, etc." were made to "dance & play hide

& seek with each other, and do acrobatics. The result is a very gay & lively little cartoon film."[22] Rather than using established techniques of stop motion or cel animation, this film was made by drawing every frame, "3,600 to be exact," directly "on clear film with India ink & a mapping pen." The resulting work was one of the first animated films made for American television. Since television ownership was quite rare at the time, McLaren had to go to a department store where televisions were on display in order to see his film shown.[23] Several months later, McLaren made a second film for W2XBS, *NBC Valentine Greeting* (1940). Beginning with the hand-drawn animated words "We love our audience," the film shows the emergence, transformation and interaction of images associated with Valentine's Day—hearts rotate, twist and go through a playful dance, interacting with and transforming into animated images of faces, lips (which kiss) and a Cupid's arrow. The film ends with the words "Will you be my valentine?" with the question mark briefly transforming into a heart. Drawing directly on film, the motions and transformations of lines and shapes take on a jittery quality, like a vitalized sketch.

McLaren's innovative approach to animation was well-suited to this exploratory and experimental period in the development of broadcast television. The idea of using animation in the nascent medium of television was a topic of considerable interest at the time. One reason for this was that animated films were "particularly well adapted to television reproduction" because the "black-and-white lines that make up the subject matter are easily reproduced by nearly any television system."[24] McLaren's filmmaking also aligned with another area of interest in the television field at the time, which was to create breaks between scheduled programming through "a system of animated abstract films that will be the counterpart of the musical interlude in an ordinary movie show."[25] McLaren's films were among the first to be used for this purpose.

William C. Eddy, who worked on special effects and animation for television, described such "tie-ins" or "bridges" as "of the greatest importance in producing a television show."[26] Such bridges could take on different forms: "inanimate or animated art work, film, miniature staging, or abstract interludes, such as kaleidoscopic pictures." With such an idea in mind, Eddy filed a patent for a "Projecting Kaleidoscope Device" just a few weeks after McLaren's Christmas film was first broadcast.[27] Eddy's invention showed "abstract designs" in motion, merging "the perfection found in geometric figures" with a "movement of the pattern as may be required to maintain the interest of the viewer." Also able to incorporate product logos or station identifications, the device combined commercialism, abstraction and animation in the new medium of television.

With NBC only able to offer limited work, McLaren sought out other jobs. He was encouraged by his contacts at NBC to meet with Bute, who ran the production company Expanding Cinema.[28] Bute had begun making films in the mid-1930s in New York, including *Rhythm in Light* (1935) and *Synchromy No. 2* (1936), that had attracted considerable commentary in the popular press and were exhibited at venues including Radio City Music Hall.[29] McLaren wrote of his first meeting with Bute in a letter to his parents, describing how she "made several abstract films, rather like some of mine. She is intensely interested in me, (is seeing my films today), she wants me to work with her... There are about 4 people in her unit, & the atmosphere just suits me, as they are congenial, and think along the same lines as I do.... So on the whole, things are looking up! Hurrah!"[30] McLaren was soon hired by Bute to work on a film that was entering production, *Spook Sport*.

This was Bute's second color film, after *Escape* (1938), and it exemplified many of the ideas that Bute was exploring at the time regarding the synchronization of color, sound, form and motion in abstract animation. As with many of Bute's films, *Spook Sport* begins with title cards that indicate its aims, translating them for a wide audience that might be mystified by its abstractions: "In the following short film novelty – color, music, movement combine to present a new type of Film Ballet." Using Saint-Saëns's *Danse Macabre* for its musical score, Bute wrote that she "designed the film very much as one would the choreography of a ballet. Thru a special process the solo figures which carry the line of the melody are painted directly on the film."[31] These figures were drawn by McLaren, evoking the music through mutability and motion—at the start, for example, two squiggling and squirming lines move in time to the music and then become a pair of abstract green ghosts, dancing with one another beside a regimented line of other ghostly figures in profile (Fig. 4.1). The fluid motion and flowing lines of these figures contrast with the start of the film, which begins with the regular movement of the hands of a clock and more rigidly linear graphic forms. While recognizable symbols of fantastic creatures and objects recur throughout, the film also presents simplified and abstract figures with a similar visual aesthetic to McLaren's television films. With the film completed in May 1940, McLaren and Bute set about "getting in touch with various probable distributors" in the hope of "selling to the highest bidder."[32] This

Fig. 4.1 *Spook Sport* (1940)

included screening it—among other films—to Gilbert Seldes at CBS television. With the major sales of the film never materializing and McLaren's work with Expanding Cinema coming to an end, he found other paid work outside of animation which included designing shop windows.[33]

McLaren continued to make films independently, working in what he called his "stutcheon" ("because it's half a studio and half a kitchen").[34] The films he worked on continued to be drawn directly onto celluloid. McLaren would later explain that, in this way of animating, "I have tried to preserve my relationship to the film, the same closeness and intimacy that exists between a painter and his canvas."[35] Using the individual frames of a film strip as miniature canvases, such work could be made without an animating studio and expensive equipment; with hand-drawn animation, "The one great advantage is that it is about *8* times as cheap as all other methods of achieving the same result."[36] The standard mode of producing animated films at the time was cel animation, used by major studios such as Disney and Fleischer. This technique had become an industrial mode of production shortly after its invention in the mid-1910s—different roles in animating were divided into different areas of expertise, such as drawing, inking and photography. With cel animation, only those parts of each frame that are meant to be in motion are redrawn on translucent cels; these cels are then placed atop other cels which have drawings on them that make up the static parts of the image, such as the background. This technique saves considerable effort, as static parts of the image don't need to drawn again for every frame of the film—this can be incredibly time-consuming because, since films are projected at 24 frames per second, thousands of entirely different images would be needed for just a couple minutes of animated film. McLaren's technique is much different, as every frame does require an entirely new drawing.

In order to create the motions that he wanted when the film would actually be screened, McLaren would need to carefully judge how each drawing differs from the previous one on the film strip. This method of production accentuated movement by its very nature: "The most effortless and easiest thing to produce by this hand-drawn method is extreme mobility; the most difficult, and almost impossible, is staticity. This is the opposite of most other animation techniques where the static image is the easiest footage to obtain, and the mobile the most difficult."[37] As an animation practice which lends itself to an aesthetic effect of constant motion, as well as a painterly mode of creation and an inexpensive means of production, hand-drawn animation combined several of McLaren's abiding concerns as an artist.

McLaren further explored the potentials of hand-drawn animation in two other films which he made during this period: *Stars and Stripes* (1939) and *Scherzo* (1939). *Stars and Stripes* shows a frenzied sequence of hand-drawn paintings and images that correspond to July 4th celebrations—with loosely drawn sketches of the American flag and fireworks—moving in time to the music of a John Philip Sousa march. For *Scherzo*, McLaren extended his creative work with the film medium by drawing directly on the optical soundtrack (a thin strip adjacent to the visual frame) to create curious noises—mainly blips and blurts—that accompanied the movements and transformations of the images. *Scherzo* was distinctive in another way as well: its images lacked any clear figurative purpose. Unlike the recognizable iconography of *NBC Valentine Greeting*, *Stars and Stripes* and *Spook Sport*, *Scherzo* presents an abstract world of shapes in motion (Fig. 4.2). The film begins with a series of small circles moving diagonally across the screen which are joined, jostled and bumped by other circles moving crossways. As the film unfolds, more and more circles form new patterns of motion, groupings and interrelationships. Some circles begin to distort, bulge, stretch and mutate, while others appear hollowed out—this strange world of simple forms in motion is brought to a close with a triangle that

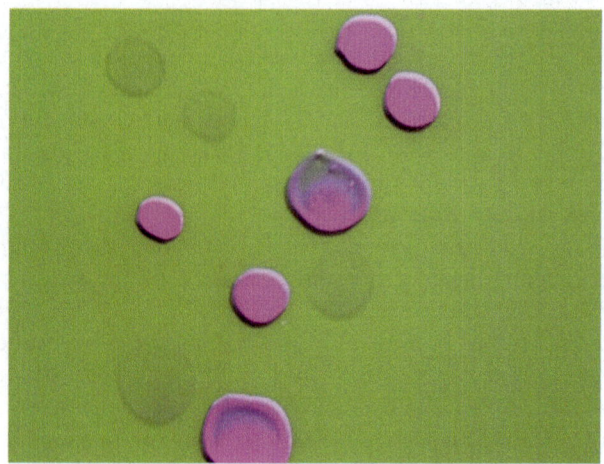

Fig. 4.2 *Scherzo* (1939)

appears, enlarges and vanishes. Rather than being structured around a particular subject matter, narrative or character, the film delightfully draws attention to variations of movement—shapes slide, spin and bounce, while odd noises are carefully synchronized with their movements.

The version of *Scherzo* that exists today begins with a title card that introduces it as "A Non-Objective Study." This was likely added to coincide with McLaren's involvement with the Museum of Non-Objective Painting and his association with Rebay, which began several months after his work with Expanding Cinema had ended. McLaren wrote to his parents about his first meeting with Rebay at "a talk on Non-Objective Paintings to a small audience in their lavish Museum in town"; he described how he "had read some rather strange articles she had written about her pet subject Non-objective Art."[38] While rather baffled and amused by her lecture—which he emphasized was just a first impression—he "went up and spoke to her after the talk, and she seemed eager to see my films, and seemed to like me. So on the following day I went to her secretary and arranged for a film show." He wrote to Rebay, describing himself as "an admirer of what you have been doing for Non-objective Art, and because I feel myself to have a contribution to make to Non-objectivity."[39] This soon led to a multifaceted association with Rebay, which included receiving a small stipend from the

Foundation for art materials so that he could make more films (in the non-objective style). In addition, as this chapter will discuss later, McLaren set up a series of film screenings and developed ambitious funding proposals for the Museum and Foundation. Each of these activities opened up new avenues for McLaren's work, which coincided with but also moved beyond Rebay's artistic values.

During this period, McLaren made two more films, *Dots* and *Loops*, which continued in the non-objective style that he had used for *Scherzo*. In a letter to his parents, he described non-objective film: "For your information, 'Non-Objective Art' is Art which does not have any recognizable objects in it, so a Non-Objective Film is a film which doesn't use objects to achieve its effect."[40] *Dots* is a clear example of this type of film, extending the play of motion in *Scherzo* while still working mainly with the simple form of the circle (or dot). From the start, the film presents different variations of motion: dots suddenly appear and then shrink as if receding into the distance; pairs of dots appear, strike one another and merge into new forms which abruptly change direction; dots and other globular or geometric shapes spin around the frame, subdividing and transforming. As the film goes on, it becomes increasingly complex in its variations of motion and transformation, with multiple shapes mutating, changing direction and moving in unpredictable ways. Different sounds, created by drawing on the optical soundtrack, accompany the motions and transformations of shapes and their interactions with one another. Without recognizable characters, objects, spaces or sounds, the flux of motion predominates. McLaren explained, "the mobile element of a film can almost always be broken down into two components, the form of a moving object, and the motion itself (divorced from the particular form that it is expressing itself through)."[41] McLaren sought to highlight "the motion itself"—"it is the mobile elements of the visuals that counts; it is the motion that speaks to us, not the image." Much like the composition of forms on the space of a canvas in non-objective painting, McLaren's films composed motion.

Rather than looking toward the rhythmic, spiritual and cosmic values of non-objective painting as Rebay had done, McLaren rooted motion in details of everyday life:

> for instance a photographed man, a cartoon man, an animal, or even a simple triangle or blob, can all leap in such a way that the viewer has an impression of joy, sadness, tiredness, youth or old age. If examined carefully frame by frame on a motion picture strip, the various movements of joy will all be

found to have a common characteristic; similarly the various movements of a tired leap will all have common factors of timing, tempo, acceleration and deceleration.[42]

In this respect, movement that is "separate from the particular thing, shape or form that moves" expresses a range of feelings in these early McLaren films. Animating the passionate interaction of two hearts, the excitement of ghosts springing into formation or the anxiety of blobs suddenly shifting direction, McLaren evoked human emotions and expressions through motion. At the same time, the use of geometric shapes, the composition of movement and the exploration of varied rhythms connected these animated films to the concerns of Rebay and non-objective painting. Much as McLaren had engaged with New York's multifaceted animation culture by adapting his artistic approach to the contexts of NBC television and Expanding Cinema, his relationship to the Museum of Non-Objective Painting offered another place for him to explore the potentials of animated motion.

McLaren continued to engage with ideas of non-objective painting in his next film, *Loops*, which was made in early 1941. While replacing the visual motif of a circle with a loop, the film begins much like *Dots* by showing a series of forms emerge, metamorphosize and diminish in size as if receding into the distance. As they do so, these looping forms curl and transform to make new kinds of shapes (Fig. 4.3). At times, these ribbons of motion suggest recognizable forms—such as a square or a heart—but their ongoing mutations never stabilize. About half a minute in, the film takes on a different tone as two loops begin an intricate and playful dance. They metamorphosize and twist around one another, fading into the distance only to come to the foreground again. One begins to orbit, like a comet, and the other breaks apart, multiplies and regathers itself into a single shape. The two forms stretch, circle, recoil and touch—other shapes come off them like droplets. Their interaction is sometimes tentative, sometimes aggressive, sometimes energized. A culmination of many of the creative ideas that McLaren had been developing, *Loops* deepened the expressive range of non-objective forms in motion.

Like the circles in *Scherzo* and *Dots*, these loops are vessels for motion without a referent. They are the basis for the film, and in this respect, they resonate with Rebay's ideas of composing non-objective paintings around a theme:

Fig. 4.3   *Loops* (1941)

In a non-objective picture the artist uses neither light, shadow and perspective nor memory and knowledge of nature. He merely uses the canvas to convey space relationship and enlivens it by creating a lovely theme. The chief beauty of a non-objective masterpiece lies in the perfect rhythm with which it presents themes so combined and related that the space used is completely organized.[43]

McLaren's films shifted this idea of compositional themes to the presentation of motions. Rather than using a theme to organize the *space* of a canvas, the themes of the circle and the loop were used to structure the *movement* of a film.

Rebay emphasized how the activity of a painter requires a cohesive overall sense of a work that is developed from the artist's "first statement of form or color" and that "continues until the space is completely, organically harmonized and all themes have been perfected and finished; the artist's concentration for continuity has to last until his intuition is exhausted."[44] Indicating a similar working practice, McLaren wrote a letter to Rebay in which he apologizes for having to decline her invitation for dinner and theater due to his work on *Loops*; this was all-consuming, with McLaren describing how he was "working on it 15 hours a day, and am so completely absorbed in it, that it would be dangerous to leave it for even a short time, because it might interrupt the Continuity, which is so impor-tant."[45] While this may have served as an excuse to politely decline an invitation, it also indicates the vital role of artistic immersion needed to create works where sensorial power and expressive richness derive from the continuity of motion itself.

DWINELL GRANT: COMPOSING ANIMATION

At the same time that McLaren was making films in New York, the artist Dwinell Grant began to develop a close association with the Museum and the Guggenheim Foundation. Before creating his first animated film, Grant's background was in painting. His work in this medium interested Rebay, who exhibited several of his paintings and offered financial sup-port.[46] Much like McLaren, who also had a background in the visual arts, Grant set about exploring the potentials of animation as an extension of existing artistic practices. For Grant, this included not only making non-objective animated films, but also theorizing how such films could be com-posed.

Before moving to New York, where he worked as an assistant to Rebay, Grant lived in Springfield, Ohio, teaching art and drama at Wittenberg College. In May 1940, he wrote to Rebay excitedly describing an artistic discovery he had made "purely by accident."[47] He explained that he had been designing the stage and lighting system for "an experimental sym-phonic drama" that was being put on by the students at the College. The set's "three-dimensional non-objective design" was illuminated by "four sets of lights on dimmers": "When completed and put in operation it was breath-taking, not only in itself, but also in the possibilities which it indi-cated." The wonder of the thing was that by controlling the color, "The whole character of the design can be changed by a simple flick of the wrist and when these changes are flowed smoothly into one another there is a non-objective composition in space and time!" While he was largely unfa-miliar with earlier works of abstract animation, Grant was aware that "all of the basic ideas involved have been used in the theater for years," and he also realized that the effect was similar to Wilfred's lumia.[48] But if such a lumi-nous world could be composed for cinema, the control of movements and changing visual compositions could lead to "far greater possibilities."[49] He excitedly asked: "What would happen if the basic design were really com-posed, instead of being built in the usual slap-dash theatrical manner! What if fifty colors were used instead of three! What if the forms were moveable!"

The potentials that captivated Grant would become central to his creative and theoretical work for years to follow.

Several months after outlining his initial ideas to Rebay, Grant completed his first film, *Themis*, with some financial support from the Foundation. Lasting only a few minutes, this striking film is based on the modulation of colors and the movement of forms—circles, square and lines made up of "small objects, cardboard, pieces of glass, and wire, etc." are animated through stop motion, which requires small iterations of movement of the objects in the frame.[50] The film's title *Themis* drew attention to how its underlying aims were closely associated with Rebay's vision of non-objective painting, referring to both a compositional "theme" and the Greek word for order, "themis."[51] The film begins with circular shapes visually emerging from a blue background; thick lines then appear, some of which spin through the frame and one of which spreads out into a square (Fig. 4.4). These curved and linear geometric objects then multiply, emerge, vanish and reposition themselves over the course of the short film, while changing hues, glinting lights and shifting shadows create a dynamic scheme of luminosity and color. Some sections of the film are dizzying in their depiction of constantly changing patterns of shapes and colors which rearrange themselves according to an obscure and sometimes unfathomable logic. Other sections offer comparatively restful pauses by

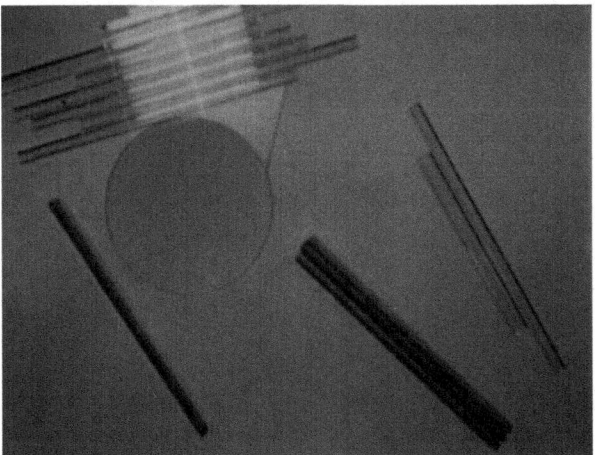

Fig. 4.4 *Themis* (1940)

gathering together forms in geometric compositions or repeating motions that are enacted by just a few shapes; the concluding passage presents a return to the simple movements of these shapes, which sway and rotate in regular patterns of motion (Fig. 4.5). Lacking a preamble explaining the film's aims or a clear overall trajectory, the film presents an otherworldly sense of animated life.

Writing to Rebay, Grant expressed his dissatisfaction with the final result: "I have just sent you the first film. I have sent it in spite of the fact that I neither think it is art nor good. It is only non-objective."[52] He went on to describe a number of problems he saw in the film, after having "studied it frame by frame": the "movement is jerky," the "colors seem a little raw" and there is not enough sense of depth. While these aesthetic elements irritated him, it was the film's compositional weaknesses that were most frustrating. He explained that the use of rhythm is sometimes "too obvious" and sometimes "completely lost." Moreover, for Grant, "the development of theme is sadly neglected" and the overall structure is flawed because "The only sequence which approaches climactic proportions comes too early in the film to have any effect but a confusing one." Despite these concerns, this "personal experiment in such a new medium" inspired Grant. "I feel very much as the inventor of a musical instrument must feel as he looks at

Fig. 4.5 *Themis* (1940)

his first successful model. Well – it works and now I can start composing for it."

Grant's central concerns regarding composition, thematic continuity, rhythm and motion corresponded closely to the interests of Rebay and McLaren. While a shared approach was evident, Rebay thought Grant's work was much more diffuse and less refined than McLaren's. In a letter to Grant describing her reaction to *Themis*, Rebay cautioned him about his limitations and immaturity as an artist, rather tactlessly adding: "A Scotchman, Mr. McLaren, showed me his films, very gifted and inventive, and soon as good as Fischinger."[53] Likely with certain aesthetic qualities of McLaren's films in mind—such as their simple visual figures and their evocation of movement in depth—she further suggested to Grant that his filmmaking "will be most effective if you use clean backgrounds and clean themes and let forms increase and decrease in space, which I found the most thrilling moment in non-objective film." But rather than following the lead of McLaren, Grant's research, writing and filmmaking—which occupied him for years—extended many of the ideas which he was developing in *Themis*.

Grant investigated technical aspects of animated films, including their production, their use of color and the production of three-dimensional films.[54] His creative and theoretical work, however, was largely focused on developing a theory of composing motion in animated film. Addressing the weaknesses of theme and structure in his first film, he suggested that a "basal theme"—a blueprint for motion—could function as "the minimum fundamental structure necessary to establish the basic character of the theme. It is the skeletal series of directions of change, perceived through the greatest economy of figures, in number and in quality, that is possible."[55] Such themes of motion could be composed, offering a way to organize movements such as patterns of acceleration and deceleration or instances of repetition and mutation.[56] In order to handle the complexity of all the ways that themes of motion might unfold over time, Grant wrote of how it was "necessary to select directions which, when combined simultaneously or in sequence, will produce a single coherent melodic line, and every direction selected must be in accordance with and regulated by the key and tempo of the movement, or part of the composition, of which it is a part."[57] This was only one of many methods of achieving a cohesive form that Grant developed over several years of working on the art of composing animation, but its borrowing from musical terminology, its emphasis on continuity and its foregrounding of motion reflected his abiding concerns as a composer of animated motion.

Since a theme moves over time, it develops. A theme can move by itself over the course of a film, generating its own dynamism, and it can also develop alongside a secondary theme. Rebay suggested this more complex development; after seeing *Themis*, she wrote to Grant, "If you start a theme, find a counter theme."[58] Further developing the implications of such a visual fugue in his next film *Contrathemis* (1941), Grant explored the potentials of counterpoint by introducing a complementary theme to generate a series of interrelated motions.[59] McLaren had introduced a similar element in *Loops*, with the appearance of a second looping form that interacted with the first. The interaction of two thematic forces could create an important quality of dynamism in the overall work: "When the relationship is one of interdependence between items and between items and the whole, the whole is proportionately less static, more dynamic."[60]

The visualization of relationships between themes could, Grant hoped, create a sense of order that would be perceived and felt by a viewer. In a draft outline for his larger project, entitled "The Non-Objective Film (A Theory of Composition)," he described the overarching premise: "The dynamic exposition of relationships can overcome conceptual chaos to produce consciousness of order."[61] Influenced not only by Rebay, but also by theorists of Gestalt psychology, Grant would emphasize how a vital sense of ordered relationships had been lost—or at least obscured—with representational art's emphasis on recognizable images, such as a still life or a portrait. A non-objective composition, on the other hand, brought the relationship between forms and colors to the foreground. Grant extended the implications of an art of interrelationships to a social context: "We find ourselves in the most complex society that has ever existed, in which the values derived from relatedness are harder to establish than ever before."[62] By experiencing an art of dynamic interrelationships, "it is reasonable to hope, at least, that the disclosure of deeper, more vital relationships will produce correspondingly more vital changes in our ability to live successfully."[63] While seemingly far removed from the concerns of the designers at the World's Fair, discussed in the previous chapter, Grant's approach to composing animation resonated with the ideas of rhythm, order and progress that Teague and Bel Geddes were exploring. Much as the Cycle of Production and Futurama used motion to display the imagined smooth workings of production or transportation, Grant was developing ideas around animation's potential to show a fundamental sense of order amid our disjointed perceptions and experiences of modern life.

Creating an artwork composed of dynamic interrelationships—integrating themes and counterthemes of motion—was incredibly challenging. This was made all the more difficult by the practice of animation, as "the composer can never have more than a fragmentary visual contact with his composition until he sees it on the screen for the first time."[64] And Grant saw the labor of animating itself, rather than the more visionary creative work of composing such a work, as "a job of complete boredom for a creative artist."[65] With such concerns in mind, Grant worked on developing systems of notation for composing animated films. One initial aim was to provide "A simple method of writing a composition so that all the detailed work and photography can be handled by persons other than the composer."[66] Another key aim was to create a sufficiently flexible method that could allow for creative intuition and not "deteriorate into a thought-out, mathematical thing."[67]

In order to effectively compose a non-objective animation, Grant saw that movement must be independent of the actual forms that it would take. For Grant, "The minute the items become images, so many association forces enter the pattern that the balance is lost."[68] Writing of how he has "taken all importance away from shapes and colors and placed it on the interval alone," Grant was exploring how motion could be the fundamental quality of a work of art.[69] This emphasis on motion led to a creative practice unmoored from established arts and ways of perceiving: "I don't have a beautiful white canvas to inspire me any more. I must project myself out into space itself and around me. There is not even the top of a mountain to stand on. One doesn't 'see' things there – one feels them with a sense that has nothing to do with physical organs." Rather than being based in objects or systems, the animated artwork becomes "as elusive as the designs we see in tobacco smoke"—fleeting and unfixed instances of ongoing motion.[70]

Underpinning these creative ambitions, Grant linked non-objectivity to urgent political and social concerns. For Grant, this was "an art that is rid of the confining, restricting bonds of race or nationality…. In the midst of the confusion of nationalistic isms here will be an art that is clear, naked and straightforward…. And it will drive into the emotions to a new depth because of the primitiveness, the directness, the fundamentalness of its expression."[71] Like Teague's emphasis on rhythm discussed in the previous chapter, Grant described how animation could become "a visual expression of a fundamental rhythm... which is based on universal constants and not limited to the narrow backgrounds of a single group of people."[72] But unlike Teague, who used rhythm as a component of design, Grant saw a new realm of rhythmic composition opening up: with non-objective animation, he would be able to present fundamental rhythms through "two means of visual expression which, for too long, have been neglected; namely, movement and light."[73] Grant's ambition was for a universal art of motion in light.

Grant's theoretical investigations and accompanying film practice were partially funded by Foundation scholarships which he needed to delay and extend numerous times, never quite realizing his ambitious plans. While working on this project throughout the 1940s, he also worked within other animation contexts: he directed animated navy training films during the war, and, shortly after the war, he turned to producing animated scientific and medical films. This latter endeavor was a response to financial necessity for Grant, and it would prove to be long-lasting and highly productive—over the course of decades, he would direct hundreds of instructional films.[74] Grant successfully navigated his way from art to science and medicine, becoming a Member of the New York Academy of Sciences in 1954. The educational potentials of animation extended many of Grant's artistic concerns into new fields, shifting his fascination with composing animation for artistic purposes to using animation for schematic and educational purposes.

A brochure for his production company, Sturgis-Grant Productions, begins by noting the wide-ranging instructional possibilities of animated film: "Many ideas in the fields of business and education involve movement and time.... Some of these ideas are communicated most efficiently by animation. For some, animation is the only possible medium."[75] The brochure went on to foreground different values of animation, noting that the "vast extent of its potential" had often been obscured by its use in comedic cartoons. But animation could do so much more: "Because all graphic art is, of necessity, a form of abstraction, animation eliminates disturbing details and provides a means of communicating anything from a simple sale pitch to a complicated technological idea with a brevity, precision and brilliance which would be hard to find in any other medium." As well as transposing Grant's interest in abstraction onto the field of instructional animation, the pamphlet also pointed out the variety of animation's potential uses. Animation could emphasize points through repetition and variation, constantly "providing views from new points"; animation could "observe an invisible world" by showing the hidden workings of nature; and animation could "simplify and clarify technical explanations" in fields ranging from statistics to theoretical physics. Coupling animation's visionary qualities with a scientific or factual basis, "the animator can extend an idea out into unknown areas, providing the research scientist with working theories on which he can base further experimentation." Animation was a springboard for new ways of expressing, perceiving and understanding—this multifaceted sense of instructional animation developed from Grant's earlier explorations of animation as a form of art.

Much like Grant's shift from an artistic to educational context for animation, the creative context for McLaren's work also changed significantly after his association with Rebay and the Museum. Even with Rebay's financial support, McLaren found himself in need of more stable employment outside of the auspices of the Museum. He found work at Caravel Films, which included writing advertising jingles and a script and storyboard for Bakelite Plastics that was to be turned into a half-hour "puppet trick film" using stop motion animation.[76] Other opportunities arose as well, including the possibility of further television work: "If the job does come off, I would have to turn out a film 20 seconds long each day all about watches or clocks, for a big watch making firm that advertised every day on television."[77] But McLaren's artistic passions lay elsewhere, and when John Grierson visited from Canada, offering him the chance to set up an animation department at the NFB, McLaren was thrilled. He wrote to his parents about this, describing it as an opportunity to "make my own special kind of trick films for publicizing things like War Savings and so on," adding that "the job seemed to be full of *artistic* opportunity, much more so than any other job I might ever get, as I would be given an almost completely free hand, [Grierson] said."[78] After considerable wrangling to get him out of his contract with Caravel—with Grierson supporting McLaren's argument "that it is their duty to release me as a request from the British government to a British subject to do war work"—McLaren moved to Ottawa in the summer of 1941 to start the animation department at the NFB, "dreaming of the sort of films I shall invent up there."[79]

At the NFB, McLaren first made instructional and propaganda films. While the projects he worked on were seemingly far removed from artistic concerns, the creative and vitalizing role of motion continued to be central to McLaren's work. In *V for Victory* (1941), for example, the letter V becomes a form through which to show movements such as walking and stretching. McLaren explained how the film's "themes are 'V' (the letter) and '• • • —'. I make a phantasy out of these simple elements. It's good fun; I am moderately pleased with the results."[80] While the symbols had considerable resonance in the wartime context—the "V" and "• • • —" (Morse code for "V") both symbolized victory—McLaren used them as an opportunity to animate different kinds of motion. Similarly, with *Dollar Dance* (1943), McLaren used the symbol of the dollar sign not only as a reference to money but also as a visual motif in order to elaborate on different potentials of motion. He elaborated on his aims in a letter to Rebay: "I am just starting on a new film called 'Dollar Dance', the main theme of which is simply a '\$'. It is really a beautiful motif to work with. The swinging, double curve, and the two strong straight lines, make excellent and exciting forms to work with."[81]

McLaren described to Rebay how other aspects of his work at the NFB were infused with similar ideas of non-objective form, extending into such seemingly inartistic contexts as "animated diagrammatic films" about "Nutrition, Agricultural Problems, Cost of Living and Price Control."[82] He explained to Rebay,

> We work very hard, and get much pleasure out of creating such films – even though they are not precisely Non-objective – because we make great use of the principle of Non-objective movement in them, from which, I'm sure, they derive great benefit. For even the most materialistic subject-matter, when it is put into movement which is suffused and pervaded with well-balanced and beautifully rhythmic motion, gains in its spiritual appeal.... there is always room for the Non-objective in even the most materialist of things.

Translating an art of themes, rhythms and motions into a filmmaking context seemingly far removed from the milieu of the gallery, McLaren's approach to animation fluidly crossed between institutional contexts while maintaining its own distinctive qualities. We have seen how McLaren had shifted between contexts—television, Expanding Cinema and the gallery—in his work in New York. McLaren's early work at the NFB continued to draw artistic motion into new contexts, instruction and propaganda, much as Grant had extended his own artistic ideas into the production of scientific and medical films. For both animators, art was not defined by a gallery space or circumscribed by an institutional context. Motion was something more fundamental—a mercurial and fluid medium.

MOVEMENT BETWEEN MEDIA

Rebay and the Museum of Non-Objective Painting engaged with animated film in ways that went beyond providing financial support and advice to individual animators. Through screenings of animated films, beginning in 1940, animation became part of the Museum. Shortly after meeting Rebay and discussing this idea, McLaren investigated the suitability of the gallery and the necessary equipment this would require.[83] This initial research soon led to a regular series of screenings of non-objective films at the Museum. Many of the films that McLaren made during his time in New York were first publicly exhibited at these screenings. The first of these, in December 1940, began with early abstract animations by Richter and Eggeling before moving on to animated films by Fischinger and McLaren. With an invitation list that included the Rockefellers, Vladimir Horowitz, Arturo Toscanini and Iris Barry, it aimed to be a prestigious affair.[84] McLaren was certainly impressed, writing to his parents:

> The Show last night at the Museum, passed off smoothly, and I think was a great success.... There were about 100 people there. And it was all very fancy. The Baroness spoke a few words between some of the films. She just loves my films, so she gave me quite a boost. After the show was over, so many people wanted to be introduced to me that I was somewhat embarrassed, and I was even more embarrassed when some people wanted my signature. I had quite a talk with Mr and Mrs Guggenheim... and some of the Rothschilds.[85]

Shown at such a major event, non-objective animation had taken on an elevated place in New York culture.

This first screening was titled a "Film Concert," a phrase that related to the films being shown in several ways. Animated film often drew upon music as a model or inspiration for its composition and its aesthetic—a "concert" emphasized this relationship between animation and music. In her introductory notes to *Diagonal Symphony* (1924), for example, Rebay highlighted how the film presented visual counterpoint and rhythm: "Here you have two fundamental form problems, the lyrical curve and the dramatic square in its purest counterpoint. This counterpoint exists and is essential to the creator of visual rhythm as well as to the creator of musical rhythm, but can be enjoyed by the layman without its fundamental knowledge."[86] In a more prosaic sense, a "film concert" also drew attention to the synchronization of music and image that was a major element of several of the films that were shown. This was particularly pronounced in

Fischinger's films, which Rebay's screening notes described as "the most advanced and artistic creations of colorful reaction and interpretation to the non-objective rhythm in music made visual" and "work of heretofore unseen rhythmic quality. No dancer ever could follow the rhythmic inter-change of music in every measure as the responsive reaction and creative interpretation of sometimes hundreds of drawings which are necessary to do justice to one single measure of music."[87] This sense of musicality was further emphasized by the titles of films, such as *Diagonal Symphony*, which would often refer to musical qualities or forms even when the film itself was silent. McLaren also referred to music in the titles of his films, first using the titles *Allegro Moderato* and *Allegro Spiritoso* for *Scherzo* and *Dots* in order to emphasize the musical tempo of motion in the films.[88]

Among the audience at the first of the Museum's screenings was the art critic for the *New York Times*, Edward Alden Jewell. Taking the name "Film Concert" as a statement of intent, he wrote a scathing critique of the screening as part of a larger discussion of the "problem of fusing aural and visual forms."[89] Responding to the films accompanied by classical music— which included Fischinger's *An Optical Poem* (1938) and *Spook Sport*—he wrote, "I was unable to witness the entire programme, but can report that of the films based on 'classical' music that I did see and hear, not one struck me as being in any significant sense successful." While the films may have effectively synchronized music and image, such a "visualization added nothing to the music, serving merely to repeat, in another medium (and often in the most trivial guise), elements that were completely expressed for the ear in the original medium." Jewell noted that McLaren's anima-tions were the "most interesting" of the films he had seen, while adding that they "proved to be of very slight consequence and, like the two 'silent' compositions – one by Richter, one a 'Diagonal Symphony' by Eggeling – never emerged from the realm of laboratory experiment." Keen to dis-tinguish between artistic forms, Jewell had little patience for the merging of media suggested by a "Film Concert" being shown at a gallery.

At the same time, Jewell saw that painting and music did share a quality of motion. Writing about painting, he noted elements which "contribute to the aggregate an artist knows as 'movement'" including "the journey of line," "the drama of color and tone" and "the repetition that helps create balance."[90] After discussing such ideas of painterly motion, he suggested that ideas of motion could be just as easily applied to music. For Jewell, the links between the motion of painting and the motion of music stemmed from rhythm: "in all of this, 'rhythm' is seen to be inextricably bound up.

It might be described as the very pulse or heart of 'movement.'" Despite these similarities between media and the parallels and analogies that can be drawn, Jewell was insistent that it was a mistake to transpose one medium into another. Animated films that combined musical and painterly qualities only muddled the distinctions between two different forms of art. He argued instead for "leaving them in their separate spheres, where they should remain." Much more successful, for Jewell, were Thomas Wilfred's clavilux recitals at the Art Institute of Light: "What the spectator beholds is visual music, composed in sequences of moving colored light. These are not themes that accompany or that are accompanied by music. They do not interpret music. They *are* music, silent music."

Rebay was somewhat taken aback by this critique, explaining to one correspondent, "The error of printing the words 'Film Concert' on the program without my consent may be responsible for the wrong attitude of Mr. Jewell to the performance. The goal in reality was to show the development of films from Richter, Eggeling, up to the great Fischinger."[91] Soon after, when she took the film exhibition to the Dock Street Theater in Charleston, the screening took on a different name: "A Festival of Rhythm."[92] While the description of the screening still used a language of intermedial connections, referring to films as "color plays" and musical "numbers," the overall tone had shifted from a combination of arts to an emphasis on "non-objective rhythmic motion in design, color, music and sound" as the underlying artistic principle.[93]

While Rebay became wary of describing the screenings of animated films in intermedial terms after Jewell's negative reaction, ideas of the musicality of painting were vital to her approach to art. The merging of different artistic forms was a longstanding interest among visual artists and filmmakers from Kandinsky to Fischinger. The combination of aesthetic elements had also been a topic of considerable interest for advertisers and exhibitors. Along with a range of other devices and techniques, polarized color displays shown at the World's Fair were seen to be offering an "entirely new" way of combining "three essentials of animation" through their depiction of "color, light, and motion."[94] In cinema, new film technologies of synchronized sound and Technicolor that had been introduced over the previous decade were transforming the aesthetics of popular animated film. As the next chapter examines in more detail, animated films were developing their synchronization of motion with music and color in dynamic ways— this was a vital feature of the popular and critical success of animated films produced by Disney and others. The relation between music, the visual arts and motion was also a central issue for the filmmakers in New York who were most closely associated with Rebay. McLaren and Grant developed projects which aimed to draw upon and expand this intermedial potential of animated film. Well aware of Rebay's own interest in the fusion of artistic forms, their ideas were a pragmatic reaction to possible funding opportunities; at the same time, their proposals extended the potentials of their own artistic ideas and creative practice.

McLaren wrote to Rebay in February 1941, outlining his plans for a highly ambitious thirty-minute film and asking if the Foundation would be able to sponsor it. McLaren envisaged the film as "a major work, with a Symphonic Structure, in three movements," which included "an Andante, in which the action is simple, bold and direct, and in which the first theme is stated, and followed by the second (or countertheme)."[95] As the film goes on, "Each theme is then developed, one against the other, and expanded into a set of variations. The second movement is a Largo; with infinitely strong, stately action the themes are modulated and developed still further, and fused with a new largo motive." The film's final third movement would be "a Presto, with lively, vigorous recapitulation of the opening themes, in which the developments and expansion of the first two movements are brought together in a brilliant rhythmic and chromatic finale." The proposal does not refer to actually having a musical score, indicating that it would be the variations of motion itself that create the symphonic structure.

While this proposal did not receive funding, the central idea of creating an extended animated film in three movements with distinct tempos of motion would later shape one of McLaren's best-known works, *Begone Dull Care*. McLaren described how he worked closely with the composer of the music, Oscar Peterson, to integrate the animation and the musical score in a manner that recalled his work making sounds by drawing on the optical soundtrack of *Dots* and *Loops*, "in which I did the percussion myself almost simultaneously with the picture."[96] In his proposal and filmmaking practice during this time in New York, McLaren was already developing ways of fusing music with animation rather than simply matching animation to existing pieces of music. In doing so, McLaren was exploring how the creation of a symphony of movement or the integration of sound and image could create new sensorial experiences rooted in motion.

Another funding proposal that McLaren made around this time, for "Automatic Mural Movies," also engaged with entwining artistic forms. But rather than developing from a musical basis, this idea elaborated on the relationship of animation to painting. His proposal was for "a method for showing mobiles (hung on a wall in a gallery) alongside 'still' painting": what initially seems to be a blank canvas would become a moving painting when an "electric circuit" registers the presence of a viewer.[97] Much like Henry Billings's moving mural at the Ford exhibit, this exhibition of a moving painting would invest a static form of art with motion:

> the illumination in part of the gallery near to the picture would dim, and at the same time the canvas would grow luminous with colour and non-objective form, which would slowly swing into rhythmic and balanced motion, making a complete evolution of non-objective action at the conclusion of which the canvas would dim and the gallery lights would return to normal.

In short, "The whole impression is one of a painting in action." Drawing images directly on film offered McLaren the opportunity to create animation like a painter working on a canvas; the idea of "Automatic Mural Movies" extended the connection between painting and animation from the production of the work to the exhibition of the work, with a framed image hung on the wall of a gallery becoming a site of animation.

McLaren would later make a series of films which elaborated on the idea of a moving painting, including *C'est l'aviron* (1944) and *A Little Phantasy on a Nineteenth Century Painting* (1946). Making "hundreds of paintings" for *C'est l'aviron*, rather than "the usual drawings on 'cells,'" McLaren explained how he would animate the individual images by "moulding them into a fluid and mobile conception, thru the way I am shooting them."[98] He described this film as a "mobile painting... in which I have completely fused my interests as a painter and as a film-maker."[99] The visual elaboration of Arnold Böcklin's painting "Isle of the Dead" (1880–1891) in *A Little Phantasy* explored a similar merging of painting and animation in which "motion replaces stillness" through an animated reworking of the original artwork: "Walls crumble, pillars shoot up and disintegrate, a great bird with spread wings materializes and a tree of flame appears and is consumed. Each movement ceases as sharply as it began, leaving no trace of its passing, and the film ends with the same lifeless island that we saw at first."[100] Similarly, his proposal for "Automatic Mural Movies" explained how the canvas could begin with what seems like a painting which would then "become luminous, begin moving, and complete a cycle, returning to a point at which the organization started, whereupon the canvas and gallery illumination would return to normal."[101] Transforming the nature of a painting by giving it motion, "Automatic Mural Movies" aimed to refashion art; in a similar manner, the idea of a symphonic film shifted musical form to animated form. In both proposals, as well as his later artistic practice, McLaren engaged with how motion could transform existing arts and, by doing so, generate new artistic forms.

Grant explored similar ideas during the early stages of his association with Rebay. Initially trained as a painter, Grant described a fusion of painterly and musical qualities in his vision of animated film's potential to be "a color art that is as dynamic and as moving as music..."[102] With such an idea in mind, and perhaps wanting to align himself with Rebay's own interests, Grant wrote notes for a funding proposal to the Foundation in 1940 that outlined a project that would examine the "innate relationship of music and painting."[103] He proposed making two kinds of films to communicate this idea. The first, a "Visual Aid for Understanding of Music" would provide "an almost literal translation of the musical artefact into color, form and movement." He planned on developing a visual representation of music through what he called a "tone-color unit" that would correspond to different musical instruments and "indicate the progress of music from beat to beat. While the ear follows the (musical) composition, the simultaneous appearance on the screen of the tone-color units will present to the eye a pictorial interpretation of the musical thought." Alongside this, he proposed an "Auditory Aid for Understanding of Painting." He planned to use a musical score to accompany the gradual emergence of a painting onscreen, with the music "interpreting audibly the elements of design, color, and rhythmic relationships contained in the complete work." In the film, "The tentative placing of basic compositional forms on the screen will be accompanied by an equally tentative sound track, as if in search of the melody. Determination of the color organization will be made audible by the consonance of the orchestration." The film would both illustrate the musical qualities of painting and highlight the "'movements' latent in the static easel painting or mural" by showing them gradually emerge. Taken together, these two films would illustrate interrelationships between painting and music through animation.

Unlike McLaren, who was keen to explore the interrelationship of different arts and who would go on to develop this in his later work, Grant began to question the relation between animation and other artistic forms. Expressing his uncertainty about transposing music or painting into animated film, he wrote to Rebay that the creative practice he envisioned "is not intended as an interpretation of any other art form, including music.

It must stand by itself, deriving its motivation from a sincere, deep feeling for aesthetic rhythms and from the qualities of the physical materials used in its composition."[104] In this respect, Grant's early funding ideas were a detour from his own creative vision of animated film. From the start, his films were silent. Shortly after seeing *Themis*, Rebay suggested that his films "*need* music. It is essential. Without music it is just one more experiment but can be done better."[105] Grant was resistant to this suggestion and he continued to avoid linking music to the image. He would later explain that the silence of his films was initially due to pragmatic reasons ("I didn't know anything about sound, and I didn't have any money at all") but later became an aesthetic choice as, in the animated films with musical accompaniment that he had seen, "it seemed to me that the visual became nothing but an interpretation of the music."[106]

Although Grant's theoretical writing was heavily indebted to a language of rhythm and composition borrowed from music and painting, he also began to question whether there was any underlying connection between animated film and the other arts. He wrote, "there is little or no relationship between this art form (non-objective film) and music. The eyes and the ears are much too different."[107] Moreover, "there is even very little relationship between this art form and painting. I have had to forget all my feeling about the composing of a canvas because the relationships which may be true in that work are no longer so when time and movement are involved." Composing non-objective animation required a very different approach than visual artists working with a static medium:

> To give an over-simple example, instead of developing a square of exactly correct dimensions, color, and texture to fit within the environment of the total painting, it is necessary to think of, say, red square revolving on its vertical axis as it changes to blue rectangle, as it diminishes in size, as it moves from upper left to lower right to disappearance in the distance, and all of this in correlation with other activities – not static environment – occurring simultaneously. This kind of thinking has not been part of their training and they should not be discouraged if achieving it requires several years of concentrated effort.[108]

The ongoing motion of animated film had led him away from thinking of artistic forms and practices as corresponding to one another: "similarities are superficial – only the fundamental aesthetic purpose can be transferred."[109] Transfixed by the potentials of accessing this "fundamental aesthetic purpose," Grant had explored connections between artistic forms only to arrive at a more singular vision of animation where its fundamental qualities were rooted in motion and change. Whether animated film was seen as a distinct medium, as it was for Grant, or a medium that could entwine itself with established artistic forms, as it was for McLaren, motion was the underlying force of artistic power.

MARY ELLEN BUTE AND KINETIC SPACE

Many of the ideas and approaches that were circulating around animation as a form of art in New York's animation culture—its relation to painting and music, the composition of motion and the primacy of aesthetic qualities rather than representational ones—were also vital to Mary Ellen Bute's filmmaking practice. In an article from 1940, Bute described her work as "Absolute Film," connecting it to other filmmakers who had used this phrase for the "famous matinee 'Der absolute Film'" that took place in Germany in 1925, where abstract animations were shown by Ruttmann, Eggeling and Richter.[110] Although situating herself within this cinematic context, her original ideas of what she termed "kinetic art" had developed independently of film.[111] While Bute, like McLaren and Grant, had a background in painting, it was in the context of New York's music culture that she delivered her first major lecture on the possibilities of entwining art with motion. Presenting a lecture entitled "Light as an Art Material and its Possible Synchronization with Sound" at the New York Musicological Society in January 1932 to an audience that included Thomas Wilfred and Leon Theremin, she outlined her ideas of an "art form of light" and "the necessity of *kinetic* art."[112] Shortly after this talk on the artistic potentials of light in motion, which covered topics ranging from modernist painting to visual music, Bute began exploring cinema as the medium for her artistic vision. With Ted Nemeth as producer and cinematographer, she soon made a series of films that explored the aesthetic and expressive potentials of motion, including *Rhythm in Light*, *Synchromy No. 2* and *Escape*. The name of her production company, Expanding Cinema, captured the sense of ambition evident in Bute's works, theoretical writing and artistic practice, advertising its productions as "Light, Form, Sound, Movement Synchronized in Abstract Film."[113]

Bute's films were aligned in many respects with the Museum and the filmmakers associated with it. Bute especially admired McLaren's work, hiring him for animation work on *Spook Sport* and describing him in 1941 as a "brilliant young Scotchman" whose work "suggests *new* dimensions in film art."[114] After attending one of the Museum's film screenings that year, she wrote to McLaren on behalf of Expanding Cinema, complimenting him on his "new study of 'Loops,' with which we were perfectly enchanted!" and also noting "We found the evening as a whole very stimulating."[115] Shortly after its completion, *Spook Sport* was shown in the Museum's screenings and a print of it was purchased by the Foundation for its nascent library of non-objective film. McLaren helped negotiate the sale, while making clear to Rebay that he wouldn't "benefit in any way financially" as he "was employed by Expanding Cinema to do Animation and Composition for which I was paid a fee; after that, my business connection with that company ceased."[116] In a letter to McLaren about the sale, Bute wrote of the Foundation as "an artistic and educational venture of the highest order" and explained how she was "completely in accord with [Rebay's] idea of establishing a non-objective color-sound film library."[117] Continuing with the flattering tone, Bute stressed her "great admiration and respect for Baroness von Rebay" and agreed to lower the film's sale price by a hundred dollars. McLaren passed along the message to Rebay, adding, "I know that the production costs on that film ran into several thousands, and I think it shows that they have real artistic interests at heart."[118]

Although Bute's work was associated with the Museum, McLaren would have been well aware that Bute's artistic aims were not entirely in accord with Rebay's rather strict notion of non-objective art. One difference from non-objective art was that Bute's films would sometimes include representational images and narrative elements. McLaren drew attention to this— once the sale of *Spook Sport* to the Foundation had been completed—in a letter to Rebay, noting that the film "though not entirely non-objective... has some merits, and for the average audience it provides a certain relief from the purely non-Objective movies."[119] Another difference from non-objective art was more a matter of emphasis—rather than bringing to the foreground qualities of order and composition (though doubtlessly important), Bute's approach at this time focused on creating a type of film that "stimulates our visual and aural senses directly with color, form, rhythm and sound." She contrasted this with other filmmaking practices, writing,

"Other motion pictures, although making use of the sensations of sight and sound, address not the eye and ear but the intellect. For example, in realistic films, the onlooker is expected to enjoy the clever imitation of nature – to be deceived into thinking the living prototype is before him." Instead, she aimed to create feeling through form and saw that an integration of kinetic aesthetic elements could most powerfully create this affect.

Bute was particularly influenced by the paintings of Paul Cézanne, writing that the "foundations" for the absolute film were "anticipated by Cézanne and his followers with whom we have an abstract art of painting taking form."[120] Roger Fry's influential discussion of Cézanne, published in 1927, had outlined how "one of his greatest contributions to art" was "his conception of colour not as an adjunct to form, as something imposed upon form, but as itself the direct exponent of form."[121] Rather than attempting to visually transcribe the image in front of him, Cézanne was seen to use "modulations" of color in a "chromatic key almost as a musician does."[122] Lawrence Gowing explains the effect of this approach, writing that "Cézanne's patches [of colour] do not represent materials or facets or variations of tint. In themselves they do not represent anything. It is the relationship between them—relationships of affinity and contrast, the progressions from tone to tone in a color scale, and the modulations from scale to scale—that parallel the apprehension of the world."[123] Bute was less interested in the particular "apprehension of the world" that Cézanne's approach offered, and more fascinated by its capacity to create an immediate visual impression through variations of color: "By stressing relationship, he lifted color from imitating objective nature to producing a visual sensation in itself."[124] Expanding this artistic approach, the relationships between colors on a static canvas could become the relationship between colors both within each frame *and* over the course of a film, coupled with other elements of interrelated movement, such as the musical score and the changing form of the images themselves. With this "richer textural range" of aesthetic elements, Bute envisioned a cinema of synchronized sensations.

Much like the emphasis that Rebay and Teague had placed on rhythm, Bute fastened on to the idea of rhythm as an underlying principle for her filmmaking practice. Fry had described how Cézanne's "extraordinary power" might be seen in his way "of holding together in a single rhythmic scheme… an immense number of small and often closely repetitive movements."[125] Bute saw that a rhythmic quality could truly come alive through motion, explaining in a press release for her first film, *Rhythm in*

Light, that "Rhythm, the development of themes in counterpoint, a variety of intensities and volume such as are used in musical composition, can only be suggested in painting, but in a kinetic visual art, one that develops in time before the eyes as sound develops before the ears—these elements of composition become actualities."[126] For Bute, rhythm could shape the composition of a film.

Bute's production notes for *Spook Sport* indicate the methodical planning that went into realizing this integration of motion with other aesthetic elements. The film itself, as noted earlier, used Saint-Saëns's *Danse Macabre* for its musical score. Unlike non-objective animations, the film had a simple story with recognizable iconography: ghosts and other creatures dance in the evening. But this premise was largely an opportunity to provide a basis for Bute's own development of synchronized forms. The production notes for the film—written before McLaren was hired to provide hand-drawn animations—explain how a "stop motion-picture technique" will be used to animate "the elements of the composition" (including "a clock, bats, macabre masks, witches, a belfry tower, a xylophone of bones and the moon") so that they will "transform and go through many of their permutations."[127] The movements of visual forms would be integrated with sound so that the "size and color of the elements of the design are related to the volume and pitch of the music." Modulations of color were noted throughout the production notes, tied in with descriptions of motion and specific musical passages. For example, Bute describes an early scene in which animated masks "expand until they touch – forming a closed circle… Simultaneously – from the 13th through the 17th bars – the lower parts of the clock's hands have turned and swung into a horizontal position… Their color changing from blue through blue violet, violet, red violet to red." With new shapes and compositions forming, colors mutating and the musical score unfolding over time, Bute aimed to integrate modulations of image and sound.

Bute's work captured the interest of Jesse Zunser, a reporter and film reviewer for *Cue*, New York's weekly guide to entertainment and culture. In 1939, Zunser wrote an article, "Kinetic Space," about Bute's work and its potential to inspire other filmmakers. With the subheading "Abstract Films are the brightest, newest variation on the 'Home Movies' hobby theme," the article described the dynamic potentials of using abstract filmmaking and animation techniques to translate music into film. Zunser wrote that making or watching such an abstract film is "one of the most thrilling experiences the motion picture affords."[128] Rather than approaching abstract filmmaking as a forbidding and complex art, Zunser suggested that Bute's approach is "so simple that any amateur can follow it" with "a camera and a little imagination." The article goes on to outline a do-it-yourself approach to making an abstract film: listen carefully to a piece of music, sketch or graph your reaction to the music, and then "plot the sequence and movement of the subject you will photograph later, counting each graph-square as a frame of film, and using various colored crayons to indicate varying intensities of tone. You plan the entire film in this fashion" (19). With this guide in hand, when it comes to filming, "you may use almost any substance you please, so long as they fit into your conception of what you wish the music and film to express." Sugar cubes, for example, are "a delight to work with as they march and recede, rise and fall, fade and emerge, or spiral with flickering lights and shadows making strangely captivating geometrical patterns and reflections." With the work completed, the article goes on to note rather optimistically, "you simply start your film and the record simultaneously, and you've got your sound-and-sight synchronized perfectly" (20).

After this breezy lesson in abstract animation, Zunser goes on to write that abstract film is the "beginning of a new and fascinating art medium" and that "Hollywood at last is beginning to catch on" with the impending release of *Fantasia* (1940) and Fischinger's involvement in its production.[129] While abstract animation was achieving an unprecedented level of attention from those working in more established artistic and production contexts, "there is no question that the future development of this extraordinary combination of sight and sound rests in the hands and in the cameras of amateurs."

The approach that Zunser described was based on various techniques that Bute had used over the preceding few years. Further drawing attention to Bute's filmmaking practice, the article ends with an extended quote from Bute that provides "a more scientific explanation" of her approach.[130] In this coda, Bute writes how "the artist creates a world of color, form, sound and movement in which the elements are in a state of controllable flux – the two materials, visual and aural, being subject to any conceivable modification." As an example of this, she describes a "mathematical system" that she is working with which guides the "intercomposition of these visual and aural materials in the time continuity." This system would "take the relationship of two or more numbers – for instance, 7:2, 3:4, 9:5:1 – fraction them around their axes, raise to powers, permutate, divide, multiply, subtract, and invert, until we have a complete composition of the desired length in numbers." This numerical composition would then be applied to different elements of the film, including its cinematography and the "shape, size, color, and luminosity of the subject – how, when and in what relationship to other elements of the composition it develops and moves." While somewhat obscure in its practical applications when creating a film, Bute's description nevertheless draws attention to the enormous possibilities and extensive planning involved in composing and interrelating aesthetic forms.

"Kinetic Space" caused something of a stir, and Fillmore Hyde wrote a follow-up piece, "More Kinetic Space." He began by noting that Zunser's article "evidently reached the heart of a sizeable group of hobbyists," adding, "The letters are still coming in. Unfortunately, they all can't be printed."[131] Hyde went on to respond briefly to the most frequently asked questions. One question was "Where can abstract films be seen?" Hyde noted, rather bluntly, that abstract films were "nowhere" to be seen at the current time, but that they sometimes appear at Radio City Music Hall or in a foreign language cinema and that it would be worth contacting Bute directly to find out if any her films are being shown in New York. Iris Barry, the curator of the Museum of Modern Art's Film Library, responded to the article, keen to emphasize that the Museum was supporting abstract film.[132] She noted that *Ballet Mécanique* (1924) had been shown regularly and that Léopold Survage's drawings for "an abstract film" were exhibited in the foyer. Moreover, "Other abstract or experimental films in our archives, including subjects by Man Ray, Marcel Duchamp, Erno Metzner, and Hans Richter, will be available for circulation to non-commercial institutions and groups." The next year, continuing this promotion of abstract animation, Barry curated the exhibition "American Designs for Abstract Films."[133] Through these public exhibitions and modes of distribution, abstract animation was presented as a form of art that was not restricted to a particular milieu but was instead open to a wide public.

Another recurring question noted by Hyde was "How does one learn to make abstract films?"[134] He suggested that aspiring filmmakers should follow Zunser's instructions, as well as "to experiment a bit, to make plenty of blunders" and perhaps join "a group of amateur movie-makers" such as the "Amateur Cinema League." He warned, "Mr. Zunser made the abstract film business seem a lot easier than it really is…. for the real abstract film, which may some day rank as one of the major art forms, you have got to go at it with more than casual interest." While sounding this note of caution, he expressed an eagerness for *Cue* to encourage such endeavors, offering the support of the magazine for those keen to start up "an abstract film society." This gesture toward democratizing what might seem to be a rarefied or specialized art form indicates how Expanding Cinema was itself expanding, becoming a medium that invited the participation of amateurs in New York's animation culture.

Not everyone was appreciative of this. These articles about abstract film received a strident reply from Joseph Schillinger which was published in *Cue*'s letter pages. Questioning the encouragement that *Cue* was offering to amateurs, he raised several objections to the article and in doing so set out his own particular theory of abstract animation. Schillinger was well-established in the New York music scene, instructing composers such as George Gershwin and Glenn Miller in his Method for Musical Composition.[135] While best known for this highly elaborate mathematical system for music, he had extended its principles of rhythmic composition to the visual arts and cinema, giving lectures, courses and interviews on the subject. Schillinger was part of the same circle of artists and inventors with whom Bute worked before she began making films, and his mathematical approach to art was a major influence on Bute's filmmaking practice. In his letter to *Cue*, Schillinger suggested that Bute had borrowed his ideas without credit in the coda to the "Kinetic Space" article where she described her current work.[136] Bute responded in the letter pages the following week, explaining how her theoretical interest in visual material and Schillinger's theoretical interest in music had coincided, and "Until the early part of 1933 my collaboration with Mr. Schillinger was a very close one."[137] Turning to "creative work" the following year, "Mr. Schillinger carried on the theoretical work and teaching. Our ways parted." Bute added that she had credited Schillinger, but this was omitted in the published article.

As well as drawing attention to his own influence on Bute's approach, Schillinger had a larger point to make. Addressing what he saw as the lack of a rigorous basis for her work, he wrote, "The chief point I wish to make in connection with your article is that the 'scientific explanation' which followed it has no relation whatever to the description of Miss Bute's film. She uses kaleidoscopic effects that are not based on any scientific theory."[138] Schillinger went on, referring to both the account of making abstract films in *Cue* and examples taken from Bute's films: "I believe it is quite obvious that shadow casting through a comb or a piece of sugar, and accompanied by music written long ago by Tchaikovsky or Wagner or Grieg, has no connection whatsoever with the scientific method of coordination of visual and auditory forms." Schillinger envisioned the rigorous application of theory—his theory, in particular—as necessary for engineering the aesthetic elements in abstract film: "In my opinion this is not a medium for haphazard experiments by amateurs. Good results can only be achieved by painstaking and precise methods. Really good abstract films can be made in no other way." The editor for *Cue*'s letter pages responded succinctly: "*Cue* believe that the field of abstract film-making should be as open to the amateur as that of watercolor painting, sculpture, woodcarving, or any of the other arts. What does Mary Ellen Bute think?"

To the question of whether "the field of abstract film making [should] be open to the amateur," Bute replied, "definitely *yes.*"[139] Rather than holding to a rigid theoretical basis, Bute was eager to encourage a multiplicity of approaches and experiments. Bute wrote in her reply that, after her initial collaboration with Schillinger up to 1934, "my position in the field of creative work has been diametrically opposed to that of Mr. Schillinger. I believe that the day of panaceas and cure-alls as Mr. Schillinger claims to have 'evolved to cover all art forms and art materials in their individual and combined forms' is over, if it ever existed."

Bute saw mathematical and theoretical systems as productive rather than determinant. *Spook Sport*, for example, relied upon a careful synchronization of sound and image for much of its effect, but the overall design—and particularly the delightful imprecision of McLaren's moving forms—was far from constrained. Similarly, Bute's next film, *Tarantella*, was highly varied in its use of formal elements. Different passages of the free-flowing musical accompaniment are integrated with an array of forms, including hand-drawn squiggles (animated by McLaren), images which suggest waveforms and lips, and contrasting curved and linear shapes (Fig. 4.6). These forms move in different ways, sometimes enlarging and shrinking, sometimes emerging onscreen or fluidly gliding by, sometimes flashing briefly or engulfing the frame. The disorienting effect is augmented by a striking use of color, with strong impressions created by single primary colors which fill the background. Sudden changes in color are coupled with more gradual shifts in hue and more balanced color schemes within the frame. While visual elements do evoke aspects of the music, the integration of form, color and motion is much more complex than a straightforward illustration of the score written by Bute's collaborator, Edwin Gerschefski. In this respect, Bute wrote that the film interrelates "mobile colour and sound" in such a way that the "complete composition is equally dependent on both materials."[140] Describing how a mathematical approach was used in the initial planning, Bute emphasized that this was only a starting point:

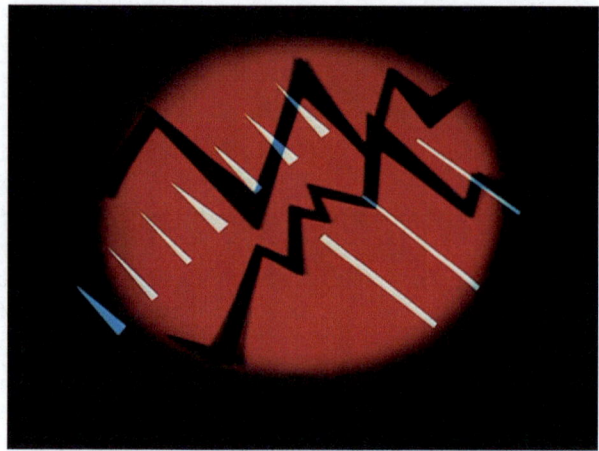

Fig. 4.6   *Tarantella* (1940)

Edwin Gerschefski, a brilliant young composer, and I developed it from a series of rhythms which we worked out arithmetically. Gerschefski translating the mathematical composition into a dance for the piano and I translating it into color and linear forms. In this case, neither of us adhered to the mathematical composition very strictly but rather used it as a spring board.

Rather than following an underlying system or order, Bute was finding new ways of interrelating aesthetic elements. Mathematics could provide a useful model for this, as could theories of musical composition. But for Bute, systems were tools in the hands of an artist—amateur or professional—and not solutions.

Rather than seeking a unifying technique for integrating color, music and motion, Bute was most concerned with creating powerful affects and sensations by combining these aesthetic elements. Since "the arts have arrived at a specialized and divergent state," bringing them back together in a single form could create new and powerful affects: "To achieve strong emotional reactions we must charge our perceptive sensual apparatus with greater and more intense exciters. In the field of art these stronger exciters are synchronized art forms."[141] The impact of such synchronized art forms could be considerable, transforming civilization:

As the embryonic state of the human mind was syncretic with emotions and intellect close and inseparable; so, too, were the early activities of mankind—closely connected and interrelated. Further development stimulated the growth of the organs of intellect and emotions so that today they are on distant planes. In order to bring them together again in forms of perception, an intense stimulation is necessary.

In one respect, as Lauren Rabinovitz writes, "Bute called for a multimedia experience (the more media the better) as the only means by which art in a modern world could overpower the conventions of realism that called for intellectual engagement and stimulate, at the level of the physiological, a pure emotional experience."[142] As well as an art of motion that could bring together intellect and feeling, this was also an art of motion that could entwine different senses and aspects of perception so that the very "materials of the art" become "the sensations of color and tone."[143] Creating sensorial impact was a driving force behind Bute's filmmaking practice.

Tarantella exemplified this idea. After a prelude which shows the credits and describes the film as a "swift moving dance presented musically and in linear forms in color," the film shows the dictionary definition of "Tarantella": "n. 1. A rapid Neapolitan dance in triplets; so called because it was popularly thought to be a remedy for the supposed poisonous bite of the tarantula. 2. The music suited for such a dance." The words "Tarantella," "remedy for" and "poisonous bite" are highlighted in different colors from the rest of the definition shown onscreen, suggesting that the film to follow is itself, figuratively, a "remedy for a poisonous bite." Perhaps a dance of animation could, in a sense, have curative powers. Perhaps art, and the "intense stimulation" generated by integrating the sensations of color, sound, form and motion, might lead us to perceive differently—a return to our senses, so to speak, made all the more imperative in light of the war that was beginning to envelop the world at the time.

* * *

Animation as art was a rich and contested idea in New York's animation culture. Rather than simply inhabiting a gallery space or drawing on an aesthetic system, the animators examined in this chapter negotiated their own sense of the extraordinary potentials of an art of motion. Bute's disregard for all-encompassing systems resonated with the views of McLaren and Grant—these animators all shared an interest in theories of composition and ways of integrating artistic forms, but they were resistant to any singular structure that would contain or define their work. The potentials of motion were too varied, open and powerful to be constrained by institutions, forms or theories of art that had been developed for other media. Shifting between contexts of television, cinema and galleries, their work was linked to different sites of exhibition. Similarly, the planning and production of their films were also multifaceted, drawing upon composition, choreography, painting, design and mathematics but never adhering to a single basis. Rather than relying upon the sense of order that Rebay saw as so vital to non-objective painting, animation became a source of open-ended possibilities that could create new relations between media, new practices of artistic creation and new sensations for spectators.

As we have seen, the relationship between art and design was a close one at the time, not only in the work of advertisers and corporate designers—who often invoked artistic values—but also in the ideas of Rebay, who sought to link non-objective painting to a wider modern world in an attempt to contribute to a sensibility based upon order, beauty and spiritual uplift. Grant's later work as an animator had also extended outward to include scientific and commercial visualizations. This was a transition from artistic concerns to design concerns—effectively expressing ideas and underlying functions through visual form. But even those animators who were seemingly less directly concerned with questions of design were still closely engaged with its potentials. For example, Bute's statement of artistic intent, "Light * Form * Movement * Sound," was published in a design journal—appropriately called *Design*—and articles relating to her earlier film *Parabola* (1938) appeared in architectural journals at the time. The visual style of *Tarantella*, with its dynamic graphic forms, also evoked contemporary trends in design. Moreover, Bute's collaborator, Ted Nemeth, would pursue instructional animation during the war, a type of design-related animation he would successfully develop for years after. McLaren also extended his animation practice into related fields of instruction and propaganda, resonating with a wider sensibility of motion's manifold possibilities, evident already in his work in New York producing television advertisements. A close relationship between animation and design was coursing through New York's animation culture.

This relationship would go on to become vital to one of the most important animation studios to emerge after the Second World War: United Productions of America (UPA). The studio produced films including the Oscar-winning *Gerald McBoing Boing* (1950) and *Rooty Toot Toot* (1952), combining—Michael Barrier writes—"strong modern design with a kind of animation whose kinetic vitality depended on the illusion of depth."[144] In these films and their wider output, UPA developed a new design-oriented aesthetic for mainstream American animated film. Much like McLaren's and Bute's films, UPA "was moving toward a style based on simplified line, flat fields of color, and collage" in the mid-1940s.[145] Norman M. Klein summarizes the effect: "With success by 1951, UPA launched something of an International Style for the industry, based on what was called then 'stylized' animation. A highly reduced surface became standard practice for cartoons in the fifties."[146] Animators working at UPA were influenced—both directly and indirectly—by the kinds of animations discussed in this chapter; for example, John Hubley, the director of *Rooty Toot Toot*, described McLaren as "a great inspiration," and McLaren visited the UPA studio and screened a print of *Begone Dull Care* in 1949.[147]

The impetus behind this turn to design also related to the experience of making animated films during the war; Giannalberto Bendazzi reprints an article written by John Hubley and Zachary Schwartz in 1946 where they describe a changing approach to animated film: "Because of wartime necessity, pigs and bunnies have collided with nuts and bolts... Many professional studios producing educational films of infinitely varied subjects soon discovered that, within the medium of film, animation provided the only means of portraying many complex aspects of a complex society."[148] This demanded new ways of using animation: "We have found that the medium of animation has become a new language... We have found that line, shape, color, and symbols in movement can represent the essence of an idea, can express it humorously, with force, with clarity."[149] Such an approach resonated with the dynamic potentials of how animated film was being explored, created and embedded within New York's animation culture.

Although their creative practice took place largely within the context of art, McLaren, Grant and Bute all shared a vision of animation that crossed boundaries, whether exploring different avenues of exhibition, investigating other art forms or supporting amateur filmmaking. Even Schillinger, who aimed for an all-encompassing system of artistic creation in his theory of kinetic composition, would be drawn in to the more free-flowing potentials of animation at this time with his invention of an "Animated Display Device."[150] After Schillinger's death in 1943, his wife Frances Schillinger filed a patent for this invention, acting as executor for his will. In her memoirs, she described it as "the 'Solidrive,' an instrument invented by Schillinger to serve as a kinetic advertising display, where objects traced their different shapes, moving at different speeds on a rotating turntable."[151] This device would combine different rhythms of motion in an integrated and automated display. In addition to the main function of showing products in motion and creating "a variety of shadow effects" in order to "attract attention to the merchandise displayed," the patent also indicated other potential uses: in "miniature theaters," "in connection with motion picture sets," "as a child's toy," "in producing scenic effects in connection with stage presentations," "in the television studio" and "in connection with the production of abstract motion pictures."[152] The scope of the device's potential uses—extending from cinema to advertising and into other cultural fields—was emblematic of how an art of animation was open to diverse paths within New York's animation culture.

NOTES

1. For details on the museum and this exhibition, see Karole Vail, "A Museum in the Making: Two Artists and Their Patron—Hilla Rebay, Rudolf Bauer, and Solomon R. Guggenheim," in *The Museum of Non-Objective Painting: Hilla Rebay and the Origins of the Solomon R. Guggenheim Museum*, ed. Karole Vail (New York: Guggenheim Museum Publications, 2009), 25–55.
2. For an account of Rebay's background, creative practice and artistic interests, see Joan M. Lukach, *Hilla Rebay: In Search of the Spirit in Art* (New York: George Braziller, 1983).
3. Hilla Rebay, *Art of Tomorrow: Fifth Catalogue of the Solomon R. Guggenheim Collection* (New York: Solomon R. Guggenheim Foundation), 6.
4. Bill Cotter, *The 1939–1940 New York World's Fair* (Charleston: Arcadia, 2009), 15.
5. Hilla Rebay, *Art of Tomorrow*, 2.
6. Hilla Rebay, *Art of Tomorrow*, 9.
7. Hilla Rebay, *Art of Tomorrow*, 7.
8. Paul Greenhalgh, *Modernism in Design* (London: Reaktion Books, 1990), 2–3.
9. Hilla Rebay, *Art of Tomorrow*, 5.
10. For an account of Rebay's interest in film and her association with filmmakers, including McLaren, see Lukach, *Hilla Rebay*, 211–225; John G. Hanhardt, "Rhythm of the In-Between: Abstract Film and the Museum of Non-Objective Painting," in *The Museum of Non-Objective Painting: Hilla Rebay and the Origins of the Solomon R. Guggenheim Museum*, ed. Karole Vail (New York: Guggenheim Museum Publications, 2009), 139–155.
11. For an account of Fischinger's career, with reference to Hilla Rebay, see especially William Moritz, *Optical Poetry: The Life and Work of Oskar Fischinger* (Bloomington: Indiana University Press, 2004).

12. Bill Mikulak, "Mickey Meets Mondrian: Cartoons Enter the Museum of Modern Art," *Cinema Journal* 36, no. 3 (Spring 1997): 65. Haidee Wasson details the activities, aims and cultural role of the film library in *Museum Movies: The Museum of Modern Art and the Birth of Art Cinema* (Berkeley: University of California Press, 2005).

13. "Museum of Modern Art Holds Exhibition of American Designs for Abstract Films," press release, April 3, 1940, Museum of Modern Art Exhibition Records 1929–1959, Museum of Modern Art.

14. For an account of Wilfred's work, see Andrew Robert Johnston, "The Color of Prometheus: Thomas Wilfred's Lumia and the Projection of Transcendence," in *Color and the Moving Image: History, Theory, Aesthetics, Archive*, eds. Simon Brown, Sarah Street, and Liz Watkins (New York: Routledge, 2013), 67–78.

15. *On Lumia, the Art of Light: Selected Articles, Criticism and Information* (New York: Art Institute of Light, Inc., n.d.), box 154, folder 69, Guggenheim Archives Collections: M0007, Series 2, Hilla Rebay papers, Thomas Wilfred, Guggenheim Archives.

16. Thomas Wilfred, "Lumia: The Eighth Fine Art," in *On Lumia, the Art of Light: Selected Articles, Criticism and Information* (New York: Art Institute of Light, Inc., n.d.), box 154, folder 69, Guggenheim Archives Collections: M0007, Series 2, Hilla Rebay papers, Thomas Wilfred, Guggenheim Archives.

17. Grant mentions his familiarity with Wilfred's work in a letter to Hilla Rebay (May 5, 1940, box 3050, folder 1, Hilla Rebay records: A0010, Series 2, Administration, Dwinell Grant, Correspondence, Guggenheim Archives). Cecile Starr notes that, before making films, Bute "became interested in the visual study of motion and assisted Thomas Wilfred" ("Mary Ellen Bute," in *Experimental Animation: An Illustrated Anthology*, eds. Robert Russett and Cecile Starr [New York: Van Nostrand Reinhold Company, 1976], 102).

18. See *Experimental Animation: An Illustrated Anthology*, eds. Robert Russett and Cecile Starr (New York: Van Nostrand Reinhold Company, 1976), 32–71.

19. William Moritz, "Non-Objective Film: The Second Generation," in *Film as Film, Formal Experiment in Film, 1910–1975*, eds. David Curtis and Richard Francis (London: Hayward Gallery and Arts Council of Great Britain, 1979), 59.

20. Dwinell Grant to Hilla Rebay, November 9, 1940, box 3050, folder 1, Hilla Rebay records: A0010, Series 2, Administration, Dwinell Grant, Correspondence, Guggenheim Archives; Dwinell Grant to Hilla Rebay, August 29, 1944, box 3050, folder 2, Hilla Rebay records: A0010, Series 2, Administration, Dwinell Grant, Correspondence, Guggenheim Archives;

and Mary Ellen Bute, "Light * Form * Movement * Sound," *Design* 42, no. 8 (1941): 25.

21. As part of a larger account of McLaren's filmmaking, Terence Dobson examines the New York period in *The Film Work of Norman McLaren* (Eastleigh: John Libbey, 2006), 99–118. Dobson provides insightful analysis and background on the films made at this time, with an emphasis on McLaren's innovations with sound and his work's relation to surrealism.

22. Norman McLaren to his parents, December 19, 1939, folder 1, Norman McLaren Archive, Correspondence, Archives and Special Collections, University of Stirling.

23. Norman McLaren to his parents, December 26, 1939, folder 1, Norman McLaren Archive, Correspondence, Archives and Special Collections, University of Stirling.

24. William C. Eddy, *Television: The Eyes of Tomorrow* (New York: Prentice-Hall, 1945), 147.

25. Leonard Cox, "Sight Effects Man," *Cue*, January 28, 1939, 17.

26. Eddy, *Television*, 188.

27. William C. Eddy, "Projecting Kaleidoscope Device," US patent 2,307,202, filed January 27, 1940, and issued January 5, 1943, 1.

28. McLaren to his parents, December 19, 1939.

29. See Lauren Rabinovitz, "Mary Ellen Bute," in *Lovers of Cinema: The First American Film Avant-Garde, 1919–1945*, ed. Jan-Christopher Horak (Madison: University of Wisconsin Press, 1995), 315–334.

30. McLaren to his parents, December 19, 1939.

31. Mary Ellen Bute, "Composition in Color and Sound," unpublished typescript for lecture presented at "Conference on Color," May 10, 1941, p. 3, box 21, folder 294, Mary Ellen Bute Papers, Yale University Library.

32. Norman McLaren to his parents, November 6, 1940, folder 1, Norman McLaren Archive, Correspondence, Archives and Special Collections, University of Stirling.

33. Norman McLaren to his parents, September 11, 1940, folder 1, Norman McLaren Archive, Correspondence, Archives and Special Collections, University of Stirling.

34. Norman McLaren to his parents, n.d., folder 1, Norman McLaren Archive, Correspondence, Archives and Special Collections, University of Stirling.

35. Norman McLaren, "Animated Films," *Documentary Film News* 7, no. 65 (May 1948): 52.

36. McLaren to his parents, December 19, 1939.

37. McLaren, "Animated Films," 52.

38. Norman McLaren to his parents, n.d., folder 1, Norman McLaren Archive, Correspondence, Archives and Special Collections, University of Stirling.

39. Norman McLaren to Hilla Rebay, October 7, 1940, box 561, folder 15, Hilla Rebay non-objective film collection: A0037, Guggenheim Archives.

40. McLaren to his parents, n.d., folder 1.
41. Norman McLaren, unpublished lecture notes, 1956, folder 1, Norman McLaren Archive, Film: Technical Notes, Archives and Special Collections, University of Stirling.
42. Norman McLaren, unpublished lecture notes, 1956, folder 1.
43. Hilla Rebay, "Definition of Non-Objective Painting," in *Solomon R. Guggenheim Collection of Non-Objective Paintings, on Exhibition from March 1, 1936 Through April 12, 1936,* ed. Hilla Rebay (New York: The Bradford Press, 1936), 10.
44. Hilla Rebay, "Definition of Non-Objective Painting," 10.
45. Norman McLaren to Hilla Rebay, January 19, 1941, box 121, folder 28, Hilla Rebay papers: M0007, McLaren, Norman, Guggenheim Archives.
46. Rebay's financial support would take different forms, including employment and fellowships. Early in their association, Rebay offered Grant a monthly stipend for painting materials (Hilla Rebay to Dwinell Grant, June 17, 1940, Dwinell Grant papers, Archives of American Art, Washington, DC).
47. Grant to Rebay, May 5, 1940. Grant had briefly corresponded with Rebay before, sharing his interest in non-objective painting and requesting the catalogue for the "Art of Tomorrow" exhibition because "past catalogs have proven of great help in teaching the principles of non-objectivism here" (Dwinell Grant to S. R. Guggenheim Foundation, July 13, 1939, box 3050, folder 1, Hilla Rebay records: A0010, Series 2, Administration, Dwinell Grant, Correspondence, Guggenheim Archives).
48. Grant to Rebay, May 5, 1940. In later correspondence with Rebay, he explained how he had not been familiar with the abstract animations of Fischinger, Eggeling and Richter: "You are so very fortunate to know these people and their works at first-hand. There is nothing here except printed reproductions in books which are nearly useless and when I was in New York, of course, I didn't know such things existed" (Dwinell Grant to Hilla Rebay, August 8, 1940, box 3050, folder 1, Hilla Rebay records: A0010, Series 2, Administration, Dwinell Grant, Correspondence, Guggenheim Archives).
49. Grant to Rebay, May 5, 1940.
50. Dwinell Grant, interview transcript, p. 1, Dwinell Grant papers, Archives of American Art.
51. The film is also known as *Composition No. 1*. Grant did not use the title *Themis* at the time of its completion, though he would later use this title for the film.
52. Dwinell Grant to Hilla Rebay, November 9, 1940, box 3050, folder 1, Hilla Rebay records: A0010, Series 2, Administration, Dwinell Grant, Correspondence, Guggenheim Archives.

53. Hilla Rebay to Dwinell Grant, November 14, 1940, box 3050, folder 1, Hilla Rebay records: A0010, Series 2, Administration, Dwinell Grant, Correspondence, Guggenheim Archives.

54. Grant's "Statement of Project for Scholarship" outlined the different areas he hoped to research with support from the Guggenheim Foundation: "Visual harmony and counterpoint for space composition"; "A simple method of writing a composition so that all the detailed work and photography can be handled by persons other than the composer"; "The range of color sensitivity of color film"; "The mechanical problems involved in the production of film"; and "Method for the production of three-dimensional film." Each research area would "be substantiated by successful experiments on film." This project proposal formed the basis of his work into the late 1940s. (Dwinell Grant to Hilla Rebay, April 11, 1944, box 3050, folder 2, Hilla Rebay records: A0010, Series 2, Administration, Dwinell Grant, Correspondence, Guggenheim Archives.)

55. Dwinell Grant, "The Structure of the Theme," unpublished manuscript, p. 36, box 3050, folder 7, Hilla Rebay records: A0010, Series 2, Administration, Dwinell Grant, Manuscripts [The Composition of the Non-Objective Film, Part III: The Structure of the Theme], Guggenheim Archives.

56. Dwinell Grant, notes, n.d., box 3050, folder 5, Hilla Rebay records: A0010, Series 2, Administration, Dwinell Grant, Manuscripts [The Composition of the Non-Objective Film], Guggenheim Archives.

57. Grant, "The Structure of the Theme," 35.

58. Rebay to Grant, November 14, 1940.

59. William Moritz situates Grant within a larger context of non-objective film, describing how, in *Contrathemis*, "where he seems consciously to use drawn figures that recall alternately the shapes used by Ruttmann, Eggeling, Fischinger and Richter, Grant combines these figures in such fresh juxtapositions, with such a subtle manipulation of structure, density and rhythm, that they are manifestly allusions integral and unique to Grant's personal idiom and discussion" (Moritz, "Non-Objective Film," 69). In the original published version, some of the paragraphs are out of order—the version of the article on the Center for Visual Music website helpfully corrects this (http://www.centerforvisualmusic.org/MoritzNonObjFilm.htm).

60. Dwinell Grant, "Art and Human Needs," unpublished manuscript, p. 51, box 3050, folder 4, Hilla Rebay records: A0010, Series 2, Administration, Dwinell Grant, Manuscripts [The Composition of the Non-Objective Film, Part I: Art and Human Needs], Guggenheim Archives.

61. Dwinell Grant, "The Non-Objective Film (A Theory of Composition)," draft outline, p. 1, Dwinell Grant papers, Archives of American Art.

62. Grant, "Art and Human Needs," 23.

63. Grant, "Art and Human Needs," 24.

64. Dwinell Grant, "Part II. The Process of Composition," unpublished manuscript, p. 78, Dwinell Grant papers, Archives of American Art.
65. Grant, "Part II. The Process of Composition," 79.
66. Grant to Rebay, April 11, 1944.
67. Dwinell Grant to Hilla Rebay, March 26, 1945, box 3050, folder 2, Hilla Rebay records: A0010, Series 2, Administration, Dwinell Grant, Correspondence, Guggenheim Archives.
68. Grant, "Part II. The Process of Composition," 60–61.
69. Grant to Rebay, March 26, 1945.
70. Grant, "Part II. The Process of Composition," 77.
71. Dwinell Grant to Hilla Rebay, June 5, 1940, box 3050, folder 1, Hilla Rebay records: A0010, Series 2, Administration, Dwinell Grant, Correspondence, Guggenheim Archives.
72. Dwinell Grant, "Statement of Project," unpublished manuscript, 1940, p. 3, Dwinell Grant papers, Archives of American Art.
73. Grant, "Statement of Project," 2.
74. Grant, interview transcript, 6.
75. "Precision Communication for Education, Science and Industry," brochure, Ansel Film Studios, Dwinell Grant papers, Archives of American Art.
76. Norman McLaren to his parents, June 14, 1941, folder 1, Norman McLaren Archive, Correspondence, Archives and Special Collections, University of Stirling.
77. Norman McLaren to his parents, July 10–11, 1941, folder 1, Norman McLaren Archive, Correspondence, Archives and Special Collections, University of Stirling.
78. Norman McLaren to his parents, July 26, 1941, folder 1, Norman McLaren Archive, Correspondence, Archives and Special Collections, University of Stirling.
79. McLaren to his parents, July 26, 1941; Norman McLaren to his parents, August 3, 1941, folder 1, Norman McLaren Archive, Correspondence, Archives and Special Collections, University of Stirling.
80. Norman McLaren to Willard Maas, n.d., container 6, Willard Maas Collection, Harry Ransom Center, University of Texas at Austin.
81. Norman McLaren to Hilla Rebay, July 30, 1942, box 3051, folder 7, Hilla Rebay records: A0010, Series 2, Administration, Filmmakers, McLaren, Norman, Correspondence, Guggenheim Archives.
82. Norman McLaren to Hilla Rebay, February 7, 1943, box 121, folder 28, Hilla Rebay papers: M0007, McLaren, Norman, Guggenheim Archives.
83. Norman McLaren to Hilla Rebay, October 19, 1940, box 561, folder 15, Hilla Rebay non-objective film collection: A0037, Guggenheim Archives. McLaren quickly followed up with further detail on renting screening equipment in a letter to Rebay on November 2, 1940.

84. "Invitations for film showing 12/27/40," n.d., box 3048, folder 9, Hilla Rebay records: A0010, Series 2, Administration, Film, Film Concerts, Guggenheim Archives.
85. Norman McLaren to his parents, December 8, 1940, folder 1, Norman McLaren Archive, Correspondence, Archives and Special Collections, University of Stirling.
86. Hilla Rebay, screening notes, n.d., box 3048, folder 9, Hilla Rebay records: A0010, Series 2, Administration, Film, Film Concerts, Guggenheim Archives.
87. Hilla Rebay, screening notes.
88. Norman McLaren to Hilla Rebay, November 14, 1940, box 561, folder 15, Hilla Rebay non-objective film collection: A0037, Guggenheim Archives.
89. Edward Alden Jewell, "Of Music and Painting: Disney 'Fantasia' Raises Anew Problem of Fusing Aural and Visual Forms," *New York Times*, January 5, 1941.
90. Jewell, "Of Music and Painting."
91. Hilla Rebay to Susan Wolters, January 11, 1941, box 3048, folder 9, Hilla Rebay records: A0010, Series 2, Administration, Film, Film Concerts, Guggenheim Archives.
92. This screening seems to have played only to meagre audiences, with the director of the Carolina Art Association, Robert Whitelaw, writing to Rebay: "It is very regrettable that the audiences for the Non-Objective motion pictures were so small but I hope that you realize, as we do, that those few who saw them enjoyed them very much. Audiences are beyond my comprehension; we though that we would have more for the films and for our recent plays at the Theatre" (Robert N. S. Whitelaw to Hilla Rebay, April 15, 1941, box 3048, folder 3, Hilla Rebay records: A0010, Series 2, Administration, Film, Correspondence: General, Guggenheim Archives).
93. "Festival of Rhythm," press release, box 3048, folder 8, Hilla Rebay records: A0010, Series 2, Administration, Film, Festival of Rhythm: Programme Notes, Guggenheim Archives.
94. James J. Ryan, "Polarized... Color Displays," *Signs of the Times*, October 1940, 11.
95. Norman McLaren to Hilla Rebay, February 19, 1941, box 561, folder 15, Hilla Rebay non-objective film collection: A0037, Guggenheim Archives.
96. Maynard Collins, *Norman McLaren* (Ottawa: Canadian Film Institute, 1976), 77.
97. Norman McLaren, "Automatic Mural Movies," in *On the Creative Process*, ed. Donald McWilliams (Montreal: National Film Board of Canada, 1991), 36.
98. Norman McLaren to Willard Maas, n.d., container 6, Willard Maas Collection, Harry Ransom Center, University of Texas at Austin.

99. Norman McLaren to Willard Maas, n.d., container 6, Willard Maas Collection, Harry Ransom Center, University of Texas at Austin. Although the film is unspecified and the letter is undated, McLaren's reference to the film having "its basis in one of the oldest most basic cradle songs of the French language" indicates that he is describing *C'est l'aviron*.

100. "A Little Phantasy on a 19th Century Painting," National Film Board of Canada, information sheet, folder 3, Norman McLaren Archive, Film, Archives and Special Collections, University of Stirling.

101. Norman McLaren, "Automatic Mural Movies."

102. Grant to Rebay, June 5, 1940.

103. Dwinell Grant, handwritten journal, n.d., Dwinell Grant papers, Archives of American Art. A handwritten note indicates that the journal is from "June (?) 1940."

104. Grant, "Statement of Project," 4.

105. Hilla Rebay to Dwinell Grant, December 3, 1940, box 3050, folder 1, Hilla Rebay records: A0010, Series 2, Administration, Dwinell Grant, Correspondence, Guggenheim Archives.

106. Dwinell Grant, interview transcript, 2 and 3.

107. Grant to Rebay, August 29, 1944.

108. Dwinell Grant, "Art and Human Needs [first draft]," unpublished manuscript, p. 76, Dwinell Grant papers, Archives of American Art.

109. Dwinell Grant, notes, n.d., box 3050, folder 6, Hilla Rebay records: A0010, Series 2, Administration, Dwinell Grant, Manuscripts [The Composition of Non-Objective Film, Part II: Field of the Composition], Guggenheim Archives.

110. Mary Ellen Bute, "Light * Form * Movement * Sound," 25; *The Promise of Cinema: German Film Theory, 1907–1933*, eds. Anton Kaes, Nicholas Baer, and Michael Cowan (Berkeley: University of California Press, 2016), 459.

111. Mary Ellen Bute, "Light as an Art Material and Its Possible Synchronization with Sound," lecture notes, p. 1, 1932, box 21, folder 296, Mary Ellen Bute Papers, Yale University Library.

112. Bute, "Light as an Art Material," 1.

113. Promotional material, box 1, folder 6, Mary Ellen Bute Papers, Yale University Library.

114. Bute, "Composition in Color and Sound," 4.

115. Mary Ellen Bute to Norman McLaren, January 28, 1941, box 561, folder 15, Hilla Rebay non-objective film collection: A0037, Guggenheim Archives.

116. Norman McLaren to Hilla Rebay, February 5, 1941, box 561, folder 15, Hilla Rebay non-objective film collection: A0037, Guggenheim Archives.

117. Bute to McLaren, January 28, 1941.

118. McLaren to Rebay, January 28, 1941.

119. McLaren to Rebay, February 5, 1941.
120. Bute, "Light * Form * Movement * Sound," 25. Bute's discussion of Cézanne in this article published in 1941 is almost identical to her discussion of his work in the lecture she gave to the New York Musicological Society almost a decade earlier.
121. Roger Fry, *Cézanne: A Study of His Development* (1927; repr. Chicago: University of Chicago Press, 1989), 13.
122. Fry, *Cézanne*, 72.
123. Lawrence Gowing, "Cézanne: The Logic of Organized Sensations," in *Conversations with Cézanne*, ed. Michael Doran (Berkeley: University of California Press, 2001), 204.
124. Bute, "Light * Form * Movement * Sound," 25.
125. Fry, *Cézanne*, 75.
126. "Film Short at Radio City Music Hall Portrays Geometry of Harmony on Screen," press release, n.d., p. 3, box 36, folder 549, Mary Ellen Bute Papers, Yale University Library.
127. Mary Ellen Bute, "Danse Macabre," production notes, n.d., p. 1, box 36, folder 554, Mary Ellen Bute Papers, Yale University Library.
128. Jesse Zunser, "Kinetic Space," *Cue*, August 26, 1939, 18.
129. Zunser, "Kinetic Space," 20.
130. Zunser, "Kinetic Space," 20.
131. Fillmore Hyde, "More Kinetic Space," *Cue*, September 23, 1939, 13.
132. Iris Barry, letter to the editor, *Cue*, October 14, 1939, 16.
133. "Museum of Modern Art Holds Exhibition of American Designs for Abstract Films," press release, April 3, 1940, Museum of Modern Art Exhibition Records 1929–1959, Museum of Modern Art.
134. Hyde, "More Kinetic Space," 13.
135. See Warren Brodsky, "Joseph Schillinger (1895–1943): Music Science Promethean," *American Music* 21, no. 1 (Spring 2003): 45–73.
136. Joseph Schillinger, letter to the editor, *Cue*, October 7, 1939, 10.
137. Mary Ellen Bute, letter to the editor, *Cue*, October 14, 1939, 16.
138. Schillinger, letter to the editor, *Cue*, 10.
139. Bute, letter to the editor, *Cue*, 16.
140. Bute, "Composition in Color and Sound," 2.
141. Bute, "Composition in Color and Sound," 1.
142. Rabinovitz, "Mary Ellen Bute," 320.
143. Bute, "Composition in Color and Sound," 1.
144. Michael Barrier, *Hollywood Cartoons: American Animation in Its Golden Age* (Oxford: Oxford University Press, 1999), 530.
145. Norman M. Klein, *7 Minutes: The Life and Death of the American Animated Cartoon* (London: Verso, 1993), 229.
146. Klein, *7 Minutes*, 230.
147. Barrier, *Hollywood Cartoons*, 531.

148. Giannalberto Bendazzi, *Animation: A World History*, vol. 2 (New York: Routledge, 2017), 10.
149. Bendazzi, 11.
150. Joseph Schillinger, "Animated Display Apparatus," US patent 2,492,241, filed September 4, 1945, and issued December 27, 1949.
151. Frances Schillinger, *Joseph Schillinger: A Memoir* (New York: Da Capo Press, 1976), 89.
152. Schillinger, "Animated Display Apparatus."

References

Barrier, Michael. *Hollywood Cartoons: American Animation in Its Golden Age.* Oxford: Oxford University Press, 1999.
Barry, Iris. Letter to the Editor. *Cue*, October 14, 1939.
Bendazzi, Giannalberto. *Animation: A World History,* vol. 2. New York: Routledge, 2017.
Brodsky, Warren. "Joseph Schillinger (1895–1943): Music Science Promethean." *American Music* 21, no. 1 (Spring 2003): 45–73.
Bute, Mary Ellen. Letter to the Editor. *Cue*, October 14, 1939.
Bute, Mary Ellen. "Light * Form * Movement * Sound." *Design* 42, no. 8 (1941): 25.
Bute, Mary Ellen. Papers. Yale University Library.
Collins, Maynard. *Norman McLaren.* Ottawa: Canadian Film Institute, 1976.
Cotter, Bill. *The 1939–1940 New York World's Fair.* Charleston: Arcadia, 2009.
Cox, Leonard. "Sight Effects Man." *Cue*, January 28, 1939.
Dobson, Terence. *The Film Work of Norman McLaren.* Eastleigh: John Libbey, 2006.
Eddy, William C. "Projecting Kaleidoscope Device." US patent 2,307,202, filed January 27, 1940, and issued January 5, 1943.
Eddy, William C. *Television: The Eyes of Tomorrow.* New York: Prentice-Hall, 1945.
Fry, Roger. *Cézanne: A Study of His Development.* Chicago: University of Chicago Press, 1989. First published in 1927.
Gowing, Lawrence. "Cézanne: The Logic of Organized Sensations." In *Conversations with Cézanne,* edited by Michael Doran, 180–212. Berkeley: University of California Press, 2001.
Grant, Dwinell. Papers. Archives of American Art, Washington, DC.
Greenhalgh, Paul. *Modernism in Design.* London: Reaktion Books, 1990.
Hanhardt, John G. "Rhythm of the In-Between: Abstract Film and the Museum of Non-Objective Painting." In *The Museum of Non-Objective Painting: Hilla Rebay and the Origins of the Solomon R. Guggenheim Museum,* edited by Karole Vail, 139–155. New York: Guggenheim Museum Publications, 2009.

Hyde, Fillmore. "More Kinetic Space." *Cue*, September 23, 1939.

Jewell, Edward Alden. "Of Music and Painting: Disney 'Fantasia' Raises Anew Problem of Fusing Aural and Visual Forms." *New York Times*, January 5, 1941.

Johnston, Andrew Robert. "The Color of Prometheus: Thomas Wilfred's Lumia and the Projection of Transcendence." In *Color and the Moving Image: History, Theory, Aesthetics, Archive*, edited by Simon Brown, Sarah Street, and Liz Watkins, 67–78. Routledge: New York, 2013.

Klein, Norman M. *7 Minutes: The Life and Death of the American Animated Cartoon*. London: Verso, 1993.

Lukach, Joan M. *Hilla Rebay: In Search of the Spirit in Art*. New York: George Braziller, 1983.

Maas, Willard. Collection. Harry Ransom Center, University of Texas at Austin.

McLaren, Norman. "Animated Films." *Documentary Film News* 7, no. 65 (May 1948): 52–53.

McLaren, Norman. Archives. University of Stirling.

McLaren, Norman. "Automatic Mural Movies." In *On the Creative Process*, edited by Donald McWilliams, 36. Montreal: National Film Board of Canada, 1991.

Mikulak, Bill. "Mickey Meets Mondrian: Cartoons Enter the Museum of Modern Art." *Cinema Journal* 36, no. 3 (Spring 1997): 56–72.

Moritz, William. "Non-Objective Film: The Second Generation." In *Film as Film, Formal Experiment in Film, 1910–1975*, edited by David Curtis and Richard Francis, 59–70. London: Hayward Gallery and Arts Council of Great Britain, 1979.

Moritz, William. *Optical Poetry: The Life and Work of Oskar Fischinger*. Bloomington: Indiana University Press, 2004.

Museum of Modern Art Exhibition Records, 1929–1959. Museum of Modern Art, New York.

Rabinovitz, Lauren. "Mary Ellen Bute." In *Lovers of Cinema: The First American Film Avant-Garde, 1919–1945*, edited by Jan-Christopher Horak, 315–334. Madison: University of Wisconsin Press, 1995.

Rebay, Hilla. *Art of Tomorrow: Fifth Catalogue of the Solomon R. Guggenheim Collection*. New York: Solomon R. Guggenheim Foundation.

Rebay, Hilla. "Definition of Non-Objective Painting." In *Solomon R. Guggenheim Collection of Non-Objective Paintings, on Exhibition from March 1, 1936 Through April 12, 1936*, edited by Hilla Rebay, 8–13. New York: The Bradford Press, 1936.

Rebay, Hilla. Non-Objective Film Collection. Guggenheim Archives, New York.

Rebay, Hilla. Papers. Guggenheim Archives, New York.

Rebay, Hilla. Records. Guggenheim Archives, New York.

Russett, Robert, and Cecile Starr, eds. *Experimental Animation: An Illustrated Anthology*. New York: Van Nostrand Reinhold Company, 1976.

Ryan, James J. "Polarized… Color Displays." *Signs of the Times*, October 1940.

Schillinger, Frances. *Joseph Schillinger: A Memoir.* New York: Da Capo Press, 1976.

Schillinger, Joseph. "Animated Display Apparatus." US patent 2,492,241, filed September 4, 1945, and issued December 27, 1949.

Schillinger, Joseph. Letter to the Editor. *Cue,* October 7, 1939.

Starr, Cecile. "Mary Ellen Bute." In *Experimental Animation: An Illustrated Anthology,* edited by Robert Russett and Cecile Starr, 102–105. New York: Van Nostrand Reinhold Company, 1976.

Vail, Karole. "A Museum in the Making: Two Artists and Their Patron—Hilla Rebay, Rudolf Bauer, and Solomon R. Guggenheim." In *The Museum of Non-Objective Painting: Hilla Rebay and the Origins of the Solomon R. Guggenheim Museum,* edited by Karole Vail, 25–55. New York: Guggenheim Museum Publications, 2009.

Wasson, Haidee. *Museum Movies: The Museum of Modern Art and the Birth of Art Cinema.* Berkeley: University of California Press, 2005.

Zunser, Jesse. "Kinetic Space." *Cue,* August 26, 1939.

CHAPTER 5

The Cinema

While animation was taking on new life in galleries, shop windows, bill-boards and exhibitions in New York, mainstream animated films were undergoing a sudden expansion by taking on feature-length form. One major impetus behind this was the remarkable success of the first feature film produced by Disney, *Snow White and the Seven Dwarfs*, which premiered in 1937 and would become the most popular film of 1938, receiving critical adulation and grossing almost half a million dollars from "manufacturing licenses" for product tie-ins.[1] It was clear to the major studios that feature-length animated films were a promising new form of cinema with huge commercial potential, and two animated features were planned for release in time for the 1939 Christmas season: *Pinocchio*, produced by Disney and released by RKO pictures, and *Gulliver's Travels*, produced by Fleischer Studios and backed by Paramount. The trade paper *Variety* reported, "A race is threatened between Max Fleischer and Walt Disney in getting to the market with their respective cartoon features."[2] Russell Holman, an executive at Paramount, outlined the urgency in a letter from September 1939, explaining how Disney was "working his head off to make the Christmas release," but there was a "great advantage in revenue to the company if the industry's second big feature cartoon to follow *Snow White* could be Paramount's *Gulliver* and not Disney's *Pinocchio*... One print in one prominent theater, like the Paramount, New York, by Christmas would decide the issue."[3] If *Pinocchio* were released after Christmas and *Gulliver's Travels* did not have to compete with the "greater prestige

© The Author(s) 2019
K. Moen, *New York's Animation Culture*, Palgrave Animation,
https://doi.org/10.1007/978-3-030-27931-8_5

of the Disney name," the financial windfall could be huge—estimated at $250,000, about a quarter of the film's budget.[4]

Paramount executives set to work to speed up the release of *Gulliver's Travels* so that it could be released for the Christmas season, going to unusual lengths to ensure its completion on time. This included last-minute scheduling adjustments so that it could be quickly scored, making special arrangements with the Technicolor Corporation so that their complex color processes would not hold things up, taking the risk of shipping undeveloped negatives by air and planning to present the New York Censor Board with a copy of the film at the last minute.[5] The studio's worries were allayed when the film's director, Dave Fleischer, submitted the final reel more than a week ahead of schedule. *Gulliver's Travels* would make its Christmas release date—even in time to have a premiere in Miami (where the Fleischer Studios was now based) before its New York unveiling.

Pinocchio had fallen behind schedule and wouldn't be released until after the holidays. An advertisement in *Variety* gleefully proclaimed: "It's a Gulliver Christmas!"[6] Depicting characters from the film in a Christmas stocking, the ad explained the excitement that was being generated around the film: "Thousands of department stores and specialty shops loaded with merchandise... the radio ringing out with the eight Gulliver hit tunes... the whole country waiting for the chance to see the only full-length feature cartoon ready for holiday release." Animated windows added to the anticipation, with the Abraham & Straus department store showcasing a window display "devoted to the antics of Gulliver and the Lilliputians" that drew in spectators curious to see the animated figures: "And how the crowds enjoy them – most of the grownups wait around for the next performance despite the children's plea that they want to see Santa Claus."[7] Complementing this spectacle, inside the department store "the very first '3-Dimensional' Gulliver show" offered added attractions.[8] This was only one location for the vast commercial promotion that circulated around the film: "Over 100 companies which have been licensed to make products in connection with 'Gulliver' are expected to spend more than $1,500,000 on material, equipment and advertising."[9] Premiering without *Pinocchio* as competition was a boon to the box office as well as a significant opportunity to rack up Christmas sales for the range of commercial products that were connected to the film. By Christmas, "it is said that every important retail outlet in the country has stocked one or more 'Gulliver's Travels' items." Released a couple of months after *Gulliver's Travels*, *Pinocchio* was accompanied by an even more extensive campaign of advertising and product tie-ins. Playing for months, unlike the regular turnover of animated shorts, feature-length animations offered substantial box office and commercial opportunities.

The feature-length animated films released in 1939 and 1940 were also part of a growing appreciation for animation's artistic and cultural value. Shortly before the premiere of *Fantasia* (1940), the third American animated feature to be released after *Snow White*, Walt Disney heralded the vast potentials of animated film, writing that "only the surface of the animation field has been scratched."[10] Rather than a subgenre of mainstream cinema, Disney described how animation "has taken its place along with the stage and motion pictures" as its own "entertainment medium." And while this medium had associations with childhood audiences, Disney emphasized its appeal to adults:

> In the beginning people were inclined to look upon the cartoon films as entertainment for children. Some people, unthinkingly, still do. But we have found over the years that it is the adults who have built and supported the productions. It is a medium which not only appeals to the child in every grownup, but invokes their imaginations. A perfect example of this is "The Three Little Pigs," which was taken up, not by the children of the world, but by the adults.

For Disney, as well as for audiences and commentators, animated film was occupying a cultural role that was much more expansive than a supporting act on film programs addressed mainly to children.

The medium of animated film was also being reshaped by significant technological developments, with the introduction of synchronized sound in the late 1920s and Technicolor in the early 1930s. Disney saw that these new technologies were vital to enlarging animation's potential: "Sound and color widened the range of animation. In our own field we have made many technical improvements. As our scope widened, better talent in drawing, drama and music have been attracted and developed. Today animation stands unique as a creative form in that it incorporates almost every other creative art."[11] In the Mickey Mouse and Silly Symphonies series produced by Disney, animated shorts such as *Steamboat Willie* (1928) and *The Skeleton Dance* (1929) had been celebrated for their interweaving of animation with sound and music, and the use of color and painterly effects were vividly integrated with animation in films such as *Flowers and Trees* (1932) and *The Band Concert* (1935). Like those filmmakers discussed in the previous chapter who were exploring the art and intermediality of animated film, popular commercial animation was embracing a fusion of media and an aura of artistry.[12]

With the release of *Pinocchio*, the Disney studios deepened animation's dynamic commercial, technological and artistic potentials, pushing the boundaries of the medium's identity and its place in culture. At first glance, *Pinocchio*'s subject matter might not appear to be the most obvious choice for these far-reaching ambitions. Writing in *The Nation*, Franz Hoellering summarized the film simply: "a free version of Collodi's fantasy; it tells the story of the puppet given life by the Blue Fairy and changed into a 'real boy' when he proves in many adventures – after initial failures – his truthfulness, courage and unselfishness."[13] While the moralism and fantasy of *Pinocchio* were partly aimed at a childhood audience—or the "child in every grownup"—its appeals also went much further. Critics marveled at the film's artistry, writing of its "sentient camera, expressive draughtsmanship, and fluent motion" and noting that "*Pinocchio* will appeal not only to the multitudes but to the aesthetes as well."[14] Admiration for its aesthetic qualities was coupled with admiration for its technical qualities, with another review noting that what is "most remarkable is the technical progress that the Disney studios have made in the last two years."[15] Disney agreed. While suggesting that the film did not have as much "heart appeal" as *Snow White*, Disney added that "technically and artistically it was superior."[16] Given these many qualities, *Pinocchio* was seen as more than a children's film: the reviewer for the *New York Post* explained, "grown-ups should on no account be allowed to think that 'Pinocchio' is exclusively for children. It probably has a higher percentage of pleasure for adults than anything Disney has ever done."[17]

Just a few months after *Pinocchio*, *Fantasia* premiered. The film was made up of seven animated sections which visualized pieces of classical music, performed by the Philadelphia Orchestra and conducted by Leopold Stokowski. These ranged from a Mickey Mouse story for "The Sorcerer's Apprentice" (Paul Dukas) to a vision of the origins of the world with "Rite of Spring" (Igor Stravinsky) to the depiction of abstract forms of motion and color for "Toccata and Fugue in D Minor" (J. S. Bach). The program that accompanied *Fantasia* spelled out its aims: "In a profession that has been an unending voyage of discovery in the realms of color, sound and motion, *Fantasia* represents our most exciting adventure. At last, we have found a way to use in our medium the great music of all times and the flood of new ideas which it inspires."[18] These aims were not only evident in the film itself, with its novel structure and form, but also in the way it was exhibited—a new sound technology called Fantasound was developed in order to create an aural experience much like attending a concert. With *Pinocchio* and *Fantasia*, the increased length of animated films was entwined with an expanding sense of what animated films could be.

An expansive vision of animation was not only evident within the films themselves, but also in how they were situated in a wider cultural milieu. Through product tie-ins, promotional strategies and intermedial extensions, animated film was escaping the confines of the cinema and crossing into department stores and galleries, book shops and record stores. Animation was also appearing as a topic for discussion in the art criticism, music criticism and society pages of major newspapers and magazines. While the animated features produced at this time were made for audiences throughout the world and were produced in Miami (where the Fleischer Studios had relocated from New York in 1938) and Los Angeles (where the Disney studios were based), New York was the central site for the expanding sense of animation that accompanied their release. Not only was New York the largest single market for these animated features, it was also the flagship location for their extravagant premieres, elaborate exhibition strategies and commercial tie-ins. Examining how New York was at the forefront of the changing cultural place for animated film in the late 1930s and early 1940s, this chapter traces how *Pinocchio* and *Fantasia* became immersed within artistic and commercial contexts beyond the cinema.

Animation's changing cultural place was similarly evident in the most prominent animated films that were screened at the New York World's Fair. While offering sales messages and industrial education, films at the Fair also explored new ways of using animation through inventive aesthetic approaches and exhibition practices, from rollicking funhouses to immersive exhibition spaces. New York was witnessing a dynamic range of new potentials being developed around animation, contributing to a culture that was taking animated film outside of its established role and reframing it as a new form of cinematic entertainment, artistic expression and commercial opportunity.

PINOCCHIO IN NEW YORK

Pinocchio's release in New York was a major cultural event. It was initially scheduled to premiere at Radio City Music Hall, where *Snow White* had been shown. Due to programming conflicts which would not allow the

Music Hall to hold the film for the "minimum engagement of ten weeks which its distributors required," exhibition shifted to the adjacent venue of the Center Theatre, which was also part of Rockefeller Center in midtown Manhattan.[19] The premiere was a grand affair, with an audience of more than 3000 in attendance. This included a host of celebrities and the "entire Rockefeller clan with the exception of John D."[20] Heightening the prestige of the opening, "formal attire was a condition of entrance." Somewhat taken aback by the pomposity of an animated film premiere requiring "black or white tie," the *New Yorker*'s "Talk of the Town" columnist wrote, "We have admired Mr. Disney's work since the first mouse, but we are opposed to this sort of promotional grandeur, now a commonplace in the moving-picture business.... We don't see why anybody has to get into tails to see an animated comic, based on a nursery story."[21] Despite the occasional skeptical response, an increasingly prestigious and rarefied aura was circulating around Disney's animated films, enhanced by their expansion into feature-length form.

Further promoting *Pinocchio* as highbrow animation, the premiere was accompanied by an exhibition in the Center Theatre's lower lounge. The exhibit showcased "200 items, including character sketches, original background paintings, etc." that were used for the production of the film.[22] Set against a wall of "rich black velour" and "protected by a velvet rope," the works were displayed as valuable works of art "guarded by two special policemen."[23] With *Pinocchio*, the Center Theatre had transformed the standard exhibition practice of displaying lobby cards that depicted scenes from a film into a full-scale gallery exhibition.

This was not the first time that drawings and cels from animated films were given the gallery treatment. In 1932, *Art Digest* reported on how Disney "is receiving his first recognition from an art organization at the Art Alliance in Philadelphia, where drawings from his 'Silly Symphonies' and the antics of 'Mickey Mouse' are being shown," further noting that "The 'Silly Symphonies' stand today where Monet and the Impressionists stood some decades ago."[24] Bill Mikulak describes how the exhibition's "opening was marked by an evening of screenings and lectures, including one titled 'The Art of Disney' by art critic and Art Alliance board member Dorothy Grafly."[25] The Philadelphia exhibition was one early example of how galleries were opening up to animated film throughout the 1930s, in the United States and internationally.[26] This related to wider conceptions of the artistry of the Disney studios; Steven Watts describes how, "By the mid-1930s, assertions that Mickey was a 'supreme artistic achievement' or that

Disney movies had gone 'almost too far beyond popular understanding' were commonplace."[27]

This appreciation of animation as art reached new heights in 1939 when the Metropolitan Museum of Art in New York hung an "original gouache on celluloid" from *Snow White*; set alongside "a glass cabinet filled with bronze and iron fittings from an Etruscan chariot of about 600 B. C.," the animation cel may have seemed rather out of place.[28] However, the museum's curator of paintings, Harry B. Wehle, was keen to defend its artistic significance, explaining how Disney is a "great historical figure in the development of American art."[29] Disney demurred: "We're working in a different medium. We have story, ideas, motion, music, narrative characters. Most of these 'fine artists' wouldn't be worth shucks to us." Nevertheless, artists ranging from Edgar Degas to Georges Rouault were influences on the studio's production and, jokingly, Disney explained how Leonardo da Vinci's experimentations, Vincent van Gogh's attention to effects of light and Eugène Delacroix's interest in painting's musicality might well have made them "great" employees for the Disney studios.

The association between Disney and galleries had also developed into a commercial endeavor. In 1938, the Courvoisier Gallery in San Francisco became the worldwide distributor for artwork and painted cels from the Disney studios.[30] The Julien Levy Gallery in New York—particularly well-known for its role in exhibiting surrealist art—became the "eastern outlet for Disney drawings," an association that would last for several years.[31] Levy made no apologies for animation's place in the gallery, declaring that "Disney animated cartoons are the only truly American Art Form" and that the works on show would appeal to adults "sophisticated enough to appreciate their naivete."

Like the Metropolitan Museum and the Levy Gallery, the Center Theatre's lobby exhibition of works from *Pinocchio* was treating animation as art. At the same time, it was deepening the association between the cinema and the gallery, entwining these two seemingly distinct spaces in a single exhibition site. The convergence of the gallery and the cinema was markedly similar to how the Museum of Modern Art and the Museum of Non-Objective Painting were displaying and screening animation. Seen as art, Disney's films were similarly blurring the boundaries between places of exhibition. Writing in the *New York Times*, Frank S. Nugent suggested that Disney's "peculiar art" was not really suitable for a museum, "except possibly in a film museum, which has a screen and a projection machine instead of wall-space and indirect lighting."[32] Taking this idea further, the artist Al Hirschfeld wrote that "animated pictures are primarily drawings, the gallery being a movie house rather than a modern museum, and this is where the art critic might perform a valuable service."[33] He described the marvelous graphic elements in *Pinocchio*: "Watch attentively the whirling of the Russian puppets. These drawings and their general conception of line and color are the finest animated work to be seen. The stylized beards and costumes lend themselves beautifully to animation. In their frenzied whirl they become spinning colors." For Hirschfeld, a scene from *Pinocchio* could be treated as a painterly expression of color and an animated film could be seen as a kinetic gallery exhibition.

Others held similar views. For example, the film critic in the *Saturday Review of Literature* wrote of how *Pinocchio*'s "wonderful world of form and color and excitement" was an example of a "new art," an "art of animated painting."[34] This notion of animation as art became an opportunity to expand *Pinocchio*'s place within the cultural and commercial spaces of New York, infiltrating galleries and transforming exhibition spaces. The *Pinocchio* pressbook, which offered promotional strategies for film exhibitors throughout the United States, took up this idea as well, exclaiming that "Art Galleries in Over 50 Cities Are Now Displaying and Selling Original Paintings from PINOCCHIO!"[35] And this gallery space could be expanded even further: "Local museums, high schools and universities are running exhibitions in co-operation with the galleries! And the galleries themselves are tying up with exhibitors when and as the engagement plays at each theater *by placing the originals on display in theatre lobbies!*" New York was the vanguard for such activities not only through the *Pinocchio* exhibition in the lobby of the Center Theatre, but also in other venues— these included a display of stills from the film "arranged for the library at Columbia University" and "a special exhibit of three Walt Disney originals at the Brooklyn Museum."[36]

Pinocchio extended beyond the cinema in other ways as well. The sites of animation culture described in Chapter 2—billboards, shop windows and educational displays—were all mobilized for the film's New York exhibition. A massive billboard of Pinocchio, located just off Times Square on 49th and Broadway, was described as "the largest head ever painted."[37] Rather than an animated spectacular, this was described as a "paint spectacular," highlighting the artistic basis of the film. Adjacent to the Center Theatre on Sixth Avenue, a more modern construction was on display: "A metal three-and-one-half story 'Pinocchio' head… with full Neon tubing around the outer edge of the medallion, all flooded by spotlights." Highlighting artistry and modern display techniques, these signs drew *Pinocchio*'s aesthetic and technical qualities into urban advertising.

Other forms of display incorporated animation into their visions of *Pinocchio*. Developing earlier display practices that had used mechanized models of Mickey Mouse and other animated figures, Loeser's department store in Brooklyn had "animated displays showing scenes from 'Pinocchio.'"[38] These were created by Old King Cole, Inc., based in Canton, Ohio, who sold "beautifully colored relief and full round reproductions of all the characters from the Technicolor cartoon feature" to dozens of department stores, including Bloomingdale's which planned to "use twelve windows with scenes from the picture and these figures."[39] Although not all such displays would be animated, motion effects would sometimes be created through "mechanical equipment which insures the efficient movement of the characters."[40] The "spirit of scenes" could also be coupled with "sound effects received from the Hollywood studios" so that the display would use synchronized sound, creating animated shows that incorporated the characters, movement, color and sound of animated films. Such spectacles appeared throughout the country and further effects continued to be developed—Gardner Displays, for example, made animated window boxes that reproduced scenes from *Gulliver's Travels* by using automated models "made of a new foam rubber which permits human animation."[41]

The New York Museum of Science and Industry, located near to the Center Theatre in the Rockefeller Center complex, joined the department stores throughout the city in its use of animation as a visual attraction with "mechanical displays" of *Pinocchio* in two of the building's windows.[42] These advertised an exhibition about the production of *Pinocchio* that was on show inside, alongside the Museum's permanent exhibitions of science and technology. In its *Pinocchio* exhibit, the Museum showcased the "process of transferring a fairy tale to the screen in the form of an animated cartoon" through "animated displays, kodachrome pictures and slides, murals and various other illustrative materials used during the making of 'Pinocchio.'"[43] The exhibit displayed a range of illustrations, models and technical devices, including "Animation drawings, story sketches, rough layouts, backgrounds, working models of clocks, music boxes and various sound effects equipment."[44] As well as exhibiting items related to the production of *Pinocchio*, the Museum also acknowledged the significant commercial culture that was circulating around the film, giving "a glimpse of its effect on industry through advertising tie-ups with manufacturers of hundreds of commercial products."[45] With the Center Theatre screening *Pinocchio*, and its gallery lobby and next door Museum joining in with displays that emphasized art and science, Rockefeller Center was a hub of *Pinocchio*-related displays. This extended to social events, including a party after the premiere upstairs in the Rainbow Room, which introduced the Pinocchio polka, and a Pinocchio-themed "ice skating carnival [that] was staged at the Rockefeller Plaza Pond."[46]

The buzz surrounding *Pinocchio* carried into nearby retail districts of New York: "Through the Sixth Avenue Association arrangements were made to fly flags welcoming 'Pinocchio,' and many merchants carried directional window stickers pointing to the Center Theatre."[47] Dozens of music stores "within 20 blocks surrounding the Center" displayed *Pinocchio* sheet music and records, while Macy's "completely furnished a children's nursery room in the furniture department, highlighted by 'Pinocchio' furniture, curtains, lamps, wearing apparel and toilet goods." This was much like the established practice of marketing films through the "cooperative advertising arrangements between merchant and exhibitor" which often "occurred at the same moment and in the proximity of department store or motion picture theater, local florist shop, hardware store, or car dealer showroom."[48] But with *Pinocchio*, the scale of such commercial activities was intensified and expanded in midtown Manhattan.

The tie-ins with *Pinocchio*, like other Disney films for much of the 1930s, were astonishing in their scope and variety. Norman M. Klein describes how such tie-ins became vital to the studio's profitability in the 1930s, as distributors were taking a considerable portion of the money that the films themselves made.[49] In 1932, Kay Kamen "reached an agreement with the studio to become director of Walt Disney Enterprises," leading to a streamlined management of the commercial merchandising circulating around Disney which was based in New York—as Watts notes, "Kamen and his dynamic organization played a key role in making Disney products a staple of American consumer consciousness."[50] With the emergence of feature-length animated films, there was an enormous effort to create tie-ins and other related merchandising opportunities. Hundreds of stores showcased Pinocchio; the commercial expansion of the film was massive, both within the city and further afield, nationally and internationally. *Pinocchio* products ranged from milk bottles to mufflers, with *Motion Picture Herald* reporting, "Almost every conceivable type of merchandise has been tied-in with the Disney production and dealers and merchants are cooperating fully."[51]

In anticipation of the Christmas shopping season, *Publisher's Weekly* reported on the interest being generated by new children's books based on *Pinocchio, Gulliver's Travels* and *The Wizard of Oz* (1939). Suggesting that these publications will be "among the most widely publicized and presented of all books for the Christmas trade," the article went on to explain their multiple appeals, including "elaborate color illustrations," "low prices," "tie-ups with the movies themselves" and "incidental publicity staged by the movie companies."[52] The marketability of *Pinocchio* as a book was suggested in the film itself, which begins with a fade-in on a large leather-bound edition of *Pinocchio* and a spotlight shining on its title. With several *Pinocchio*-related books released over Christmas, publishers "started rolling up sales that are all the more impressive because the picture has not yet been released, though publicity for it has been heavy for several weeks; nor will it be released in time for Christmas.... The pulling power of the Disney name and of 'Pinocchio' seem to do the trick." Shop displays for these publications would sometimes include other *Pinocchio*-related material, with "toy departments, book departments and many other departments... all using 'Pinocchio' as a theme."

The commercial activity circulating around *Pinocchio*, as well as other Disney films and characters, was a significant source of income for Walt Disney Productions. In the company's September 1940 annual report, the total income generated by extra-cinematic activities—including product licensing, publishing, music royalties and comic strips—was more than half a million dollars, about a quarter of the combined film rental income for *Pinocchio* and Disney's short subjects in the same year.[53] The report noted, "Names and characters created by the Company and licensed for use on merchandise, etc. continue to have a widespread appeal. Royalties from this source, from books and music, and revenue from comic strips and art sales, constitute a substantial portion of the income of the Company."[54]

The tie-ins did more than just bring in money—the advertising that circulated around galleries, music and publications associated with *Pinocchio* reminded the audience about the film and generated further interest in its release. Products functioned as miniature advertisements, with the *Pinocchio* pressbook declaring how "1500 Pinocchio items each reaching millions of buyers, all advertised and displayed locally, are working hand in hand with your box office."[55] It was if each item served as a "mute twenty-four sheet" poster for the film, so that "Every conceivable field of trade is fully covered!"

The tie-ins would highlight how the film itself offered many different kinds of appeals, including artistry, musicality, appealing characters and an enchanting story. These could potentially attract diverse audiences with different areas of interest. The pressbook for the film engaged with these multifaceted appeals of *Pinocchio*—in addition to typical information about the film and its production, it also presented stories for different sections of the newspaper, including "Art Features," "Music Features," "Animation Features," "For the Woman's Page," and "Children & Pet Stories." This multiplicity extended also to the coverage of *Pinocchio*'s premiere, with movie critics for New York newspapers joined by "photographers, society, music, book and feature writers."[56] While Disney's short films had also emphasized a range of appeals, the extended length and scope of the feature-length animated film offered further opportunities for immersing an animated film within a wider cultural milieu. The animated feature could become a compendium of different allures and forms, each with their own cultural values and commercial opportunities. And this encouraged a multifaceted expansion beyond the cinema: the gallery, the bookstore, the music shop, the library, the city street, the department store and the Museum of Science—all hosting *Pinocchio*.

FANTASIA AS A NEW FORM OF CINEMA

In the same year that *Pinocchio* premiered in New York, *Fantasia* was released. *Fantasia*'s cultural role has been a subject of abiding interest among historians and animation scholars, including Steven Watts and Moya Luckett.[57] The film's formal and technological innovations, coupled with its overt references to high culture and its visualization of classical music, were extraordinary for a mainstream feature film at the time. While discussing these aspects of *Fantasia*, I want also to foreground how it related to a broader idea of animation's expansiveness in New York. In many respects, its distinctive presentation and aesthetic ambitions were immersed within a larger network of ideas circulating around the place of animation in New York's animation culture.

While *Pinocchio* was extending outwards into other cultural spaces, *Fantasia* aimed to transform cinema itself with Fantasound, a "revolutionary technique in sound reproduction" that was developed for the film's exhibition in conjunction with RCA.[58] An article in *Scientific American* detailing this sound technology explained how Disney was "working toward a two-fold change in the entertainment world."[59] The first change was evident in the film's distinctive form, which used animated film to illustrate and embellish works of classical music. The second change, "perhaps of more genuine significance," was the development of the Fantasound technology, described as a "sound reproduction system for movies which would bring to motion-picture audiences this great music in all its glory, in a form closely approximating that enjoyed by the privileged few who attend symphony concerts." As the first location for Fantasound, New York presented *Fantasia* in its initial run as a new form of animated music.

Fantasound offered a number of innovative effects. It allowed for a significantly increased volume range (from 35 decibels to 75 decibels) and "a correspondingly increased range of tonal frequencies and hence quality of reproduction" in order to better capture the effect of a symphony orchestra.[60] With speakers placed throughout the cinema, and not just adjacent to or behind the screen, Fantasound could also create a mobile, stereophonic and immersive experience of sound. New sound recording techniques were needed; these involved the division of the orchestra into different sections so that the musical elements could "be blended at will and reproduced through the required loudspeaker."[61] The projection of the sound also required a change to existing technologies. While a normal optical soundtrack was attached to the film as a backup, the effects of Fantasound were created through "a second strip of standard movie film" that was made up of "*four* individual sound tracks," including three tracks for the sound and one for an "auditory perspective" that guided the movement of sound.[62] This "auditory perspective" allowed sound to move within the cinema, "So when Mickey Mouse appears on the right, a control mechanism switches on the loudspeaker directly behind him and veers the sound to another speaker when he moves."[63] In this manner, Fantasound could create "a complete third-dimensional effect of sound and music" that "causes sound actually to move with all action on the screen." Moving sound by placing it in different parts of the cinema was seen to offer considerable aesthetic possibilities: "'Fantasound' succeeds in taking music and sound out of its customary accessory or incidental role in the theater, and elevates it to the position of an important tool in the hands of the dramatist." The dramatic and musical potentials of Fantasound were seen to be far-reaching, filled with transformative possibilities for cinemagoing.

Cinemas had to be refitted for Fantasound—this included substantial changes to the projection facilities and the introduction of an elaborate network of speakers in the auditorium. *Fantasia*'s first run in New York required considerable work at the Broadway Theater, which involved the installation of "a total of 90 speakers, 36 of them being located back-stage and the remainder distributed throughout orchestra and balcony of the-ater."[64] This led to a dispute between unions in New York over who would be contracted to do the work—the union responsible for installing new equipment or the union responsible for its operation.[65] Soon after this was resolved, enabling *Fantasia* to premiere in New York in November 1940, another problem arose. Due to a flood of government orders for RCA radio equipment, "Defense production is holding up openings of Walt Disney's 'Fantasia' in cities outside of New York."[66] Rather than fol-lowing on swiftly from its New York premiere as was originally planned, any distribution of *Fantasia* outside of New York was delayed until the end of January 1941. Wider distribution beyond a select number of cities con-tinued to be limited almost a year after *Fantasia*'s initial release. Moving the equipment from theatre to theatre was a burdensome task—weighing "approximately 15,000 lbs," it "required one-half of a standard freight car space" to ship.[67] With such considerations in mind, a "simplified sound sys-tem" that enabled overnight installations was soon developed in order to allow for a more widespread release.[68] Even this created financial and logis-tical strain, and soon after the soundtrack was "re-recorded for standard sound systems and [the film] will be generally road-shown and distributed by RKO."[69] Fantasound was no more, never to return. Despite all of these challenges, the initial exhibition was a considerable success; in New York, *Fantasia* played for longer than *Gone with the Wind* (1939).[70]

Not only did *Fantasia* require the transformation of existing cinemas, it also required new approaches to cinema as an industry. An article in *Variety* pointed out that *Fantasia* "is not only a new kind of sound pic-ture; it also must create its own channels of exhibition."[71] Partly due to the non-standard exhibition practices involved, Disney would be taking the unusual step of circumventing the regular distributor of Disney films, RKO, and instead "going into the distribution field, with direct bookings through his own organization."[72] Moreover, the film "is so different from other pictures that it will require a selling technique all its own." Aware of the many challenges involved with this new venture, Disney approached *Fantasia* as the first instance of a much larger "entertainment enterprise" that could transform the ways in which animated films were shown.[73]

Turning away from any suggestion that *Fantasia* could be divided and shown as separate short films, Disney described how it is "best appreciated when it is presented on a program of its own" as "the audience is in an entirely different mood."[74] Moreover, *Fantasia* could transcend a typical cinemagoing experience:

> The quality may not be obvious to a lot of people the first time, but I believe they will come back a second time. The second time you relax and really enjoy it because the music that is coming from the screen is the greatest music that has ever come from any screen. If the public does not like the pictures they can close their eyes and still go out satisfied they have had their money's worth.

The suggestion that music is "coming from the screen" highlights the musical qualities of the film and its projection of sound, while also gesturing toward a changing conception of what it means to "watch" a film.

Fantasia was an attempt to establish a new kind of animated cinema, with New York as its initial test case. "Fantasia Forever!" declared an article in the *Los Angeles Times*, explaining, "One of Disney's projects is a sort of perpetual 'Fantasia,' in which new subjects will be constantly added to the present eight, like new 'editions' of a revue."[75] In this vision of *Fantasia*'s future, the cinema would become a space that would host changing shows of animated music: "Roy Disney, Walt's brother and business manager, amplified this plan further. It is the studio's hope, he said, to encourage certain key exhibitors to put on continuous 'seasons' of cartoon works – in Fantasound, of course, for this is the only way in which production and equipment can be made to pay for themselves." The paper's music critic added, "These daily and nightly concerts will be given at film theaters with constant variations continuously devised so that people can drop in and listen to their favorite music and see the color and watch the artists' ideas come to life and be happy for moments or inspired forever, as the case may be."[76] In order to extend the life of *Fantasia* in such a way, with "evenings of light concerts and more dramatic compositions to suit all types of music lovers, and incidentally bring repeat customers to the box-office," Disney began planning and developing animated films for musical works including "Clair de Lune" (Claude Debussy), "Peter and the Wolf" (Sergei Prokofiev) and "The Swan of Tuonela" (Jean Sibelius).[77] These ambitious ideas for an ongoing *Fantasia* did not materialize for a range of reasons which, as Robin Allan writes, included "the studio's financial troubles," along with its "strike, loss of foreign markets and America's own entry into the war."[78] But for a brief period, *Fantasia* was pointing toward a transformation of animation aesthetics, sound technology, film exhibition and distribution, and the cinematic experience.

Reviewers described *Fantasia* as the "inauguration of a new art form" and a "mountainous achievement of motion picture art" in a "remarkable new medium."[79] Presenting Disney with the Irving G. Thalberg award at the 1942 Academy Award ceremonies, David O. Selznick referred to Disney in glowing terms as "the very first artist of the motion picture" who, with *Fantasia*, had "created a new art form."[80] Integrating music with animation was common to animated films at this time, suggested by the titles of animated series such as "Silly Symphonies" and "Merrie Melodies." But with its distinctive structure and increased emphasis on animation's musicality, Disney championed *Fantasia* as "a new medium of expression which, for the first time, will enable an audience to 'see' music."[81] In its more experimental form, however, this was an existing area of cinematic exploration for a number of artists and animators—Bute had been publicizing her films as "seeing sound" since the mid-1930s and Fischinger's participation in the production of *Fantasia* drew upon his background creating visual music through animation. Perhaps with even earlier works and ideas of visual music in mind, Disney acknowledged that *Fantasia* was not quite so new, noting that "The effort to combine sight and sound artistically is almost as old as time itself." While linked to earlier artistic practices and contemporary filmmaking in a number of ways, *Fantasia* was still a uniquely prominent combination of music and animation, coupling the new form of the feature-length animated film with cinematic and technological innovations.

Fantasia became a subject of considerable fascination within New York's animation culture. Writing in the *New York Times*, Edward Alden Jewell took *Fantasia* as the starting point for his review of the more experimental works shown in the "film concert" at the Museum of Non-Objective Art. Jewell wrote that the aim of combining the different arts of painting and music in film "has been widely, even heatedly, discussed of late – ever since the advent of Walt Disney's 'Fantasia.'"[82] As the previous chapter discussed, Jewell wrote of how painting and music shared qualities of movement, such as rhythmic form and dynamic composition. However, for Jewell it was a mistake to think that artistic forms could be unified in an animated film. Painting and music should be left "in their separate spheres, where they should remain." Saving his most strident criticism for the attempts to merge images with music in the abstract animations shown at the Museum of Non-Objective Painting, Jewell was sympathetic to *Fantasia*. He thought its ambitions were actually quite modest and that it was best "to approach this extraordinary film on its own terms – terms that to me seem only to ask that one accept or reject it on the basis of its entertainment value, as a glorified and technically improved 'silly symphony.'"

Other major critics were more open to the idea that the aesthetic of painting and the aesthetic of music could be combined in animated films. Lewis Jacobs—who had worked with Bute and Schillinger on an unfinished abstract animation in the early 1930s—devoted a chapter to Disney in his major survey of American film history, *The Rise of the American Film* (1939). Published shortly before the release of *Fantasia*, Jacobs writes, "Disney like all gifted directors employs movement as the basis of his structure. Sound and color have not impeded his structural movement, but have themselves become integrated with it."[83] He goes on to discuss a range of ways in which sound and color "function as mobile units" within Disney's films, such as the "rhythmic pattern" of sound effects and how color is "seldom static… always taking on a new hue with each of the emotional developments and moving with the images and sound." Jacobs concludes his chapter on Disney, writing, "His contributions in the application of sound and color to movement have added new concepts – still to be formulated into principles – to the body of film knowledge on which the medium will now progress further" (505).

The combination of image and sound in Disney's films also attracted the attention of major composers, with George Antheil, in a regular column for *Modern Music*, writing in 1938 that "Disney, as has been long evident, turns out the most consistently good scores here. His music department should be recognized by serious American musicians as the most ingenious in the motion picture centre."[84] This quality stemmed partly from the ways in which these animated films were produced to carefully synchronize music, image and motion. In another of his columns, Antheil described an encounter with Stokowski: "One day as he was leaving the Walt Disney headquarters, I said that I considered the scores of his studio by far the best in town. 'How can they help but be,' he replied. 'They are the only scores in town planned in advance of shooting.'"[85] The practice of building an animated film around or in conjunction with a musical score was not unique to Disney by any means, but the studio's films were the most celebrated and well-known films to entwine animation with musicality.

Joining art, film and music critics, Disney participated in the conversation circulating around the integration of painting and music through animation. He wrote that *Fantasia* is a film in which "the musical compositions suggest the mood, the pictorial pattern and even the individual phases of action.... The fact that music, by its nature, is in constant movement affords a plan for the movement of the picture."[86] With *Fantasia*, the relationship between music and animation had taken on new feature-length life—rather than another Silly Symphony, here was a film that Disney described in more exalted terms as a "concert picture."[87]

Fantasia explored new forms of animated film in other ways as well. An article in *Variety* described the film's distinctive presentation: "Total unconventionality of the picture, the producer declared, is expected to work in its favor. It's different, even to the lack of a main title. Name of the picture and the credits do not appear on the screen. Like a concert, it opens with music. Credits are in the program."[88] Foregoing standard practices, *Fantasia* was fashioning a new kind of cinematic experience. Arthur Beach, writing for the *National Board of Review Magazine*, discussed the novelty of the film's structure—a string of short animations connected by Deems Taylor's commentary—in emphatic terms, "To such a work it is useless to apply the ordinary rules of the cinema.... The framework of conductor, commentator and orchestra, for all its possible charm, is an obvious mechanical device to afford the only unity that a picture like *Fantasia* could have.... It is not a cinema, it is a series of cinemas."[89] In a similar vein, Beach also suggested that *Fantasia* "has no unity, dramatic or modal; its component parts are as distinct from one another as canvases lined up side by side in a gallery, or, more aptly, as the numbers in a ballet concert." Associating the film with other cultural spaces in a manner like Hirschfeld's discussion of *Pinocchio* as akin to a gallery of moving paintings, Beach saw *Fantasia* as a film that bridged different arts. This suggested an intermedial experience somewhat like the Museum of Non-Objective Painting's exhibition of films within a gallery—the initial description of these screenings as a "film concert" may have been a nod toward *Fantasia*.

Fantasia's experiments with the form of animated film extended even to its tie-in publication, *Walt Disney's Fantasia* (1940).[90] Rather than following the typical format of retelling the film's stories or recounting its production, the book integrated text and image with a visual design that evoked motion and music. Color paintings depicted scenes from the film while sketches of different animated characters danced and marched across the pages. Musical passages appeared alongside the text and as graphic elements, with staves curling and twisting around the page or forming expressive visual abstractions of the music. "The most unusual music book of the season," this was apparently the "first Disney book for adults"; the buyer's guide in *Publisher's Weekly* described it as a "book-symphony" that offered "a new and original art form."[91] This new kind of publishing tie-in was part of the wider sense that *Fantasia* was blurring boundaries between media forms. Developing new avenues for animation, *Fantasia* was seen to be fashioning an artistic experience that was not—or not *only*—cinema. This ambitious approach resonated with the expansion of *Pinocchio* into other cultural fields. With these feature-length films, animated film's identity was being disrupted. The well-established space of the cinema could no longer contain the different visions and offshoots of animation that were developing around the feature-length films produced by Disney. New artistic and commercial paths were opening up, and New York became the most prominent site for this expanding sense of animation.

Animated Film at the Fair

Although operating on a smaller scale than the major features appearing in New York at the time, a number of films at the World's Fair embraced the same spirit of animated experimentation and expansion. Alongside a dizzying array of "sub-standard projectors with their endless belts of colour cartoon extolling chewing gum, pickles, coffee, ham and eggs, motor tyres," new forms, technologies and exhibition practices were being explored.[92] Such films were part of a host of other motion pictures projected at the Fair which were, as Haidee Wasson explains, being shown "in venues that could in no way be deemed theatrical but instead made up of walls, floors, ceilings, small booths and boxes as sites for images big and small, continuous and discontinuous, silent and not."[93] Sometimes part of "elaborate multi-medial exhibits" and sometimes "partial elements of much larger and elaborate themed environments," moving images were integral to the "World of Tomorrow" on display at the Fair. A press release from the Department of Feature Publicity explained how "motion pictures are used in new and striking fashion, and for many new purposes."[94] Animated films were front and center, providing key examples of "the latitude in technique and approach," the "enhanced appreciation of the medium" and the "new imagination" that was evident in films at the Fair. Turning from animated features to animated films at the Fair, we can see that a sense of experimentation was by no means restricted to major studios. Rather, this was part of a larger movement toward new approaches to exhibition and aesthetic form in New York's animation culture.

One of the most striking animated films at the Fair was *In Tune with Tomorrow* (1939), which demonstrated "phenomenal developments in the art of motion picture production applied to showing in a dramatic way the engineering advancements incorporated in today's Chrysler, Dodge, De Soto and Plymouth automobiles."[95] Through stop motion animation, the film depicted a car being constructed—its various parts operating as "actors" who were "endowed with the power of locomotion and completely released from the force of gravity. With gay élan, they jumped, marched, turned, wheeled, ran and sailed through the air, singly and in precise formation, assembling themselves into a complete car."[96] Viewed through polaroid glasses, the film created startling three-dimensional motion effects. Showing objects swinging toward the viewer and receding into the background in a display of automation, "Action that occurs in the foreground of the picture seems not to remain on the screen, but to leave the stage and take place immediately in front of the eyes of the visitor, no matter where he sits."[97] Animation lent itself to the dynamism of the subject matter, given a striking visual impact through the use of three-dimensional film. Moreover, like *Fantasia*, the film aimed to create an immersive experience for the spectator—but rather than being surrounded by mobile sound, a viewer was placed in the midst of moving images that came at them directly. As a malleable medium that had been lauded for its use of the new film technologies of synchronized sound and three-strip Technicolor earlier in the decade, animation was particularly well-suited to offering new cinematic experiences.

While the technological innovations at the Chrysler exhibit were aligned with the Fair's corporate and industrial themes, new routes for animated films were also being developed for advertising. *Mickey's Surprise Party* (1939) was among the most popular animated films at the Fair, a status largely due to being one of the first Mickey Mouse films to advertise a product. Writing in the *New Yorker*, John Mosher was thrilled that "Mickey Mouse has, so to speak, gone into trade. He has left his lofty and haughty tower at last and, like many another artist, has turned commercial."[98] Mickey's advertising film was a tremendous success; it was described as the "outstanding feature" of the National Biscuit Company's exhibit and seen by more than a million visitors just a few months after the Fair opened.[99]

Running almost the length of a regular Mickey Mouse short, the film begins with Minnie preparing homemade cookies as a surprise for Mickey. Unfortunately, unbeknownst to Minnie, her pet dog Fifi accidentally spills

popcorn kernels into the mix. Soon after, Mickey and Pluto arrive at Minnie's home. They smell something burning—rushing into the kitchen,
Mickey and Minnie see that the cookies have been burnt and, taking them
out of the oven, the kernels begin popping and the cookies shoot around
the room. Once this scene of dynamic mayhem ends, Minnie is reduced
to tears at her failed attempt at a delightful surprise. Luckily, Mickey has
an idea. He dashes out and quickly returns with an assortment of Nabisco
products. "Surprise!" he exclaims, and Minnie lists the various products on
full display: "Oh, Mickey, Nabisco! Lorna Doone, social teas and Oreos."
Mickey adds, "my mother used to buy them all the time" and brings out
his favorite, fig newtons. While overt in its advertising aims, the film offers
many of the same appeals as more artistically minded Disney short films.

As well as drawing Disney into the advertising field, *Mickey's Surprise
Party* was embellished by a spectacle of animation that took place outside
of the building: "An animated display of puppets designed by Tony Sarg
march around the exterior of the theater behind glass."[100] In this "brightly
lighted puppet parade… gaily colored animated puppets enact the Mad
Hatter's tea party from 'Alice in Wonderland', 'Old King Cole and His
Fiddlers Three', 'The Old Woman in the Shoe', and forty-one other scenes
dear to the heart of childhood; and all of them very cleverly promoting the
desire for National Biscuit products."[101] This puppet parade was much like
other motion displays used for advertising, creating animation through a
"quick-acting pendulum motor" so that "marionettes may be made to perform through mechanical agitation, in a way which quite closely resembles
manual manipulation."[102] *Mickey's Surprise Party* and the National Biscuit
exhibit extended animation: from a Disney film to a Disney advertisement
and from animation in a cinema to animation outside of the theatre itself.

The designer of the marionette parade, Tony Sarg, was embedded in
a wider network of visual and commercial culture that intersected with
animation in multiple ways. While his early work was as an illustrator, he
was best known as a puppeteer, staging a longstanding and widely praised
series of marionette shows. This had extended to other fields over the previous decades; in the 1920s, his work ranged from producing the animated silhouette film series *Tony Sarg's Almanac* to designing the balloons
for Macy's Thanksgiving Day Parade (a job that he continued with for
decades). At the World's Fair, in addition to designing the National Biscuit
display and illustrating the official "Pictorial Map" for the Fair, his "Enchanted Forest" exhibit used live actors and mechanical figures to create "a
miniature illusion show depicting a realistic woodland scene, with sound
and polarized light creating eerie, fantastic effects."[103] Sarg's creative work

also involved illustrating the advertising campaign for the radio show "Adventures of Pinocchio" which had begun broadcasting in 1939, likely in an attempt to take advantage of the pre-publicity surrounding Disney's *Pinocchio*.[104] Sarg's wide-ranging work was emblematic of the multiple strands of New York's animation culture, engaging with different media, popular characters, spectacular effects, fantastic themes and display techniques all associated with animation.

The relation between puppetry and animation was a well-established trope in animated films; *Pinocchio* was part a longstanding tradition in which marionettes, toys, dolls and other inanimate figures become animated. The composer Virgil Thomson highlighted the link between puppetry and animation in a more conceptual manner in an article written shortly after the release of *Pinocchio*: "The esthetic of the animated cartoon is not a new thing. So far as I can figure it out, it is identical with that of the Marionette theater."[105] He goes on to suggest, "'The Sorcerer's Apprentice,' in *Fantasia*, might just as well have been done by Tony Sarg." Thomson's idea of the close relation between animated films and marionette shows reflected how these arts were being entwined in New York's animation culture. Exhibits and displays, as we have seen, were automating the motion of animated figures through new devices and technologies. Some were even self-consciously combining animated films and animated figures as two distinct—but similar—spectacles of motion.

This combination of animated film, animated displays and puppetry was evident in early plans for a Popeye exhibit at the Fair. The proposal for this exhibit pointed to the enormous appeal of Popeye, with his comic strip, product tie-ins and animated films reaching millions. Popeye was immersed in a range of media and forms of popular entertainment, much like *Pinocchio* and other animated features. An early idea developed by publicity staff for King Features, which owned the rights to Popeye, was to combine different media in a specially designed "House of Popeye" with a "Popeye Marionette Show and a screening of one or two Popeye movie reels."[106] Planning eventually shifted to more of a funhouse atmosphere, with a "Cartoon Ship" building that would "consist of 15 scenes, all animated and synchronized" featuring Popeye and other comic strip characters, along with "a Funny Marionette Show."[107] Like Sarg's wide-ranging creative work, the Popeye exhibit combined graphic arts, motion display, puppetry and film.

Alongside the exhibits that combined different animated forms, different techniques of depicting motion were combined in films at the Fair.

One of the films screened in the special theatre at the Ford exhibit for the Fair's second season, *Symphony in F* (1940), coupled documentary footage of a Ford assembly plant with fanciful stop motion animation, including marching purchase orders, the metamorphosis of a V8 emblem into a dancing wooden puppet, and car parts which form a parade and then assemble themselves. Rather than drawing sharp distinctions between animated scenes and actual footage of the production process, the film fluidly shifts between modes of representation. As part of its animation, scenes of the moving figures in the Cycle of Production display, discussed in Chapter 3, were integrated into the film (Fig. 5.1). The animated figures were shown individually away from their place on the rotating display and then gathered together at the end, appearing in their stations upon the Cycle of Production for the climax of the film. *Symphony in F* presented its industrial subject matter through multiple forms of interrelated motion: documentary footage of laborers and automated production processes, stop motion animation, and live-action footage of animation that had been created through mechanical devices. This was part of a larger turn toward combining animated forms that was taking place at the time, from animated figures within and outside the National Biscuit exhibit to the mixture of animated films and animated figures in the plans for the Popeye funhouse.

Fig. 5.1 *Symphony in F* (1940)

Another prominent animated film at the Fair, *Pete-Roleum and His Cousins* (1939), also combined different approaches to animation aesthetics, exhibition and audience address in order to create a novel animated experience. Funded by "fourteen major oil companies" as part of the Petroleum Industry Exhibition, which offered a "tribute to and explanation of the petroleum industry," the film presented a celebratory message of petroleum's value to society.[108] Rather than presenting this information in a typical instructional manner, the film illustrated different facets of the petroleum industry through the stop motion animation of "little rubber puppets" that resemble drops of oil.[109] Publicity for the film explained, "The cinema has a sensational new 'find' – no Scandinavian glamor girl this time, but a humorous new type of flexible rubber figurine to be featured in a Technicolor puppet film which promises to be as new to the film world as was 'Snow White,' according to Joseph Losey, its producer" (1).

The production of *Pete-Roleum* drew together an impressive range of talent: its music was composed by Hanns Eisler, who had scored several of Bertolt Brecht's plays; it was animated by Charley Bowers, who had been creating astonishing and inventive animation since the 1920s; it was edited by Helen van Dongen, a political documentarist who worked as an editor with Joris Ivens and Robert Flaherty; and it was directed by Joseph Losey, whose later work would establish him as a critically acclaimed filmmaker.[110] Merging animated fantasy and industrial education, *Pete-Roleum* depicted everyday uses of petroleum—from the running of cars to the manufacturing of soap to the waxing of apples—in order to dramatize its value. Early scenes show how oil had transformed society, from a sickly horse dragging a carriage to the early days of the automobile to a streamlined city in the modern age (Fig. 5.2).

The film is structured around Pete-Roleum's narration, which includes scenes of direct address where he is set against a stark black background or a field of oil derricks. These scenes are interwoven with short vignettes, instructional interludes and a narrative framework where the anthropomorphic oil characters leave the earth, only to return after their critic—an offscreen heckler—pleads for them to come back after realizing the devastation that the absence of oil would cause. The visual design is striking, with dynamic framing and a creative use of abstraction. Losey expressed particular admiration for Howard Bay's contribution to the film, describing the "miniature sets" as "brilliant" and noting that the "oil drop figure" designed by Bay (Fig. 5.3) "has remained a symbol of the oil companies – I think Shell – ever since."[111] (Losey almost had it right—it was a character

Fig. 5.2   *Pete-Roleum and His Cousins* (1939)

Fig. 5.3   *Pete-Roleum and His Cousins* (1939)

later used in Esso's advertising, Happy the Oil Drop Man, who was based on Bay's design.) Later reflecting on his work on the film, Losey described how it "consumed a great deal more time than it should have and was an extremely painful and lengthy experience."[112] He summarized the project somewhat ruefully: "It was planned as an entertainment promotion that would tell 'the story of petroleum's usefulness to the human race' (Seems a bit ironic now)."

Although Losey may not have remembered the film fondly, accounts at the time greeted it with fascination. A preview in the *New York Times*, before the film was completed, suggested that it had "a novel, experimental nature and may very likely point the way toward an innovation in the field of fantasy films."[113] *Pete-Roleum* was hardly unprecedented in its use of animation, and Losey curated a "survey of the development of the animated cartoon and puppet film" at the Museum of Modern Art shortly after *Pete-Roleum* premiered at the Fair.[114] With one reel of the film shown in a program that included films produced by Disney, Emile Cohl, Walter Lantz, Charley Bowers and Len Lye, alongside stop motion films by Wladislaw Starewicz and George Pal, *Pete-Roleum* was situated in a longer history of animation, as well as the artistic context of the gallery. In "Discussion of Three-Dimensional Animations," an article likely written to coincide with this screening, Losey wrote a "history of the technique and its practitioners, starting with the work of Méliès."[115] He described *Pete-Roleum* as "the most ambitious experiment of its kind to date."

While its animation techniques were not quite as novel as publicity and reviews at the time suggested, *Pete-Roleum* was a strikingly original animated film in other ways. *Pete-Roleum* drew upon Losey's background as a theatre director for the Living Newspaper Unit in New York. Losey transposed some of the dramatic ideas from that context into an animated film. Colin Gardner explains that in the living newspaper, "The objective was to present the topics – housing, syphilis, co-operatives, labour unions, flood control, famine – as objectively as possible. Each scene was usually based on a researched document, statistic, or conversation."[116] Such topics would be shown

> as the problem of the average person, so that the production took on a didactic role, giving the man or woman in the street a chance to understand the social, political, and economic forces that affected them. In this way, each problem found its root cause in recent history and social conditions: in short, the result of a private enterprise system that exploited human needs.

Although these leftist and political aims hardly chimed with the petroleum industry, *Pete-Roleum's* emphasis on daily experiences and factual information was seen to resonate with the approach of the living newspaper, with a press release for the film noting how it "presents in 'Living Newspaper' expository fashion the facts as to price, production, wages, employment, profits, competition, conservation, and the material advances made possible by Petroleum."[117] Drawing key aims of the living newspaper into industrial propaganda and animated fantasy, *Pete-Roleum* fused together different arts and forms.

The experimental approach of *Pete-Roleum* was further developed through plans for an exhibition that drew upon characteristic features of living newspaper plays, with their staging's "fluid dynamism" and "overall dialectical movement."[118] A dialectical clash was to be shown in *Pete-Roleum* by contrasting the celebration of oil products taking place onscreen with an offscreen heckler who loudly criticized this celebration. It was originally planned that this conflict would be given greater impact by having the character of Pete-Roleum appear both as an animated figure onscreen and in the auditorium as an "an 8-foot marionette," leaping "from screen to stage and back again, carrying the running thread of the production, and arguing with a Heckler's Voice from the audience, in a humorous running dialogue."[119] While never fully realized, the innovative plans to cross between animation and puppetry, with the film combining the "technique of Walt Disney and Tony Sarg" as one article from the time described it, was testing the boundaries of animation's form and aesthetics in ways that resonated with wider trends at the time.[120]

Another way that the film aimed to express a clash of views was through its use of sound: "There are two separate, interlocking sound tracks, one representing the voices of the screen characters and the other blaring forth the taunts of a heckler in the audience."[121] The effect of this was hampered by the venue, with the film "projected on a screen suspended at least fifty feet above the heads of its audience" in which "sound scampers elusively around the hall with a harsh, hollow sound from which the chest and middle tone has been removed, vainly in order to counteract the acoustical absurdities of the premises."[122] While *Pete-Roleum's* use of multiple tracks was similar to *Fantasia's* use of Fantasound, it lacked the bespoke exhibition space and technological investment needed in order to really work. However, *Pete-Roleum* and *Fantasia* were considered together in another way: a press release reported how Stokowski—who had played such a major onscreen and offscreen role in *Fantasia*—has a "deep interest in these new screen characters as a possible interpretative medium for music."[123] While Stokowski's interest may well have been fanciful, the suggestion that one of the most well-known conductors of the time could be so intrigued by stop motion animation indicates the cultural resonance—and adaptability—of animated film in this period.

Combining different forms of motion, experimenting with new technologies and exhibition practices, and playing with established media, *Pete-Roleum* shared the same exploratory spirit as other animations in the World's Fair and New York's wider animation culture. Much like the displays and exhibits that this book has examined, the cinema as a place of exhibition was alive to the impact, multiplicity and transformative potentials of animation.

NOTES

1. "'Bagdad' Also Will Have a Commercial Licensing Hookup," *Variety*, December 27, 1939, 8.
2. "Fleischer-Disney Race," *Variety*, February 1, 1939, 5.
3. Russell Holman to A. M. Botsford, September 19, 1939, Paramount Picture production records, *Gulliver's Travels*, Margaret Herrick Library.
4. Russell Holman to A. M. Botsford, September 30, 1939, Paramount Picture production records, *Gulliver's Travels*, Margaret Herrick Library.
5. Louis R. Lipstone to Lou Diamond, November 3, 1939; Chas. P. West to Richard Murray, October 6, 1939; Chas. P. West to Mr. Freeman, November 3, 1939; Chas. P. West to Mr. Freeman, November 3, 1939. The correspondence is held in the Paramount Picture production records, *Gulliver's Travels*, Margaret Herrick Library.
6. Advertisement, *Variety*, December 6, 1939, 17.
7. Dorothy Coburn, "A Preview of Santa's Pack: On a Trip Through Brooklyn's Toyland," *Brooklyn Daily Eagle*, November 30, 1939.
8. Advertisement, *Brooklyn Daily Eagle*, December 3, 1939.
9. "Setting Final Policies on 'Wind,' Cartoons 'Gulliver,' 'Pinocchio,'" *Motion Picture Herald*, December 9, 1939, 15.
10. Walt Disney, "Cartoons Look to New Horizons, Find Them Happily Limitless," *New York Herald Tribune*, September 16, 1940.
11. Disney, "Cartoons Look to New Horizons."
12. See Steven Watts, *The Magic Kingdom: Walt Disney and the American Way of Life* (Columbia: University of Missouri Press, 1997); Robin Allan, *Walt Disney and Europe* (London: John Libbey, 1999); and Esther Leslie, *Hollywood Flatlands: Animation, Critical Theory and the Avant-Garde* (London: Verso, 2002).

13. Franz Hoellering, "Films," *Nation*, February 17, 1940, 261.
14. Archer Winsten, "Disney's 'Pinocchio' at the Center Theatre," *New York Post*, February 8, 1940; William Boehnel, "Pinocchio Stamped with Disney's Genius," *New York World-Telegram*, February 10, 1940.
15. Rose Pelswick, "'Pinocchio' Opens at Center Theatre," *New York Journal-American*, February 8, 1940.
16. Michael Barrier, *Hollywood Cartoons: American Animation in Its Golden Age* (Oxford: Oxford University Press, 1999), 266.
17. Archer Winsten, "Disney's 'Pinocchio' at the Center Theatre."
18. *Walt Disney Presents Fantasia* (New York: Walt Disney Productions, 1940), 9.
19. "Center Theatre to Revert to Films for 'Pinocchio,'" *New York Times*, January 12, 1940.
20. Lee Mortimer, "Mr. Puppet Pinocchio Bests Mr. Clark Gable," *Daily Mirror*, February 8, 1940.
21. "Notes and Comment—The Talk of the Town," *New Yorker*, February 17, 1940, 13.
22. "Screen News Here and in Hollywood," *New York Times*, February 3, 1940.
23. "'Pinocchio' Campaign Covers Every Angle," *Showmen's Trade Review*, February 17, 1940, 13.
24. "Comedy Relief," *Art Digest*, November 1, 1932, 10.
25. Bill Mikulak, "Disney and the Art World: The Early Years," in *Animation: Art and Industry*, ed. Maureen Furniss (New Barnet: John Libbey, 2012), 114. Mikulak provides further details on this exhibit, as well as exhibits at the Los Angeles County Museum in 1940 and the Museum of Modern Art in 1942.
26. Exhibitions of drawings and cels from the Disney studios had appeared in a range of galleries in the 1930s, including the Kennedy Galleries in New York in 1933 and the Leicester Galleries in London in 1935 ("Mickey Mouse Invades Gallery," *Art Digest*, May 1, 1933, 12; "Art of Mr. Disney," *The Times*, February 13, 1935).
27. Watts, *The Magic Kingdom*, 121.
28. Louise G. Burroughs, "Notes," *The Metropolitan Museum of Art Bulletin*, February 1939, 50; Frank S. Nugent, "Disney Is Now Art—But He Wonders," *New York Times*, February 26, 1939.
29. Nugent, "Disney Is Now Art—But He Wonders." The work on display—like virtually all of the "Disney" works appearing in galleries—was not created by Disney himself but was rather produced by others working in the Disney studios.
30. "World-Wide Disney," *Magazine of Art*, September 1938, 546. See also, Mikulak, "Disney and the Art World," 125.
31. "Fifty-Seventh Street Mouse," *Cue*, September 17, 1938, 9.

32. Nugent, "Disney Is Now Art—But He Wonders."
33. Al Hirschfeld, "Disney Versus Art," *New York Times*, March 17, 1940.
34. Thomas Burton, "Walt Disney's 'Pinocchio,'" *Saturday Review of Literature*, February 17, 1940, 17.
35. Pressbook for *Pinocchio*, Cinema press books [microform], reel 90, Performing Arts Research Collections, New York Public Library.
36. "'Pinocchio' Campaign Covers Every Angle," 13.
37. "'Pinocchio' Campaign Covers Every Angle," 13.
38. Dorothy Coburn, "A Preview of Santa's Pack." For an account of earlier uses of Mickey Mouse in department store displays and shop windows, see Richard deCordova, "The Mickey in Macy's Window: Childhood, Consumerism, and Disney Animation," in *Disney Discourse: Producing the Magic Kingdom*, ed. Eric Smoodin (New York: Routledge, 1994), 205–207.
39. "Over 70 Stores Contract For 'Pinocchio' Displays," *Showmen's Trade Review*, December 9, 1939, 17.
40. *Display Animation, 1938: The Year Book of Motion Displays*, ed. I. L. Cochrane (New York: Reeder-Morton Publications, 1938), 131. These animated displays anticipated the later use of Audio-Animatronics in Disneyland. Disney explained how those animated figures were "just another dimension in the animation we have been doing all our lives" (Watts, *The Magic Kingdom*, 413).
41. *Display Animation, 1939–40: The Year Book of Motion Displays*, ed. I. L. Cochrane (New York: Reeder-Morton Publications, 1939), 202.
42. "'Pinocchio' Campaign Covers Every Angle," 13.
43. Douglas W. Churchill, "Screen News Here and in Hollywood," *New York Times*, February 8, 1940.
44. "Hollywood News and New York Screen Notes," *New York Herald Tribune*, February 1940.
45. Churchill, "Screen News Here and in Hollywood."
46. "'Pinocchio' Campaign Covers Every Angle," 13.
47. "'Pinocchio' Campaign Covers Every Angle," 13.
48. Jane Gaines, "The Queen Christina Tie-Ups: Convergence of Show Window and Screen," *Quarterly Review of Film and Video* 11, no. 1 (1989): 38.
49. Norman M. Klein, *7 Minutes: The Life and Death of the American Animated Cartoon* (London: Verso, 1993), 53.
50. Watts, *The Magic Kingdom*, 149.
51. "'Pinocchio', 'Tom Edison' Bow In; MGM Dates 'Wind' in 279th City," *Motion Picture Herald*, February 10, 1940, 31.
52. "Juveniles from Movies Selling for Christmas," *Publisher's Weekly*, December 9, 1939, 20.

53. The report summarized the related income: "Fees for licensing of cartoon characters: $289,829.57"; "Income from art work for books and periodicals: $92,245.09"; "Music royalties: $24,388.51". In addition, the comic strip income was $105,210.78 ("Walt Disney Production Statement of Income and Earned Surplus for the Year (52 Weeks) Ended September 28, 1940," report, p. 10, Margaret Herrick Library).

54. "Walt Disney Production Statement of Income," 5.

55. Pressbook for *Pinocchio*.

56. "'Pinocchio' Campaign Covers Every Angle," 13.

57. Watts, *The Magic Kingdom*; Moya Luckett, "Fantasia: Cultural Constructions of Disney's 'Masterpiece,'" in *Disney Discourse: Producing the Magic Kingdom*, ed. Eric Smoodin (New York: Routledge, 1994), 214–236.

58. "Disney's 'Fantasia' Is Really Revolutionary," *American Cinematographer*, December 1940, 558. In *Walt Disney and Europe*, Robin Allan describes how ideas for Fantasia's exhibition were even more ambitious in its early planning, including using "3D (with special glasses)" in the abstract Bach section (108) and having "scents and the smell of flowers and incense" in the cinema to accompany the Schubert section (168).

59. A. P. Peck, "What Makes 'Fantasia' Click," *Scientific American*, January 1941, 28.

60. A. P. Peck, "What Makes 'Fantasia' Click," 28.

61. "Disney's 'Fantasia' Is Really Revolutionary," 558.

62. A. P. Peck, "What Makes 'Fantasia' Click," 29.

63. "Disney's 'Fantasia' Is Really Revolutionary," 558.

64. A. P. Peck, "What Makes 'Fantasia' Click," 29.

65. "'Fantasia's' Spot Between IATSE and IBEW Scrap," *Variety*, October 30, 1940, 7.

66. "U. S. Defense Demands Stall RCA-Disney on 'Fantasia' Equipment," *Variety*, November 20, 1940, 4.

67. William E. Garity and Watson Jones, "Experiences in Road-Showing Walt Disney's Fantasia," *Journal of the Society of Motion Picture Engineers* 39 (July 1942): 13.

68. "With Simplified 'Fantasound,' RKO Probably Will Distrib 'Fantasia,'" *Variety*, April 16, 1941, 7.

69. "General Distribution for Disney 'Fantasia,' Minus 'Fantasound,'" *Motion Picture Herald*, May 3, 1941, 47.

70. "'Fantasia' Sets A Run Record," *Motion Picture Herald*, September 20, 1941, 44. The same article indicated that *Fantasia* had made a profit in its initial run against a budget of $2,200,000, although acknowledging that it was difficult to "determine accurately." An earlier article in *Motion Picture Herald* reported that *Fantasia* had earned more in its initial exhibition in eleven cities than *Snow White* had earned in the same markets ("General Distribution for Disney 'Fantasia', Minus 'Fantasound,'" 47).

71. "Fantasia," *Variety*, November 13, 1940, 16.
72. "Disney's Own Distrib for 'Fantasia,'" *Variety*, August 21, 1940, 6.
73. "Disney Won't Tell About 'Fantasia'—But I. P. Will," *International Projectionist*, April 1940, 12.
74. "The November Conference," *National Board of Review Magazine*, December 1940, 4.
75. Philip K. Scheuer, "Town Called Hollywood," *Los Angeles Times*, January 12, 1941.
76. Isabel Morse Jones, "The Week's High Note in Music," *Los Angeles Times*, January 26, 1941.
77. "Music to Suit Audience Mood for 'Fantasia,'" *Variety*, February 19, 1941, 2.
78. Allan, *Walt Disney and Europe*, 104.
79. Kate Cameron, "Disney's 'Fantasia' a Work of Film Art," *Daily News*, November 14, 1940; Thomas J. Fitzmorris, "Films," *America*, November 30, 1940, 223.
80. "Speech Delivered by David O. Selznick at the Academy of Motion Picture Arts and Sciences Dinner of Thursday, February 26, 1942," Irving G. Thalberg and Norma Shearer Papers, Margaret Herrick Library, Los Angeles.
81. Disney, "Cartoons Look to New Horizons."
82. Edward Alden Jewell, "Of Music and Painting: Disney 'Fantasia' Raises Anew Problem of Fusing Aural and Visual Forms," *New York Times*, January 5, 1941.
83. Lewis Jacobs, *The Rise of the American Film: A Critical History* (New York: Harcourt, Brace and Company, 1939), 501. For a discussion of Jacobs's assessment of Disney in terms of art, see Watts, *The Magic Kingdom*, 129–130.
84. George Antheil, "On the Hollywood Front," *Modern Music*, January–February 1938, 118.
85. George Antheil, "On the Hollywood Front," *Modern Music*, November–December 1938, 64.
86. Walt Disney, "Cartoons Look to New Horizons."
87. "Walt Disney Doubts 'Fantasia' Will Ever Show Him a Profit," *Variety*, November 13, 1940, 4.
88. "Walt Disney Doubts 'Fantasia' Will Ever Show Him a Profit," 4.
89. Arthur Beach, "Fantasia," *National Board of Review Magazine*, December 1940, 11.
90. *Walt Disney's Fantasia* (New York: Simon and Schuster, 1940).
91. Gladys Burch, "Musical Christmas," *Publisher's Weekly*, November 23, 1940, 1957; Alice Hackett, "P. W. Forecast for Buyers," *Publisher's Weekly*, November 2, 1940, 1776; "Deems Taylor," *Publisher's Weekly*, November 30, 1940, 2071.

92. Thomas Baird, "The World's Fair: Its Films," *Cine-Technician*, September–October 1939, 86.

93. Haidee Wasson, "Selling Machines: Film and Its Technologies at the New York World's Fair," in *Films That Sell: Moving Pictures and Advertising*, eds. Bo Florin, Nico de Klerk, and Patrick Vondereau (London: British Film Institute, 2016), 54. See also, Haidee Wasson, "The Other Small Screen: Moving Images at New York's World Fair, 1939," *Canadian Journal of Film Studies* 21, no. 1 (Spring 2012): 81–103.

94. "Motion Pictures at the New York World's Fair 1939," New York World's Fair 1939 Department of Feature Publicity, June 28, 1939, p. 1, box 781, folder 28, New York World's Fair 1939 and 1940 Incorporated Records, PR0.2 New Film Releases, New York World's Fair Motion Picture (1939), New York Public Library.

95. *Official Guide Book: The World's Fair of 1940 in New York* (New York: Rogers, Kellogg, Stillson, 1940), 29.

96. *Exhibition Techniques* (New York: New York Museum of Science and Industry, 1940), 66.

97. Press release, box 381, folder 4, New York World's Fair 1939 and 1940 Incorporated Records, P1.200 Chrysler Corp. (1939), New York Public Library.

98. John Mosher, "The Current Cinema," *New Yorker*, July 13, 1940, 51.

99. *Official Guide Book of the New York World's Fair 1939* (New York: Exposition Publications Inc., 1939), 110; S. N. Holliday (Advertising Department, National Biscuit Company) to Edward Carlin (Department of Exhibits and Concessions), September 21, 1939, box 459, folder 10, New York World's Fair 1939 and 1940 Incorporated Records, I. Central Files—I. D. Participation, P1. Private Enterprises—P1.5 Comfort, National Biscuit Co. (1939), New York Public Library.

100. *Official Guide Book of the New York World's Fair 1939*, 110.

101. *Display Animation, 1939–40*, 100.

102. I. L. Cochrane, *Motion Display Mechanics* (New York: Reeder-Morton Publications, 1939), 89.

103. *Official Guide Book of the New York World's Fair 1939*, 56.

104. "Big Promotion Drive Arranged for Pinocchio," *Broadcasting*, October 15, 1939, 68.

105. Virgil Thomson, "Composing for the Movies," *National Board of Review Magazine*, January 1941, 5.

106. Dick Hyman and Chester Weil, memorandum, June 24, 1937, p. 1, box 541, folder 1, New York World's Fair 1939 and 1940 Incorporated Records, P1.630 Side Shows, King Features Syndicate, Inc. (1939), New York Public Library.

107. Memorandum, n.d., New York World's Fair 1939 and 1940 Incorporated Records, P1.630 Side Shows, King Features Syndicate, Inc. (1939), box 541, folder 1, New York Public Library.

108. "The Exhibits: An Amazing Array," *New York Times*, April 30, 1939.
109. Petroleum Industry Exhibition, press release, n.d., p. 2, box 349, folder 16, New York World's Fair 1939 and 1940 Incorporated Records, P1.03 Power, Petroleum Industry Exhibition, Inc. (1939), New York Public Library.
110. Rob King discusses *Pete-Roleum*, including its relation to the films of Charley Bowers and the World's Fair, in "The Art of Diddling: Slapstick, Science, and Antimodernism in the Films of Charley Bowers," in *Funny Pictures: Animation and Comedy in Studio-Era Hollywood*, eds. Daniel Goldmark and Charlie Keil (Berkeley: University of California Press, 2011), 191–210.
111. Michel Ciment, *Conversations with Losey* (London: Methuen, 1985), 57.
112. Joseph Losey to Raymond Borde, April 3, 1981, Joseph Losey Collection, British Film Institute.
113. Bosley Crowther, "Films for the Fair; Motion Pictures Will Play a Big Role in the Flushing Flats This Summer," *New York Times*, March 5, 1939.
114. "Tracing History of Cartoon, Puppet Film," *Motion Picture Herald*, June 24, 1939, 56.
115. David Caute, *Joseph Losey: A Revenge on Life* (New York: Oxford University Press, 1994), 68.
116. Colin Gardner, "The Losey-Moscow Connection: Experimental Soviet Theatre and the Living Newspaper," *New Theatre Quarterly* 30, no. 3 (August 2014): 256.
117. Petroleum Industry Exhibition, press release, 2.
118. Gardner, "The Losey-Moscow Connection," 256.
119. Petroleum Industry Exhibition, press release, 2.
120. "'Pete Roleum' and His Cousins to Picture the Story of Oil at Fair," *New York World-Telegram*, October 15, 1938.
121. "Films of Fact," *The Times*, August 1, 1939.
122. *TAC, A Magazine of Theatre, Film, Radio, Music, Dance*, July 1939, 30, Joseph Losey Collection, British Film Institute. Losey noted that the two-track experiment with sound "never worked" (Joseph Losey to Raymond Borde, April 3, 1981. Joseph Losey Collection, British Film Institute).
123. Petroleum Industry Exhibition, press release, 1.

REFERENCES

Allan, Robin. *Walt Disney and Europe*. London: John Libbey, 1999.
Antheil, George. "On the Hollywood Front." *Modern Music*, January–February 1938.
Antheil, George. "On the Hollywood Front." *Modern Music*, November–December 1938.

"Art of Mr. Disney." *The Times*, February 13, 1935.

"'Bagdad' Also Will Have a Commercial Licensing Hookup." *Variety*, December 27, 1939.

Baird, Thomas. "The World's Fair: Its Films." *The Cine-Technician*, September–October 1939.

Barrier, Michael. *Hollywood Cartoons: American Animation in Its Golden Age*. Oxford: Oxford University Press, 1999.

Beach, Arthur. "Fantasia." *National Board of Review Magazine*, December 1940.

"Big Promotion Drive Arranged for Pinocchio." *Broadcasting*, October 15, 1939.

Boehnel, William. "Pinocchio Stamped with Disney's Genius." *New York World-Telegram*, February 10, 1940.

Burch, Gladys. "Musical Christmas." *Publisher's Weekly*, November 23, 1940.

Burroughs, Louise G. "Notes." *The Metropolitan Museum of Art Bulletin*, February 1939.

Burton, Thomas. "Walt Disney's 'Pinocchio.'" *Saturday Review of Literature*, February 17, 1940.

Cameron, Kate. "Disney's 'Fantasia' a Work of Film Art." *Daily News*, November 14, 1940.

Caute, David. *Joseph Losey: A Revenge on Life*. New York: Oxford University Press, 1994.

"Center Theatre to Revert to Films for 'Pinocchio.'" *New York Times*, January 12, 1940.

Churchill, Douglas W. "Screen News Here and in Hollywood." *New York Times*, February 8, 1940.

Ciment, Michel. *Conversations with Losey*. London: Methuen, 1985.

Coburn, Dorothy. "A Preview of Santa's Pack: On a Trip Through Brooklyn's Toyland." *Brooklyn Daily Eagle*, November 30, 1939.

Cochrane, I. L. *Motion Display Mechanics*. New York: Reeder-Morton Publications, 1939.

Cochrane, I. L., ed. *Display Animation, 1938: The Year Book of Motion Displays*. New York: Reeder-Morton Publications, 1938.

Cochrane, I. L., ed. *Display Animation, 1939–40: The Year Book of Motion Displays*. New York: Reeder-Morton Publications, 1939.

"Comedy Relief." *Art Digest*, November 1, 1932.

Crowther, Bosley. "Films for the Fair; Motion Pictures Will Play a Big Role in the Flushing Flats This Summer." *New York Times*, March 5, 1939.

deCordova, Richard. "The Mickey in Macy's Window: Childhood, Consumerism, and Disney Animation." In *Disney Discourse: Producing the Magic Kingdom*, edited by Eric Smoodin, 203–213. New York: Routledge, 1994.

"Deems Taylor." *Publisher's Weekly*, November 30, 1940.

Disney, Walt. "Cartoons Look to New Horizons, Find Them Happily Limitless." *New York Herald Tribune*, September 16, 1940.

"Disney Won't Tell About 'Fantasia'—But I. P. Will." *International Projectionist*, April 1940.

"Disney's 'Fantasia' Is Really Revolutionary." *American Cinematographer*, December 1940.

"Disney's Own Distrib for 'Fantasia.'" *Variety*, August 21, 1940.

Exhibition Techniques. New York: New York Museum of Science and Industry, 1940.

"Fantasia." *Variety*, November 13, 1940.

"'Fantasia' Sets a Run Record." *Motion Picture Herald*, September 20, 1941.

"'Fantasia's' Spot Between IATSE and IBEW Scrap." *Variety*, October 30, 1940.

"Fifty-Seventh Street Mouse." *Cue*, September 17, 1938.

"Films of Fact." *The Times*, August 1, 1939.

Fitzmorris, Thomas J. "Films." *America*, November 30, 1940.

"Fleischer-Disney Race." *Variety*, February 1, 1939.

Gaines, Jane. "The Queen Christina Tie-Ups: Convergence of Show Window and Screen." *Quarterly Review of Film and Video* 11, no. 1 (1989): 35–60.

Gardner, Colin. "The Losey-Moscow Connection: Experimental Soviet Theatre and the Living Newspaper." *New Theatre Quarterly* 30, no. 3 (August 2014): 249–268.

Garity, William E., and Watson Jones. "Experiences in Road-Showing Walt Disney's Fantasia." *Journal of the Society of Motion Picture Engineers* 39 (July 1942): 6–15.

"General Distribution for Disney 'Fantasia,' Minus 'Fantasound.'" *Motion Picture Herald*, May 3, 1941.

Hackett, Alice. "P. W. Forecast for Buyers." *Publisher's Weekly*, November 2, 1940.

Hirschfeld, Al. "Disney Versus Art." *New York Times*, March 17, 1940.

Hoellering, Franz. "Films." *Nation*, February 17, 1940.

"Hollywood News and New York Screen Notes." *New York Herald Tribune*, February 1940.

Jacobs, Lewis. *The Rise of the American Film: A Critical History*. New York: Harcourt, Brace and Company, 1939.

Jewell, Edward Alden. "Of Music and Painting: Disney 'Fantasia' Raises Anew Problem of Fusing Aural and Visual Forms." *New York Times*, January 5, 1941.

"Juveniles from Movies Selling for Christmas." *Publisher's Weekly*, December 9, 1939.

King, Rob. "The Art of Diddling: Slapstick, Science, and Antimodernism in the Films of Charley Bowers." In *Funny Pictures: Animation and Comedy in Studio-Era Hollywood*, edited by Daniel Goldmark and Charlie Keil, 191–210. Berkeley: University of California Press, 2011.

Klein, Norman M. *7 Minutes: The Life and Death of the American Animated Cartoon*. London: Verso, 1993.

Leslie, Esther. *Hollywood Flatlands: Animation, Critical Theory and the Avant-Garde*. London: Verso, 2002.

Losey, Joseph. Collection. British Film Institute.

Luckett, Moya. "Fantasia: Cultural Constructions of Disney's 'Masterpiece.'" In *Disney Discourse: Producing the Magic Kingdom*, edited by Eric Smoodin, 214–236. New York: Routledge, 1994.

"Mickey Mouse Invades Gallery." *Art Digest*, May 1, 1933.

Mikulak, Bill. "Disney and the Art World: The Early Years." In *Animation: Art and Industry*, edited by Maureen Furniss, 111–129. New Barnet: John Libbey, 2012.

Morse Jones, Isabel. "The Week's High Note in Music." *Los Angeles Times*, January 26, 1941.

Mortimer, Lee. "Mr. Puppet Pinocchio Bests Mr. Clark Gable." *Daily Mirror*, February 8, 1940.

Mosher, John. "The Current Cinema." *New Yorker*, July 13, 1940.

"Music to Suit Audience Mood for 'Fantasia.'" *Variety*, February 19, 1941.

New York World's Fair 1939 and 1940 Incorporated Records, New York Public Library.

"Notes and Comment—The Talk of the Town." *New Yorker*, February 17, 1940.

Nugent, Frank S. "Disney Is Now Art—But He Wonders." *New York Times*, February 26, 1939.

Official Guide Book of the New York World's Fair 1939. New York: Exposition Publications Inc., 1939.

Official Guide Book: The World's Fair of 1940 in New York. New York: Rogers, Kellogg, Stillson, 1940.

"Over 70 Stores Contract For 'Pinocchio' Displays." *Showmen's Trade Review*, December 9, 1939.

Paramount Picture production records, Margaret Herrick Library.

Peck, A. P. "What Makes 'Fantasia' Click." *Scientific American*, January 1941.

Pelswick, Rose. "'Pinocchio' Opens at Center Theatre." *New York Journal-American*, February 8, 1940.

Performing Arts Research Collections, New York Public Library.

"'Pete Roleum' and His Cousins to Picture the Story of Oil at Fair." *New York World-Telegram*, October 15, 1938.

"'Pinocchio' Campaign Covers Every Angle." *Showmen's Trade Review*, February 17, 1940.

"'Pinocchio', 'Tom Edison' Bow In; MGM Dates 'Wind' in 279th City." *Motion Picture Herald*, February 10, 1940.

Scheuer, Philip K. "Town Called Hollywood." *Los Angeles Times*, January 12, 1941.

"Screen News Here and in Hollywood." *New York Times*, February 3, 1940.

"Setting Final Policies on 'Wind,' Cartoons 'Gulliver,' 'Pinocchio.'" *Motion Picture Herald*, December 9, 1939.

TAC, A Magazine of Theatre, Film, Radio, Music, Dance, July 1939. Joseph Losey Collection, British Film Institute.

"The Exhibits: An Amazing Array." *New York Times*, April 30, 1939.

"The November Conference." *National Board of Review Magazine*, December 1940.

Thalberg, Irving G., and Norma Shearer Papers. Margaret Herrick Library, Los Angeles.

Thomson, Virgil. "Composing for the Movies." *National Board of Review Magazine*, January 1941.

"Tracing History of Cartoon, Puppet Film." *Motion Picture Herald*, June 24, 1939.

"U. S. Defense Demands Stall RCA-Disney on 'Fantasia' Equipment." *Variety*, November 20, 1940.

"Walt Disney Doubts 'Fantasia' Will Ever Show Him a Profit." *Variety*, November 13, 1940.

Walt Disney Presents Fantasia. New York: Walt Disney Productions, 1940.

Wasson, Haidee. "Selling Machines: Film and Its Technologies at the New York World's Fair." In *Films That Sell: Moving Pictures and Advertising*, edited by Bo Florin, Nico de Klerk, and Patrick Vondereau, 54–70. London: British Film Institute, 2016.

Wasson, Haidee. "The Other Small Screen: Moving Images at New York's World Fair, 1939." *Canadian Journal of Film Studies* 21, no. 1 (Spring 2012): 81–103.

Watts, Steven. *The Magic Kingdom: Walt Disney and the American Way of Life*. Columbia: University of Missouri Press, 1997.

Winsten, Archer. "Disney's 'Pinocchio' at the Center Theatre." *New York Post*, February 8, 1940.

"With Simplified 'Fantasound,' RKO Probably Will Distrib 'Fantasia.'" *Variety*, April 16, 1941.

"World-Wide Disney." *Magazine of Art*, September 1938.

CHAPTER 6

Conclusion

In New York's animation culture, the uses of animation were extraordinarily diverse. Animation was drawn into commercial activities, combining and creating artistic forms, contributing to an expanded cinematic experience, offering a vivid form of education and illustrating the dynamism of modern life. Here was a seedbed for new technologies of three-dimensional sound and vision, alongside other new ways of creating and exhibiting animated film that would be taken up by mainstream studios and experimental practitioners alike. This was the laboratory in which new technologies of the photoelectric cell, polaroid film and miniaturized motors were geared toward popular entertainment. This was a central site for new strategies for film merchandising, new links between design and art and new ways of envisioning advertising and display. This multiplicity was taken up across different cultural fields, generating a hub of creative activity. With America's entrance into the war, this animation culture subsided, shifting into war-related activities and largely becoming an afterthought in the face of more pressing everyday concerns. While New York's animation culture was a passing moment within a longer history, it can help illuminate the vibrant potentials of animation itself. New York's dreams of a kinetic future demonstrated the power of motion, its capacity to open up new ways of thinking, creating and seeing.

New York's animation culture embraced an exploratory spirit, pushing the limits of where animation belonged and what it could be. The animated works on display offered lively experiments with aesthetic form, innovations

© The Author(s) 2019
K. Moen, *New York's Animation Culture*, Palgrave Animation,
https://doi.org/10.1007/978-3-030-27931-8_6

in how technologies and materials could be used to create animation, an expanding sense of the places where animation could be exhibited and different ideas of animation. These are all features of animation cultures more broadly, and New York's distinctive engagement with them helped create a particularly rich moment in animation history in which boundaries between different uses of animation were becoming blurred. For example, the *Daily News* suggested that one of the more experimental sequences in *Fantasia* (1940), "a series of lines and color in various forms, a visual abstraction of the artists' interpretation of the Bach music," was itself perhaps "inspired by the fountains at the World's Fair, as the color and line suggest the waterspouts that were played in harmony with the tinted lights and music in Flushing Meadows during the exposition."[1] While any direct influence is unlikely, the willingness to connect the musicality, color and motion of *Fantasia* with fountains at the Fair indicates the kind of overlapping ideas of animation coursing through New York. Seeking out new effects of motion, artists, animators, designers, advertisers and educators embraced new technologies in their creation of cinematic experiences and kinetic arts. Technology helped transform animation in many ways, allowing for new relationships between media to be developed and contributing to a context in which static forms were enlivened by motion. But technology did not determine or shape the directions that animation would take. Instead, it facilitated new ideas and forms within a larger creative and cultural sphere.

Throughout this book, we have seen how different ideas of animation allowed for seemingly distinct cultural fields to be transformed and reimagined by motion. The notion that animation could be a form of art, for example, underpinned the use of motion in Fifth Avenue shop windows, gallery shows and screening spaces alike. Similarly, animation was entwined with different media in often unexpected ways—for example, the animated windows designed by James Gosling and the animated spectaculars designed by Douglas Leigh were both compared to the emergent medium of television, which was itself a promising new site of animated film for Mary Ellen Bute and Norman McLaren.

Taking a much less open-ended approach, Joseph Schillinger, the music theorist discussed in Chapter 4, argued for a more cohesive and delimited use of animation. In response to the many "requests for his opinion and analysis" of *Fantasia*, Schillinger wrote a short "statement" on the film.[2] He was highly critical, arguing that "the media of paralleling music by visual images are both inadequate to the character and form of music with which they are synchronized, and employ the visual images belonging to totally different categories, such as animated cartoons, ballets, fairy tales, and abstractions" (192). Rather than this erratic approach, a much more scientific method was needed, specifically his own system for engineering visual compositions. While Schillinger was hardly alone in his criticism of *Fantasia*, his vision of animation as something that should abide by a precise method of composition was distinctly different from the wider understanding of animation in New York's animation culture. While some of the institutional contexts and prominent figures in this culture did call for particular uses of animation—whether as part of an overall composition of shop windows on Fifth Avenue or as a type of non-objective art in the Museum of Non-Objective Painting—the paths that animation took were wonderfully varied. Rather than a discrete aesthetic form with its own distinct functions, animation was seen to be open to new and expansive possibilities, crossing borders rather than abiding by them.

This fluidity of animation was certainly not unique to New York at this time. One recurring theme in this book has been how New York's animation culture drew upon earlier forms and practices of animation. These included recent events such as the turn toward motion display at the Century of Progress Exposition which ran from 1933 to 1934, the rise in the cultural prominence of animated films most visibly evident in the popularity of films produced by Disney, such as *Snow White and the Seven Dwarfs* (1937), and the shift in industrial design toward an emphasis on motion and dynamism. The influences on New York's animation culture also went back further in history, to practices of abstract animation from the 1920s, to an interest in using static art forms to evoke movement that had been attracting considerable attention since the turn of the century and to an array of mobile media—from moving panoramas to film—that had emerged in the previous century or even earlier. All of these precursors had a powerful impact on New York's animation culture. However, this animation culture did not simply develop from these earlier practices in some kind of coherent historical narrative or straightforward lineage. Instead, a range of influences were intermingled with an eagerness to embrace new forms, techniques and potentials of animation.

Although the interactions between different animators, such as McLaren and Bute, helped generate these ideas and creative practices, New York's animation culture tended to be less rooted in individuals and more closely associated with spaces, institutions and cultural fields. While appearing in different parts of the city, much of the creative energy circulating around animation at this time was located in three hubs of activity: Rockefeller Center, the World's Fair and the art galleries in midtown Manhattan. These central locations of New York's animation culture were new ventures and as such were likely more open to the novelty of animation than other more established locations. At the same time, there was considerable financial and cultural capital behind each of these places that allowed for a significant—and sometimes quite costly—engagement with animation. These sites offered a microcosm of animation's extensions into entertainment, education, culture and commerce. For example, Rockefeller Center's dynamic Hall of Motion was in the same building complex as the exhibition venues for the first Disney features and the offices of Douglas Leigh. Similarly, galleries in midtown Manhattan offered a multifaceted engagement with animation: screening a range of animated films, supporting animators, developing film libraries and exhibiting production material. The Fair also drew together different forms of animation, from films to displays, entwining motion with modern life in hugely popular exhibits. Rather than adhering to a single conception of what animation should be, these three sites hosted a variety of animated forms.

While no overarching purpose or approach shaped this animation culture, there were recurring themes evident within it, as the Introduction discussed: a cultural fascination with the impact of motion itself, a deep interest in animation's capacity to cross between media or create new media and an exploration of the aesthetics of motion. Individual animators were sophisticated and ambitious in the ways that they engaged with these different facets of animation, whether developing ideas for animated symphonies or integrating color with movement. Such themes also went beyond individuals to encompass the discourses and activities that circulated around animation, where new arts of motion were heralded in newspaper advertisements and new commercial endeavors were being generated around animation.

After 1940, some of the major figures in this culture would continue to seek out new ways to expand animation. Norman Bel Geddes, who had explored the use of motion in his creative practice and design work, had cosmic ambitions for animation when he became interested in applying his dramatic sense of design to the Hayden Planetarium in the early 1940s. Dismayed by the poor quality of the Planetarium's shows, Bel Geddes wrote a scathing letter to Roy Chapman Andrews, the Director of the American Museum of Natural History:

There is nothing imaginative or convincing about the show you are putting on at the present moment. The Planetarium as conceived, and on which a considerable sum of money was expended, and as originally presented to the public, had to a high degree the four basic elements of drama: light, movement, sound and imagination. The latter three elements are completely lacking in the present performance.[3]

Perhaps thinking of *Fantasia*'s critical success with synchronizing motion, color and sound, Bel Geddes began to develop a project to improve the planetarium's shows with Disney in mind: "In my opinion there is every reason to make a great, popular theater out of the Planetarium – a theater of a totally new kind, just as Mr. Disney has developed a theater of a totally new kind."[4] From the highway system of Futurama to the cosmos of the planetarium, Bel Geddes aimed to create new dramatic spaces through motion.

Bel Geddes was not alone in observing how the movement of the heavens resonated with animation. An advertisement for the Zeiss Planetarium Projector, used in the Hayden Planetarium, was discussed at the start of the first of I. L. Cochrane's *Display Animation* yearbooks. Cochrane wrote, "Every displayman should visit one of the four Planetaria located in this country, and realize how puny in comparison is the best commercial displaymanship."[5] This interest in planetaria as a model for animation indicates the extent to which motion was becoming seen as a form of immense value, sometimes tied in with cosmic and universal qualities. Other participants in New York's animation culture were drawing upon such ideas in more philosophical ways. In her promotion of non-objective art, Hilla Rebay saw enormous potentials for animation—particularly through its use of rhythm—to present a carefully composed world of motion that resonated with spiritual values. Similarly, Walter Dorwin Teague saw rhythm as a universal value that could be powerfully expressed through animation. Such far-reaching potentials of motion contributed to and helped shape the ambitious nature of New York's animation culture.

Others were more interested in a comparatively down-to-earth sense of animation's potentials. One later example of this, drawing together key participants in New York's animation culture, took place in Times Square in the early 1960s. At this time, Leigh had remained a key figure in New York advertising, and while the animated spectaculars that used Epok were no longer the thrilling novelty they had been in the 1930s, they continued to draw the attention of pedestrians. Decades after living in New York,

Fig. 6.1   *New York Lightboard Record* (1961)

having become a world-renowned and Oscar-winning animator, McLaren designed the animated show for one of Leigh's signs. Using the same Epok panel as the Wilson Whiskey sign discussed in Chapter 2, *New York Lightboard* (1961) visualized the wonders of Canada for potential American tourists. Filled with delightful animations that displayed and promoted characteristically Canadian attractions, this work embraced the same lively motion and mutability as McLaren's early films. Here, in Times Square, was a bravura performance of McLaren's style, using a soundless, colorless and blocky Epok aesthetic that was a return to basics, seemingly a world away from the further explorations of animation that McLaren had made since leaving New York. With its metamorphoses of moving words and forms, the animated sign was captivating: in a characteristically fluid section, a maple leaf transforms into a sun, which then becomes an image of trees and a canoe, part of a seemingly endless flow of moving and changing imagery on a continual loop (Fig. 6.1). Set beside a billboard for Planter's Peanuts, with its regular lighting changes and the monotonous movement of Mr. Peanut's cane, McLaren's animated spectacular was an exceptionally vivid depiction of animation's dynamic potentials.

A short film made about this sign, *New York Lightboard Record* (1961), coupled footage of the sign with footage of spectators watching its animated show—gazing upward, some look on seriously, some become distracted as

Fig. 6.2 *New York Lightboard Record* (1961)

they walk along and others smile and laugh; a man with an 8 mm home movie camera films the sign and a woman seated behind a window watches its endless permutations (Fig. 6.2). Each viewer's reaction is different, but those looking up are transfixed—at least for an instant—by the luminous motion, like a fireworks display or a comet in the night sky. From the movement of the stars in a planetarium to an animated sign on Times Square, the sight of motion fascinates and captivates. The dynamism of New York's animation culture is one vibrant instance of just how much creativity, thought, effort and passion could be generated by the enthralling power of motion.

Notes

1. Kate Cameron, "Disney's 'Fantasia' a Work of Film Art," *Daily News*, November 14, 1940.
2. Frances Schillinger, *Joseph Schillinger: A Memoir* (New York: Da Capo Press, 1976), 191.
3. Norman Bel Geddes to Roy Chapman Andrews, October 8, 1941, box 29, folder 444.1, Norman Bel Geddes Theater and Industrial Design Papers, Hayden Planetarium, Correspondence, Harry Ransom Center, University of Texas at Austin.

4. Norman Bel Geddes, "Miscellaneous Notes on Planetarium Job," November 24, 1941, p. 2, box 29, folder 444.1, Norman Bel Geddes Theater and Industrial Design Papers, Hayden Planetarium, Correspondence, Harry Ransom Center, University of Texas at Austin.
5. *Display Animation, 1936: The Year Book of Motion Displays*, ed. I. L. Cochrane (New York: Reeder-Morton Publications, 1936), 9.

References

Bel Geddes, Norman. Theater and Industrial Design Papers, Harry Ransom Center, University of Texas at Austin.

Cameron, Kate. "Disney's 'Fantasia' a Work of Film Art." *Daily News*, November 14, 1940.

Cochrane, I. L., ed. *Display Animation, 1936: The Year Book of Motion Displays.* New York: Reeder-Morton Publications, 1936.

Schillinger, Frances. *Joseph Schillinger: A Memoir*. New York: Da Capo Press, 1976.

INDEX

Printed by Printforce, the Netherlands